Delimitation and States Reorganization

AF519419

'Democracy is the theory that the common people know what they want, and deserve to get it good and hard.'

—H.L. Mencken

Advance Praise

'The constitutional arrangements in a democracy need to be reformed from time to time for adjustment to emergent challenges and for dealing with the varying rate of population growth in different areas. In *Delimitation and States Reorganization: For a Better Democracy in Bhārat*, Gautam Desiraju and Deekhit Bhattacharya propose coupling the overdue delimitation of constituencies to the formation of new states so that their powers are relatively balanced. This book is a worthy sequel to Desiraju's pioneering *Bhārat: India 2.0* in which the fault lines related to federalism, secularism, and caste-based reservations were noted and solutions proposed.'

Subhash Kak, Regents Professor, Oklahoma State University

'It is said that in the Mahabharata 108 kings participated in the Great War from either side. Each of them represented a distinct cultural zone of the great land mass called Bhārat. It is interesting that in this compelling book, the authors, taking a different and modern approach, are advocating smaller states almost akin to those times.'

Pawan Gupta, SIDH, Mussoorie

'An incisive and timely contribution to the discourse on Bhārat as a civilizational state. At a moment when the nation faces the critical challenge of delimitation, Gautam Desiraju and Deekhit Bhattacharya provide a visionary roadmap for equitable electoral and federal reforms. Rooted in dharmic principles and the essence of Bhārat's diversity, the book addresses foundational questions of representation, state reorganization, and parity. This work is essential reading for policymakers, scholars, and citizens invested in ensuring Bhārat's democracy evolves to reflect its civilizational ethos and future aspirations.'

Shobhit Mathur, Vice Chancellor, Rishihood University

'Dozens of books have been written about the idea that Bhārat is a "civilizational state". This book actually explains how a civilizational state should be governed in the 21st century. It should be read by every practically minded political reformer. The most pernicious legacy of Indira Gandhi's twenty-one months of Emergency rule isn't the presence of the words "socialist" and "secular" in the Constitution. It's the fact that the representation of Indians in the Lok Sabha has been frozen at 1971 levels for more than fifty years. With a delimitation exercise now looming and a national census long overdue, Gautam Desiraju and Deekhit Bhattacharya argue that it will only be possible to restore the principle of equal representation of the people ("Each Vote Same Value") if at the same time India's state boundaries are redrawn to create better balanced political units ("Each State Same Heft"). They thus propose a radical reorganization—they rightly call it a "rational reorganization"—of a divided India into a united Bhārat. Their proposed map of seventy-five states, each sending a dozen or so representatives to the Lok Sabha, would promote responsive politics while retarding linguistic chauvinism and other forms of identitarian division. Desiraju and Bhattacharya present a lucid case for constitutional renewal that should be read by every practically minded political reformer. This book is a comprehensive blueprint for constitutional renewal and is highly recommended.'

Salvatore Babones, Associate Professor, University of Sydney

'The struggle to reclaim democracy in the Indian *ganrājya* will remain a non-starter without an understanding of historical context and current realities. The discourse must also acknowledge and tackle the "ontological monopoly", as the authors call it, that the West holds over these terms. Similarly, a recognition of "neocolonial ideological vestige(s)" that define Western conceptions of democracy and institutional functioning as undebatable universalisms is required, for without challenging such dogmas a truly workable solution will remain a non-starter. The delimitation exercise, on hold for nearly fifty years, will unleash a torrent of discussions and debates, marked more by cacophony than reason. This book is an important contribution to ensuring the imminent discourse is marked by a modicum of knowledge and understanding. It deserves to be read and discussed widely.'

Abhinav Agarwal, author

'This book describes the transition of civilizational Bhārat into the nation-state of India after a hiatus of several centuries. However, this is work in progress, for while the edifice of democracy has worked and India has seen elected governments change at regular intervals both at the centre and in the states, there are two major fault lines of our democratic process—the differential value of each individual vote and the asymmetry among states which constitute the Union of India. Desiraju and Bhattacharya point out that "one person one vote" does not, ipso facto, translate into "each vote same value" for the value of a vote in Kerala is 1.8 times that of a voter in Rajasthan. With eighty seats in the Lok Sabha, UP exercises unparalleled heft in the political economy of the country. The freeze on delimitation from 1976 has aggravated both these issues, but hopefully, if after the next census, a delimitation exercise is undertaken, the authors propose that India should be reorganized into seventy-five states "de novo" to ensure that the value of each vote and the power of each state in the affairs of the Union replicate to the extent possible the provisions of Article 81(2), which states that (a) there shall be allotted to each state a number of seats in the House of the People in such manner that the ratio between that number and the population of the state is, so far as practicable, the same for all states; and (b) each state shall be divided into territorial constituencies in such manner that the ratio between the population of each constituency and the number of seats allotted to it is, so far as practicable, is the same throughout the state. So even if the authors' call for the restructuring of Bhārat into seventy-five states may appear slightly farfetched, there is substantial merit in their argument, and it is certainly an issue that needs to be pondered over and discussed at length if we want our democracy to be as deep, effective, meaningful, and civilizational as we want it to be!'

Sanjeev Chopra, author

'India is embarking on a much-delayed census shortly, which will be the base for a statutory delimitation exercise that will redefine politics and political power in India. With north India having a higher share of total population now compared to the south, political power will shift more to the Hindi belt due to increased seats in Parliament "punishing" the south for its higher growth and a better educated low fertility population. Further, 33 per cent of the increased seats will be reserved for women, dramatically expanding their role in Parliament. The bigger issue will be the shift of political power to urban areas from rural areas with urban and semi-urban areas getting possibly around 50 per cent of the increased seats from around 21 per cent based on the 1991 census. This will also impact the seats in the state legislatures with urban areas gaining massively. All these factors will reshape the future of our democracy and political power. Some states with a huge population are increasingly becoming ungovernable too. In this new book, the authors examine this issue in depth, question the need for large states, and ask for a redefinition and modernization of the entire political structure in India.'

T.V. Mohandas Pai, Chairman, Aarin Capital Partners

'A thought-provoking and lucid read by Gautam ji and Deekhit. India needs more states to be better governed, as some of them are rather large and unwieldy. At the same time, considerations of the fine line between healthy and diverse subnationalisms and anti-dharma activism have to be kept in mind; in this manuscript, they have been. This may not be the last word on the topic, perhaps, but certainly one of the most eloquent beginnings.'

Harsh Madhusudan, author

'*Delimitation and States Reorganization: For a Better Democracy in Bhārat* by Gautam R. Desiraju and Deekhit Bhattacharya is a groundbreaking book that offers a compelling vision for reimagining Bhārat's democratic structure through nationwide delimitation of constituencies and state boundaries. The authors present a masterly analysis of Bhārat's unique civilizational democracy, challenging Western notions of liberal democracy and advocating for a system that better reflects Bhārat's cultural and historical context. The book aims to address longstanding imbalances in Bhārat's electoral system and governance by proposing smaller, more uniform states and equitable representation. The Desiraju and Bhattacharya proposals for "Each Vote Same Value" and "Each State Same Heft" offer a roadmap for transforming Bhārat's political landscape to ensure fair representation and effective governance. This book is essential reading for anyone interested in Bhārat's democratic future and the evolution of governance in civilizational states.'

Abhijit Chavda, podcaster

'*Delimitation and States Reorganization: For a Better Democracy in Bhārat* is the latest and a welcome addition to a growing body of literature exploring various aspects of the Indian democracy from a civilizational standpoint. For a book of a comparatively small size, it packs in an impressive wealth of technical information and a well-thought-out analysis on an area that is often overlooked in mainstream discourse. It powerfully argues for a new approach and stresses on the need for delimitation and reorganization of states in view of the developments more than seventy years after India attained independence. The authors have delved in detail about the hasty and reckless manner in which India's states were "created" on the basis of languages in the 1950s even as India was preparing for democracy. It makes for painful and alarming reading, but it is a warning that couldn't have come at a better time. Desiraju and Bhattacharya also make a compelling case for reorganizing the Indian Union into about seventy-five smaller states using a wealth of data, statistics, precedents, and gleanings from our cultural heritage. Overall, this book is a valuable contribution to both an assessment and a reassessment of the manner in which we think about Indian democracy. It challenges long-held myths and opens up new avenues for reform.'

Sandeep Balakrishna, author and founder, *The Dharma Dispatch*

'This book is a great addition to the discourse on modern India in light of political developments in 2024. The ideal model of governance is one of the toughest codes to crack. This book uses examples from our past and present to show how the more decentralized India becomes the easier it will be to govern. With an asymmetry of populations and fertility rates, how can we achieve the objective of "Each State Same Heft"? The book insists that unless each Indian state has a similar population, we can never achieve our desired goal of "Each Vote Same Value". The book makes you think hard about what are the potential problems that face India in light of demographic spread and offers some unique solutions for the same.'

Kushal Mehra, author and podcaster

'Gautam Desiraju and Deekhit Bhattacharya make a compelling argument for uniform state sizes and equal representation in order to remove disparities in how states like Uttarakhand and Bihar are treated by the Union. An important work on moving the dialogue forward on how to effectively manage a country as large as India.'

Arun Krishnan, author, the Vathapi trilogy

Delimitation and States Reorganization

For a Better Democracy in Bharat

Gautam R. Desiraju
and
Deekhit Bhattacharya

ink | OCCAM

Copyright © 2025 Gautam R. Desiraju and Deekhit Bhattacharya

Gautam R. Desiraju and Deekhit Bhattacharya assert their rights under the Indian Copyright Act to be identified as the authors of this work.

All rights reserved under the copyright conventions. No part of this publication may be reproduced or transmitted in any form or by any means, electronic or mechanical, including photocopying, recording or any information storage or retrieval system, without the prior permission in writing from the publisher.

This book is solely the responsibility of the author(s) and the publisher has had no role in the creation of the content and does not have responsibility for anything defamatory or libellous or objectionable.

BluOne Ink Pvt. Ltd does not have any control over, or responsibility for, any third-party websites referred to in this book. All internet addresses given in this book were correct at the time of going to press. The author and publisher regret any inconvenience caused if addresses have changed or sites have ceased to exist, but can accept no responsibility for any such changes.

ISBN: 978-93-6547-842-6

First published in India 2025
This edition published 2025

BluOne Ink Pvt. Ltd
A-76, 2nd Floor, Sector 136, Noida
Uttar Pradesh 201301
www.bluone.ink
publisher@bluone.ink

Printed and bound in India by Thomson Press India Ltd.

Kali and Occam are imprints of BluOne Ink Pvt. Ltd.

ink | OCCAM

To the silent voters of Bhārat

Contents

सत्यमेव जयते

Dr Murli Manohar Joshi
Former National President, Bharatiya Janata Party
Padma Vibhushan Awardee

A NOTE ON DELIMITATION AND STATES REORGANIZATION

In their latest book, 'Delimitation and States Reorganization' the authors Gautam R. Desiraju and Deekhit Bhattacharya, taking a clue from science and realizing that Bharata is a civilizational state and is a complex system, aver and argue that electoral delimitation and states reorganization must be held simultaneously so that "Each Vote Same Value" and "Each State same Heft" can be achieved without continuous political interference. The authors on purely mathematical grounds, conclude that the states of Bharat must be roughly of the same size to obtain true economic and political democracy.

Without social and economic democracy, political democracy had no meaning therefore, from political democracy, we must progress to economic democracy which "means working for a certain measure of equality of opportunity in the economic sphere". The concept embodied in our Preamble assures equality of status and opportunity, which incorporates all the legal, social, political and economic aspects. All citizens are equally entitled to enjoy the political rights to vote and participate in the process of governance without any distinction. The concept of equality of status and opportunity has been given concrete substance and shape in the constitution.

Members like Shri Kamalapati Tripathi regretted that draft had drawn inspiration mainly from foreign Constitutions alone and had not cared to cast even a glance at the historic spirit and culture of India and its approach towards life. Many other members were unhappy with this draft as the draft Constitution did not in the least pay attention to the political philosophy and situation of this ancient country, Several members were disappointed to find that the draft constitution did not reflect Gandhi's views regarding the rural India and Panchayati Raj and decentralization of power to the last man in the ladder.

Former Union Minister Govt. of India : • Home Affairs • Human Resource Development • Science & Technology • Ocean Development
Former Chairman : • Public Accounts Committee • Estimates Committee

6, Raisina Road, New Delhi - 110001 Tel. : (011) 23718444, 23326080 Fax : (011) 23711772 email : murli@sansad.nic.in

It was young Deendayal Upadhyaya who, though, at that time was not associated with any political party, wrote an article pointing out that the draft suffered from a fundamental deficiency as it did not reflect the civilizational consciousness of Bharat. He also suggested that a commission be appointed for reorganizing the map of the states. It may be of interest to note that Bharatiya Jana Sangh with Pt. Deendayal Upadhyaya as its founding General Secretary adopted a resolution in its very first plenary session (1952) suggesting the reorganization of the proposed adhoc provincial units (states) into smaller autonomous administrative units (Janpad) based on administrative, economic, developmental and security considerations. The Vajpayee government. did carved out three states viz. Uttarakhand, Jharkhand and Chhattisgarh on this principle.

If may be recognized that the ancient Indian thinkers believed that the problems of democratic republican polity were essentially moral. Democracy to use an idiom of "mathematics" is a function of various factors, a resuscitation of so many variables. The most important quality needed for democratic functioning of a society is to have strong moral fiber and a firm belief in the fundamental equality of all human beings, and respect for other opinions and tolerance.

Emphasizing the urgency for creating an ethical democratic society Jayaprakash Narayan (JP) had said that a word that figures boldly on the ancient sign post is Dharma. Indian polity held that the State was subject to the Dharma, and it was its duty to uphold and protect Dharma. He also believed that unless life in India is again organized on the basis of Dharma democracy will remain distantly removed from the life of the people.

In JP's Opinion the problem of devising the right kind of polity was obviously a part of the larger problem of social reconstruction. The task also is one of social engineering, needing the help of the State; of scientists, experts, educationists, businessmen, experimenters, of men and women, young and old. It is a task of dedication; of creation; of self-discovery. It is a task that defines India's destiny. It spells a challenge to India's sons and daughters. Will they accept the challenge?

There is no doubt that channels of representation of the commons in the political affairs were not only prescribed in the Indic law books but also put into practice by polities. Altekar observes: It should, however, be noted that our ancient Indian constitutional thinkers had advocated and brought about an extensive decentralization of government functions and powers by investing village councils, town committees and district boroughs with a very wide administrative powers and functions.

According to R.S. Sharma, Panini's Ashṭadhyayi, gives an exhaustive account of the republics, their functioning, their locations, and above all their characteristic typology, has no parallel.

Burton Stein has stated that, the peasant societies of medieval South India are more ancient, durable and, yes, elegant than most in the world.

Recently, Dr. Jitendra Bajaj has drawn my attention. The Chola Inscription Kulottunga I ry 19 AD 1089, which records a sale of 200 kuli of waste land and a quarter of a house-site to the temple of Sri Rajendrachola-vinnagar alvar at Sri Rajendrachola-chaturvedimangalam, a taniyur of Kaliyur-kottam in Jayangondachola-mandalam, by the perunkuri-sabha of the village. this inspiration brings out a very important aspect of the power and functioning of the sabha. Since the lands sold were to be converted to a flower-garden with the same Kulottunga-Cholan, the sabha decided not to levy any tax on the lands made it tax-free. Those who ignored the decision should incur the wrath of brahmadeya and the tirukkulam. Even after this if the king's officers tried to exact the taxes, the sabha itself would pay the same. This indicates that the Sabha enjoyed high degree of autonomy.

In sum, it may be suggested that so far as channels of political representation in the State affairs were concerned, micro-region continued to occupy central stage in Vijayanagara.

This exhibits the expression of dissent by the commons which is the hallmark of modern democracy, and also indicates that the republican spirit and character of the Indian people continue to survive despite they were at times subjected to the autocratic/monarchical/imperialistic rule.

In this backdrop, the present book demands that modern Bharata should formulate its polity that best suits her civilizational consciousness as proud members of the millennia old civilization and play its destined role in the modern world.

In my opinion. This book has provided a roadmap which needs a serious discussion at various levels by the intelligent opinion makes of all hues and shades of this country. Such literature is the need of the hour, for which I congratulate the authors.

Dr. Murli Manohar Joshi

New Delhi
15th December, 2024

Preface

Bhārat, the world's largest democracy, concluded its largest ever election (to date) in 2024, with 64.2 out of a possible 96.88 crore voters exercising their franchise in seven phases of voting stretching across six weeks. Counting was swift and completed in a day. The results were declared using the first-past-the-post system. The National Democratic Alliance (NDA) obtained a historic third consecutive mandate, securing a comfortable majority in the Lok Sabha with its major constituent, the Bharatiya Janata Party (BJP), obtaining 240 seats in the 543-member lower house with a 36.5 per cent vote share. Indians take the democratic exercise seriously, and the general election of 2024 was no exception. Political equations were dissolved and recrystallized over the course of the elections and later, representing the myriad thoughts which animate the country's political life.

Bhārat is a civilizational state that respects differences and tolerates them, imbued with a core of spiritual fraternity based on *dharma* (not to be conflated with the much narrower concept of religion) that enables debates on the meaning of words like 'liberty' and 'equality'. Although the history of India during the past 500 or so years has been chequered and unfortunate, Bhārat has comfortably entered the comity of mature democracies today, and it is an object lesson for other democracies, even those in the Americas and Western Europe. In a recent statement, the US White House has said that there are 'not too many more vibrant democracies in the world than India'.[1]

No two democracies are exactly the same. One size does not fit all. No country is as diverse as Bhārat. Democracy here is ever improving because the country respects and tolerates all manner of differences. This parallels the essence of Indian philosophy, which is rooted in dharmic thought, which embodies the universal timeless principle of cosmic order, *Rta*. This really is the true origin of democracy in this country.

Yet 'One Person One Vote', or put differently, 'Each Vote Same Value', is the fundamental principle on which all democracies are based. This fundamental principle was embedded in the Indian Constitution adopted on 26 January 1950. However, deviations from this principle have taken place. A strange set of political circumstances have resulted in the sizes of parliamentary and assembly constituencies remaining largely fixed for fifty years. Delimitation has essentially been frozen for half a century.

Possibly because population has increased with different rates in different states, each vote in Kerala is now worth nearly 1.8 votes in Rajasthan, while each vote in Tamil Nadu is equivalent to 1.6 votes in Bihar.[2] Similarly, a vote in Andhra Pradesh, Odisha, and Telangana is worth more than one in Delhi, Haryana, Madhya Pradesh, and Uttar Pradesh. Each state is not the same in these matters. These aberrations have not attracted attention either in India or abroad. Unequal representation seems to have gone unnoticed because, by and large, the states getting extra representation are on the whole better educated and more affluent. This is the so-called north–south divide, the dangers of which had been identified as early as in 1955 by Dr B.R. Ambedkar, the chairman of the drafting committee of the Indian Constitution. The south and the west on the whole seem to be ahead of the east and the north in matters of the economy.

While unequal representation is not new in evolving democracies, the redrawing of constituencies, or delimitation, is always controversial, accompanied as it usually is by allegations of gerrymandering. However, the exercise is always carried out in democracies at regular intervals as the population changes—India has been the exception. The country also needs a census badly, and this has not been held since 2011.

Delimitation for us is closely linked to parity in the way the Union of India deals with its constituent states, especially in matters concerning economics. Ideally, no state should be more or less important in the eyes of the Union. 'Each State Same Heft' should be the principle. If the populations of the states are more or less comparable, it will solve two refractory problems almost simultaneously. The representation of each state in Parliament would be nearly the same, and delimitation would become a smooth, ongoing exercise independent of which political party is in power at the Centre. The manner in which any state interacts with the Centre would become nearly the same, and there would be no question of some states dominating the national discourse, in effect heightening the inequality between them. The idea of smaller states is not new. However, systematic discussions as to why states ought to be uniformly small have been few and far between, with links to constituency delimitation not explored. Simultaneously, a number of pressing economic issues arise from the way the country is politically organized, in terms of both efficiency and equity.

The proposals contained in this book do not concern themselves with the political party or coalition gracing the country's administration at any point in time. In this sense, this book is not about politics. The imperfections and the inherent inaccuracies of the delimitation status quo has punished and favoured many, if not all, sides of the political divide quite capriciously. Regrettably, these imbalances have come to impose inequities of all sorts on the people of the country by distorting their true electoral choices—and all that follows. The proposals contained herein pertain to a healthy constitutional and institutional functioning of Bhārat, for democratic choices to reflect accurately in its electoral system without fear or favour, and where each citizen can genuinely have an equal say. Each citizen must have the same say as any other citizen, and each state must have the same say as any other state.

This book deals with the idea that only if constituency delimitation is taken up along with reorganization of state boundaries would the whole effort lead to a coherent reality. In other words, we are suggesting a nationwide delimitation of constituencies along with a nationwide delimitation of the state boundaries themselves. This, in our view, would be a workable answer to one of the serious challenges that face the presently elected NDA government. Execution of these goals would lay the ground for a completely fair electoral procedure and governance system in the years to come.

CHAPTER I

What Is Democracy?

'The job of a citizen is to keep his mouth open.'

—Günter Grass

Democracy, at its simplest, is any system of collective governance adopted by people who would like their individual views to contribute to the way in which they are governed. It is trite to mention the etymology of the term as arising from the Greek *demos* meaning village or people and *kratos* meaning rule, but the origins of democracy probably stretch far before the time of the ancient Greeks. As humans assembled in small agglomerations or the earliest villages, they would have appreciated that there were some issues, such as scarcity of food, security of hearth and home, and fear of natural calamities. In such cases, it would become necessary for them to act as a group if they were to cope with an otherwise 'nasty, brutish, and short' life per Thomas Hobbes.[1] To preserve their individual interests and their families, however, they would also have begun to realize that there would need to be some measure of notional parity amongst them, at least to an extent that the opinion of an individual would be considered by the group. Societies which would provide some sort of system where the views of all are at least voiced would heighten the collective survival of all, since useful ideas may emerge from unlikely quarters, and each person would be able to give a fitting perspective based on what she or he specialized in. One hesitates to use the word 'equality' in this context because the mathematical rigour of this word is scarcely applicable to complex social issues and hierarchies, pertaining to interactions between people and the way in which an individual gives up a part of his will for the larger good of the group.

Why Democracy?

All societies need some method of sorting through the opinions of individuals and the sundry pressure groups or factions that proliferate political life. Democracy, with its countless manifestations across history, serves this purpose well.[2] Giving some say and a modicum of political participation to identified members of a society, that is, citizens, allows a society to maintain cohesion while navigating the pressures emerging from individuals, families, tribes, clans, and various other groups. A successful counterbalance to potential secession or anarchy from factions which are able to achieve enough traction to destabilize society would have been to introduce some measure of balance in considering the opinions and wishes of individuals and groups.[3] In essence, democracy is simply a convenient umbrella term for mechanisms which allow citizens and their groupings to have some systematic say in the governance of their society.

Democracy, through the innumerable iterations with which it has persisted, also has a more evolutionary effect. Apart from being effective in preventing grievances from snowballing into civil wars, democracy serves two very important functions. Firstly, as societies and their contexts evolve, the power of social groupings over society waxes and wanes.[4] Historically, priests have given way to warriors, who in turn were followed by landlord aristocrats. Then, businessmen displaced the aristocracy, and today we see a fugue or a point–counterpoint between professional politicians and big business worldwide. Each of these transitions and the conflicts they spawned could only be managed through systems which provided a negotiatory forum between power groups, while reflecting the changes occurring in society. Democracy as a means of facilitating socioeconomic transitions without enforcing stagnation or giving in to irredeemable fission has been responsible for the successes of many nations, including the United Kingdom. We will address this idea later in this chapter.

Secondly, there is a long-term link between democracy and innovation. At an intuitive level, giving a voice to everyone would allow a far greater range of ideas to reach the rest of the group, which would enable the group to consider courses of action which would otherwise be unfathomable. Democracy evolves and abhors statism simply because humans are adaptive animals. Democratic forms of governance lead to institutions that are inclusive in nature, mirroring the inclusivity inherent in the institution of democracy itself. Inclusive institutions are those that allow and encourage participation by the bulk of the populace in economic activities that make the best use of their talents and skills roughly in accordance with their choices. This was one of the founding principles of the USA in 1776. These inclusive institutions enable inclusive markets, and inclusive markets foster competition—a prerequisite for sustained innovation.[5] It is also not difficult to see why democratic political systems lead to innovation-friendly economic institutions such as secure private property, a working legal system which accords sanctity to promises,[6] and public services. Back of the envelope calculations confirm this hypothesis—democracy measures such as V-Dem and the Economist Intelligence Unit's Democracy Index have a generally positive relationship with many measures of innovation, including the Global Innovation Index, resident patent applications per million of population, and expenditure on research and development.[7]

What Is Democracy?

Democracy has come to mean various things to various people over the course of history, but inherent to it is the assumption that an individual has some sort of say in how she or he is governed within a group. However, from the very beginning, it must have been apparent to individuals in small agglomerations that they would need to, for practical reasons, vest power in one of their group, possibly a stronger or more authoritative person with an ability to hold people together. Such a person was endowed with the responsibility to maintain the essential concerns of the group, especially during difficult times brought about by issues such as food scarcity, aggression by enemies, or acts of God. From the earliest days, therefore, all were not strictly equal. This procedure in which one person was designated as the first among equals would imply some kind of choice or *election* by the people or by a subsection thereof (such as the elders of tribes), of a chieftain, progressing to a minor king or *rājan* as the agglomeration grew in size. As numbers in a population swelled, they required some system of having intermediaries who would elect the chieftain for them. In most circumstances, the elders of the tribe would represent their families and designate or advise the chief. The election is, therefore, a basic conjoint to any democracy and is a form of linking the individual with the nation, and other groupings within it.

One notices that the Vedic people evolved political systems, which were tightropes between the various groups within the society and the demands of the times they lived in. Before they established towns or, in other words, when they were pastoral people, the *rājan* was a republican figure who had to symbolically display a notional equality vis-à-vis the priesthood (i.e., Brahmins), the officer corps (i.e., Kshatriyas), and the common folk (i.e., Vaishyas). So much so, that before a war, the *rājan* and Kshatriyas had to affirm the notional equality of all members of the tribe by breaking bread in the same plate with the common folk. As society became more settled, sophisticated, and even hierarchical, the now monarchical *rājan* was still required to balance power groups and maintain democratic political elements. The later Vedic era, as shown by passages in the later mandalas of the *Rigveda* and the *Atharvaveda*, had a fourfold system of councils. The Sabhā had tribal elders and select advisors stationed within the palatial compound as a check on the *rājan*. The Samiti, a much broader body, was a folk assembly where common folk would transact business and deal with the priesthood for communal rituals. Most importantly, the *rājan* had to be elected and re-elected by the Samiti, even if this was done symbolically. The Vidatha was an even broader body, in which commoner women too had the right of participation and could transact all sorts of social, economic, and military business. The Gana was a special purpose body, which was an assembly of men ready to wage war, and was formed only prior to armed action. The Gana would thus centralize an otherwise decentralized system and is somewhat analogous to the governance system of countries during a declared emergency. The Vedic age also required re-election campaigns; yajnas such as the *rājasuya* were required to be performed by a *rājan* to prove his suitability for the role. Even when society had ossified on the lines of *jāti* and with the *rājan* at the helm of an absolutist system, democratic traditions continued in a muted and sometimes morphed version. The Mauryans and Guptas sanctioned and devolved power to various guilds and bodies, each of which had democratic elements and self-governance. Towns had municipalities with elected representatives, and villages evolved similar systems. Many of these systems, in some shape or form, survive to this day. Thus, even as contexts changed, the principle of democracy remained embedded within Bhāratiya society, until it was irretrievably disturbed by foreign invaders.

As one progresses towards larger and more powerful kingdoms and empires, the ideas of democracy, and also republicanism, become more sophisticated. Two examples become particularly important: the city state of Athens in ancient Greece and the Mauryan Empire in India. Fascinatingly, Swami Vivekananda has outlined how two different streams of political thought emanated from these two ancient civilizations which were, in a sense, related. He said in a meeting in Triplicane, Madras, in 1896, 'Two curious nations there have been—sprung of the same race, but placed in different circumstances and environments, working out the problems of life each in its own particular way. I mean the ancient Hindu and the ancient Greek.'[8]

Both these societies made a conscious choice to enshrine the principle of representation in their governance systems. It is unlikely that there was much communication between Athens and Pataliputra initially—the sheer geographical separation would have precluded this. Therefore, neither society borrowed these concepts from the other until the advent of Alexander on the banks of the Indus.[9] Yet, the fact that similar democratic impulses existed in both places suggests that these are fundamental instincts in a matured society. The Greek city states had a multitude of representative bodies throughout their histories, each embodying varying metrics of responsibilities and eligibilities. Even the relatively more militaristic and oligarchic Sparta had systems of representative governance. We see here the early intersection of a democracy and a republic. The very concept of a written constitution had emerged from the need to properly frame the functioning of these bodies, which was heralded by the constitution of Draco (ironically, the person who has lent his name to the term 'draconian'). Bhāratiya principalities were also equally, if not more, interested in experimenting with a mix of hierarchy and representative governance.

Ancient India's ideas of democracy and republicanism were rooted in religion and influenced by communication systems within the country. Republics flourished in regions that were difficult to access and, therefore, not suited to be a part of a bigger monarchy. The unique feature in ancient India was that democracy, republicanism, and monarchy were integrated under the overall canopy of dharma, the universal law, in which they mostly coexisted. The integration of these ideas was unique to ancient India and a result of the common aspirations and inclinations of people in governance. Accordingly, India's systems of governance were flexible, and it was not always necessary or expedient to classify them into silos.

An interesting observation about India's historical experiences with democracy, republicanism, and monarchy is that we tried to shuffle these various forms of government around the same times as other countries. In India, attempts at democracy and republicanism were made approximately between 500 BCE and 100 CE. This corresponds with developments in Greece and Rome during those times. These gave way to different forms of monarchy for about 1,500 years more, similar to what prevailed in the Roman Empire. Clearly, these societies in widely separated parts of the world were economically comparable, for the mode of thinking in any society is primarily governed by its economic condition. Around the same time, trade relations became more frequent between these great civilizations, and each viewed the modalities of the other with curiosity and amazement. Even then, all these various systems would at times coexist to suit the conditions and predilections of peoples; the princely state of Jammu and Kashmir, for example, had a constitutional monarchy in 1947, ensconcing within itself principalities which ranged from tribal councils presided over by chieftains to self-governing republics, hardly having a Westphalian analogue.[10]

The futility of trying to define a principle like democracy through mechanisms within which it may manifest can be seen as follows. As one traces the course of history, we find that concepts such as democracy, monarchy, republicanism, and their variants have a great deal of overlap, and strict definitions are all but impossible. Democracy, in particular, is the government of the people, as Abraham Lincoln has said. People are paramount in any democracy, and the interests of the State are subservient to the wishes of the people. Using the stratagem of the election, democracies in modern times elect small numbers from among themselves to govern them for limited time periods—much like how in statistics a properly picked sample of data from a larger universe approximates the make-up of such a universe. Hence, one arrives at the considerable overlap between a democracy and a republic.[11] Similarly, the institution of a constitutional monarchy introduces elements of overlap between a democracy and a monarchy. When the people, as a principle, are collectively provided primacy over decision-making, it is only natural that the exact mechanism by which they are to determine their choices are also up to the people.[12] The process in which a society slowly transitions from aristocratic modalities of governance to more democratic modalities is unique not only to the vagaries of history but also the varied ways in which a people and constituent individuals conceive themselves. Strict definitions are, at best, conceptual crutches for unique and evolving ways in which a society negotiates its governance over changing times.[13]

In light of the above, it is fallacious to equate democracy with the manner in which certain Western nations manifest democracy in their own workings, because these institutional norms themselves are the outcome of their peculiar arrangements arising from their unique historical and socio-economic experiences. Democracy is what the people and institutions of a particular nation make of their experiences; adjudging whether a country is democratic or not, based on the normative benchmarks of alien peoples is antithetical to democracy itself, considering that such a frame privileges the views of unconnected foreigners over a people attempting to democratically exercise self-determination in how they wish to be governed. Labelling governance systems as inherently illiberal or undemocratic, isolated from the social, economic, and cultural context underlying such systems, is an anti-democratic expression of neocolonial tendencies. What is liberal, and what is democratic, and if a society even finds it worthwhile to label with the appellation of 'liberal', are decisions that are best taken by such societies themselves, engaging their own particular decision-making mechanisms arising from their unique contexts. Thus, what is to be deemed undemocratic or illegal must gain legitimacy from each society's own social discourse, at each society's own terms. Challenging the West's ontological monopoly over terms such as democracy is a necessity for nations to chart their own courses, free of the institutional pressures which attach to the West's conceptualization of political terminology.

How Did Democracy Evolve?

Republicanism appeared in Europe much later than in the old civilizations. It can be seen in Florence during the Renaissance or early modern Britain under Oliver Cromwell's commonwealth. This was perhaps due to the fact that European feudalism was closely related to the way in which European militaries were organized, where standing armies were rare, and feudatories were responsible for the upkeep of troops. The American colonies of Britain broke away from the mother country during the American Revolution of 1776 and formed a federal republic, primarily due to a lack of representation and the economic pitfalls of the same. In many ways, the thirteen colonies which formed the United States were the continuation of the Cromwellian experiment. With the French Revolution in 1789, the idea of the republic was firmly ensconced in contemporary political life, along with the post-enlightenment concept of political equality and a value framework centred around citizens' rights. A similar parallel course was followed by Asia but slightly later due to colonial pauses in the 18th and 19th centuries. Nevertheless, there is no denying that in the 20th century, the English parliament, the US federation, the French Revolution, and Marx's socialism[14] served as constitutional models, inspiring in turn the Chinese republic, the Japanese constitutional monarchy, Ataturk's Turkey, and the Indian freedom movement.

This begs the question as to how the Western democracies evolved into the patterns they now display. For this, one needs to consider the three primary democratic models of the Western world: Britain, the USA, and France. The Western model is important because in one way or another it has become the principal framework for more than half the countries of the world today, the somewhat patronizingly termed 'functional democracies',[15] to fashion their modes of governance. What is lost in the conversation is that liberal democracy, by whatever name it is called, is only a particular methodology of actualizing the democratic principle that has emerged from the peculiar historical, social, and economic issues which the West faced. The idea that the West's conception of democracy and institutional functioning is universally applicable to peoples having distinct temperaments, histories, and needs, and that any other alternative institutional arrangement is anti-democratic, is self-contradictory. It is a neocolonial ideological vestige, a project which is oddly reminiscent of the infamous conception of the white man's burden. India inherited, or shall we say defaulted into, the liberal democratic model simply because of the urge to 'modernize', a term which was once synonymous with adhering to a supposedly superior Western mode of political life and a sentiment paramount in countries that had been colonized or were parts of autocratic monarchies. Unfortunately, and as we see in India today, intellectual colonization long outlasts political colonization.[16]

Liberal Democracies of the West

Modern democracy, or what may also be called 'liberal' democracy, is marketed as a system of government in which power is vested in the people, allowing them to participate in decision-making processes directly or through elected representatives, however constrained, within the ideological rubric of liberalism. This form of government originated in Europe and America over the last 250 years or so and in many ways has been thrust upon the world as a benchmark (implicit at times and enforced by the West through its informational levers at others) for other countries that term themselves democracies. Arguably, its fundamental principles include some measure of equality, freedom of expression within limits, and the protection of individual rights, again within certain limits. Each of these attributes may be qualified from one form of democracy to another, but, in a broad sense, these ideas are adhered to. Democracy, as has been stressed earlier, promotes accountability through regular elections, ensuring that leaders govern with popular consent. Other features of democracies include respect for the rule of law, protection of minority rights, and mechanisms for peaceful conflict resolution, to the extent that all citizens are treated on a level playing field. Overall, democracy fosters civic engagement, pluralism, and the pursuit of common welfare, reflecting diverse voices and fostering a society where citizens have a say in shaping their collective destiny. *Vox populi, vox dei.*[17]

Over the past millennium, the evolution of democracy in the Western world has been a complex and multifaceted process, shaped by historical events, philosophical ideas, and sociopolitical movements. Key milestones in this journey include the Magna Carta in Britain, the French Revolution in France, and the establishment of the American Constitution in the United States. Additionally, the ideas of philosophers like François-Marie Arouet (better known by his nom de plume, Voltaire) have played a significant role in shaping the concept of democracy and individual rights.

The Magna Carta, acceded to by King John of England in 1215, marked an important moment in the development of democracy. It established the principle that the monarch was subject to the law and had to govern according to established customs and rights. While initially a document aimed at protecting the rights of the nobility, the Magna Carta laid the groundwork for the idea that rulers were accountable to their subjects and helped to limit the power of absolute monarchy. It is worth noting that this idea, namely that the king is accountable to his people, was developed in quite a sophisticated way in Bhārat, at least 2,500 years before the Magna Carta.[18] Our scriptures say that both the ruler and the ruled are accountable to a higher power, that is, dharma and the duties of a king towards his people was as much a political task as it was a mode of worship.

Democracy, as it had emerged in the West, was a sort of power-sharing and troubleshooting mechanism between feudal lords. One notices that the history of democracy in continental Europe as well as in the United Kingdom is intimately tied to the internecine feudal warfare which ravaged the continent. With every round of destruction and bloodletting, the surviving lords had to come up with new institutional ideas to reduce the possibility of the war continuing, and to compete on an economic basis instead. The Thirty and Eighty Years' Wars found an end in the Treaty of Westphalia, in which the concept of borders, jurisdictions, and equality of states was enunciated. This treaty, more than any other, limited the power of the Vatican in European affairs and became the harbinger of secularism, through which Caesar broke free from the shackles of the Pope. With the resultant relief obtained, the empires of Europe were able to progress because they could develop scientifically and venture into new worlds across the oceans, leading ultimately to their rapid economic growth.

Britain's constitutional history has undergone significant transformation, evolving from an autocratic monarchy to a liberal democracy over the past 1,000 or so years.[19] Following the Magna Carta, further developments established limitations on royal authority and laid the groundwork for the rule of law. The English Civil War of the 17th century resulted in the execution of King Charles I and paved the way for the Glorious Revolution of 1688, which led to the establishment of parliamentary supremacy and constitutional monarchy.[20] Slowly, the House of Commons gained preponderance over the House of Lords, and by the early 20th century, the latter was reduced to a ceremonial body. The gradual expansion of suffrage, the development of political parties, and reforms such as the Reform Acts of the 19th century further democratized the system. Today, Britain is a liberal democracy with a constitutional monarchy, characterized arguably by the rule of law, representative government, and protection of individual rights.

The French Revolution of 1789 was another pivotal event in the evolution of liberal democracy as it challenged the entrenched power of the monarchy and aristocracy. The revolutionaries espoused principles of liberty, equality, and fraternity, leading to the overthrow of the monarchy and the establishment of the First French Republic. The Declaration of the Rights of Man and of the Citizen, inspired by Enlightenment ideals, proclaimed the rights of individuals and laid the foundation for modern democratic principles. Unlike the British, who were more concerned with the management of their immediate feudal lords and changes in the economy, the French chose to prioritize a set of values based on the concept of natural rights, that is, rights which accrue to man simply due to the fact that they are men. Accordingly, they held that these values were universal in nature.

Simultaneously, in the United States, the American Revolution and the subsequent drafting of that constitution in 1787 led to the creation of a democratic republic. The US Constitution established a system of government with checks and balances, dividing power between the executive, legislative, and judicial branches, and enshrined principles of popular sovereignty and individual rights.[21] This document has become the blueprint for many constitutions of democracies all over the world, and its importance is of the first magnitude. It stresses an 'American Dream' that goes far beyond the pursuit of happiness and economic well-being in that it envisages a world populated by a better type of human being. The Bhārat of yore seems to have arrived at this idea too in the form of the Upanishads that cover the entire gamut of human behaviour and experience and even more, rather than being specific to any age, country, or circumstance.

Jean-Jacques Rousseau, a key figure of the Enlightenment, played a central role in shaping modern democratic thought with his ideas on the social contract and the sovereignty of the people. Rousseau argued that legitimate political authority arises from the consent of the governed and that individuals have inherent rights that must be protected by the State. His emphasis on the primacy of the individual and the collective will of the people laid the groundwork for liberal democracy in the West, influencing subsequent political thinkers and movements. In this context, the Enlightenment emphasizes and promotes individualism to such an extent that in its high noon in the 20th century it led to the delegitimization, or even decimation itself, of society as an entity, including traditional family structures and values. The West is yet to devise any system as stable and sound as the one it had replaced, even as it emphatically advocates for Enlightenment and post-Enlightenment values to be imposed on others, by force if necessary.[22]

In summary, the evolution of democracy in the Western world over the last 1,000 years has been characterized by a gradual expansion of individual rights and freedoms, guided by key historical events, legal documents, and philosophical ideas. These have now been rendered dogmatic, practically shaping these sets of values into a religion unto itself, and the total economic domination of the world by the West over the last 100 years has made it arrogant and supercilious towards all those that it does not deem as being like it.

Typically, the so-called liberal West has had its own ways of evaluating democracies and has liked to propagate the idea that its version of democracy, a kind of 'Christianized' (of the Protestant variety) democracy[23] in which one places individual rights above all else, is the best form of democracy. The critic would argue that today's liberal democracy of the West has degenerated into wokeness and also into a crude bypassing of the fact that other countries, who also call themselves democracies, might have evolved forms of governance that are not to the complete liking of the West. Wokeness itself is the logical end of zealousness for the individual and his supposedly innate right to be completely unrestrained from the evil known as the community, its institutions, or nature itself, and the West continues in its relentless quest to convert the world to this new creed through all means necessary. The Western liberal is usually the most illiberal.

The trite demarcation of the world as the First, Second, and Third Worlds during the Cold War era seems absurd today. The First World, the so-called 'free' world, was supposedly the democratic ideal. In reality, it was just a euphemism for an economic scheme wherein the USA and its vassals, the G7 of today, held the world in a stranglehold. We may call this economic scheme the Amerisphere. The so-called Second World, supposedly groaning under the Soviet jackboot, was defined as having no democracy at all, but it was deemed a dangerous adversary. So clearly, the West recognized that their form of democracy was not the only way to achieve global power and hegemony. The only thing they felt they might have had that the Second World did not was a kind of 'moral' superiority, whatever that might have meant. The so-called Third World of those times, now politely referred to as the Global South, is an equally meaningless term.[24] This group, containing the poorest nations in the world, were supposed to 'behave themselves' within the so-called 'rules-based order' of the West, in their attempts to become more like the First World. How they were supposed to do this in an economic system that was severely skewed towards the rich Amerisphere is hard to fathom. The United Nations, a creation of the Amerisphere, became populated with experts from the Third World who were paid the highest of First World salaries to 'study' their poor countries and prepare bulky reports about why they stayed poor. Ranging from the excesses of Pinochet's 'Chicago boys'[25] to the architects of the 'shock therapy' which followed the Soviet Union's dissolution,[26] the outcomes of such 'expert' interventions have had a chequered past.

Going against this scheme of things, the two most populated countries in the world who also belonged to this so-called Third World, figured out their own way to finesse themselves economically upwards and are now projected to be among the top three world economies by 2030. Apparently, this is not to the liking of the West, and they now term one of them an electoral autocracy and the other a closed autocracy. China under Deng Xiaoping broke through economically in the 1980s, and so did India under P.V. Narasimha Rao after 1991. However, India remained in a mezzanine state, where the reform impetus which was forced by the country's bankruptcy petered out with complacency, excess, and apathy. The next systemic revamp came with Narendra Modi on 18 May 2014, a day which the *Guardian* newspaper has referred to as the date when the British finally left India.[27] In this spirit, India is more accurately called Bhārat after this date.

Labelling other countries according to value judgements that prioritize some criteria that are found in Western democracies alone, the Amerisphere tries to impose some kind of 'moral' authority with respect to modes of governance. This is a futile attempt to establish their above-mentioned 'rules-based order', in which the rules are Western, the base of such determination is Western, and the order is that which the West prefers. To this end, there are a number of think tanks in the West that keep issuing rebukes and diktats couched in reports at frequent intervals, rating various countries according to what they believe are ideal democratic credentials. Take, for example, the Gothenburg based V-Dem Institute which, according to its Democracy Report 2024, categorizes India as an 'electoral autocracy'. This body categorizes countries into four regime types based on their 'score' in the Liberal Democratic Index (LDI). Naturally, if a system is parameterized in a particular way, it will only yield outputs that are in consonance with the input parameters, that is, one can decide what outcome to have first, and then simply pick parameters which can justify such a pre-decided outcome.[28] An easy way to understand this through an example is by taking the case of how Sri Lanka was outshining India in most socio-economic indicators per the 'experts', until of course it went belly up and had to depend on its poorly rated northern neighbour for survival.[29] According to V-Dem, governments are, in descending order, liberal democracies, electoral democracies, electoral autocracies, and closed autocracies. To this end, India has been consigned to the third category. This is apparently justified because, according to V-Dem, freedom of expression, clean elections, and freedom of association are compromised here. Perhaps V-Dem is unaware of our nightly television jousts which are inaccurately termed debates, or of the constant political churn on Indian social media. In general, the manner in which our recent general election was conducted, the largely free and fair nature of the exercise, the fact that not a single candidate in the 543 constituencies was murdered during the process, and the fact that all the political parties involved, whether winners or losers, accepted the verdict of the citizens calmly and without demur, hardly suggest that Bhārat is anything other than a mature democracy.

V-Dem claims that liberal democracies are the most ideal because in addition to free and fair elections, which are enjoyed by electoral democracies too, they have robust mechanisms for judicial independence and constraints on executive overreach, along with rigorous protection of civil liberties and equality before law. Apparently, these features are not present in India. Consideration of the matter will, however, demonstrate that the above contentions are ill-founded. If anything, India is a country where irate politicians run to courts instead of running in elections.

It is interesting to compare the Indian Constitution with others in the world. According to the Comparative Constitutions Project, developed at the University of Texas at Austin and the University of Chicago, we do not rank that high in the level of executive power conferred by the constitution. France, Poland, Russia, Spain, and Thailand, on the other hand, figure very high in this respect. Executive power can lead to executive overreach, and an objective determination indicates that this is not a real danger in India. Judicial independence supposedly ranks very high in liberal democracies, but the Comparative Constitutions Project states that our judiciary is distinctly more powerful than that in the US. What is indeed impressive is the level of judicial independence in India. The country ranks alongside Argentina, Brazil, Italy, and a few other countries, raising questions as to the limits of judicial independence's utility. Also of note is that most of our legislation is subject to judicial review. In terms of individual liberties, the scope and breadth of our fundamental rights is truly impressive, and the all-important Article 32 gives a citizen the right to appeal to a court if (s)he feels that these rights are being transgressed upon. In summary, even if we are termed an electoral autocracy, ours is a reasonable constitution if it is compared with the constitutions of liberal democracies.

Electoral Democracy: India as a Unique Experiment

From the first Lok Sabha election in 1952 in which 489 seats were allotted across 401 constituencies, right up till the eighteenth general election in 2024 in which 543 members have been sent to the lower house, the Indian citizen has been smart about how (s)he votes. Circumstances have changed considerably over the last seventy-two years. The early years of our democracy saw a nation impoverished by 150 years of British rule. The international community doubted whether India was even capable of maintaining a democratic form of government considering her poverty levels. India demonstrated convincingly even in those hard times that democracy is not a luxury of the rich.

The period between 1967 and 2014 was one of uncertainty, experimentation, and hesitation. The various ruling dispensations during this interregnum, whether they were of a single-party type or a coalition, were always trying to balance the competing pulls of the rich, the middle class, and the underprivileged sections of a bewilderingly diverse society living in a huge country and struggling under an overall shroud of poverty and disentitlement. This was the period disparagingly referred to as having the 'Hindu growth rate'. This balancing of interests was almost never successful, and it was easier for politicians to become corrupt. Crass political considerations often ruled the roost. The country was held to ransom by a gaggle of regional, linguistic parties that propagated dynastic rule. There was a refreshing inflection point in 2014 brought about by an election in which the contradictions of the governing regime were too many to sustain it any longer. Fortunately, the modern post-2014 Bhārat has become at least aspirational, if not yet affluent. It remains to be seen if these trends continue after the 2024 election.

Through all these phases the largely disadvantaged Indian voter was always considering various options while also realizing that (s)he might have little contact with the person elected for a full five years, given the huge sizes of our parliamentary constituencies. The landmark elections of 1971, 1977, and 2014 have shown that even without stressing the importance of the individual in the strident manner the liberal democracies of the West do, the Indian voter has demonstrated adequately the power of the vote—exactly the same for each and every eligible voter. If 1971 and 2014 were decisive mandates for a strong ruler—almost a presidential election—1977 showed what happens when the strong ruler exceeds her brief. The 2024 election has shown that the electorate can re-elect a ruler but place some constraints on him. As always, the voter is the king.

This is nothing short of remarkable and testifies to the acumen and savvy of the Indian voter. The Nigerian author Chinua Achebe has said that a functioning, robust democracy requires a healthy, educated, participatory followership.[30] India shows that the degree of health and education in our country is at least at the level where meaningful democracy has been possible. About the participatory nature of our democracy, there never was any doubt. Maybe we realized what a precious gift we had got in the form of democracy when we secured our independence in 1947.

Important policy changes followed the 1971 and 2014 elections. It is almost as if our elections are more about giving validation to a single individual whose vision has captured the imagination of society at large. Important elections in India seem to be more about vesting this individual with a huge responsibility and concomitant authority to take the nation forward, but with a caveat—the authority can be taken away just as easily by the same electorate if the ruler fails to deliver the goods. We have here the essence of an *electoral democracy*, an institution that is more characteristic of a country where society, rather than the individual, plays a pivotal role in directing the course of events. In other words, this is a civilizational state as opposed to a nation state.

Unlike in the West, the majority of old countries, especially in Asia, have never seen their history in a negative light and have always been proud of it. However, given their long and arduous journey out of colonialism and exploitation by the West, they were never able to confidently discuss it in public forums. It was not possible to do so in the West-centric and anti-civilizational post-World War II liberal international order for fear of being misinterpreted as being against modernity. Recently, however, countries that have been hesitant to embrace their history have started to do so with pride. Bhārat and China stand out in this regard. This phenomenon has not been properly acknowledged in international forums. This is only to be expected because the West has had long-standing concerns about the term 'civilization' itself.

As the economic focus of the world shifts to Asia, our ideas of democracy, so far only measured against Western liberal democracy, will be redefined by a move towards the civilizational paradigm. Most non-Western countries are culturally and civilizationally diverse. However, the West disregards their democratic and governance systems even when their legislators are fairly elected. The liberal Western worldview is not compatible with the democratic systems seen in the majority of non-Western countries because these countries are civilizational democracies. In the West, family and society are subordinated to the individual and to human rights. In Asia, family and society are civilizational assets—social capital.

Ancient civilizations like India and China are characterized by the fact that their long and unbroken history has had a deep impact on the way in which people think. Historical memory is very strong in these old countries. It is indeed these thousands of years of history that have laid the foundations of what we may today term as the Civilizational State. The West, in contrast, internalized the concept of the Dark Ages—a break in their history as it were—and through this stratagem it arrived at a working definition of modernity. Basically, the modern era in the West is what followed the Dark Ages, beginning with the Renaissance and Giotto, Copernicus, or whatever you will. In this way they distanced and detached their past from their present. Paganism gave way to Christianity. Their excursions into democracy are strictly a feature of their modern era and may have begun with the ideas of Rousseau, although a somewhat ornamental obeisance is paid to the Magna Carta which came several centuries before. In this way modernity was defined by the West, and they continued to hold 'the Rest' to this artificial standard.[31]

This Western definition of modernity was intended to overcome history—more specifically to concoct a historical discontinuity within Europe pre and post the Roman collapse. The ancient and the modern were artificially disconnected—a civilizational break—by the so-called Dark Age theory. With the USA of today having no civilization of its own, we may conclude safely that the American-led rules-based world order today has never had any (ancient) civilizational sense. However, the rest of the world does have a civilizational continuity and a high sense of civilizational memory. These two ways of thinking, the civilizational and the Western, are, therefore, utterly different in every possible way. The West and the Rest are actually two different worlds. Rather than speak about the obsolete First, Second, and Third Worlds of the Cold War, it is more accurate to speak about the two conflicting worlds of today: the civilizational and the Western. Samuel Huntington was wrong when he spoke about the clash between the Western and Islamic worlds.[32]

The real conflict is the one between civilizational states and nation states—the first with civilizational consciousness, continuity, and connect, and the latter without them.

In the context of democracy, it should be emphasized that all civilizations need not be the same. The civilizational identity of a state flows from the thinking of its people. Accordingly, any particular civilization may be either *democracy compatible* or *democracy incompatible*—whatever be one's definition of democracy. China, which is civilizationally aware, has been an autocracy for the greater part of its history. On the other hand, India, which also has civilizational foundations, has generally upheld democratic values, except during the periods of Islamic and British rules. Ancient India always had a democratic underpinning. In practical terms and with respect to governance, sovereignty of the people was paramount, and it rested in the moral law, also called dharma. This law held the people and their monarchs responsible to the higher calling. Dharma or righteousness is the monarch of monarchs.[33] To preserve dharma, kings govern, and even give their lives. This sovereign of sovereigns rules both the rulers and the ruled. Bhārat is a wonderful example of the fact that political consciousness is compatible with democracy because of the philosophy that drives it.

Now let us return to the idea of modernity. The West believes that modernity is something that has been uniquely defined by them. This idea went unchallenged for around 200 years following the French Revolution. One suspects that this was mostly because the West was also economically dominant during this period. It became an issue when the Rest began asserting that there were other origins of modernity and started questioning the notion that the West was the only intellectual source of enlightenment for nations and people.

They started pointing out that there was a fundamental error in the way the West has looked at itself and also at the rest of the world.[34] The Rest is actually several times bigger than the West in geographical area and population; it has a diversity and now an economy that is much bigger and poised better than the West. The continuing error in the thinking of the West is their failure to understand the Rest, and this is why surveys like the one by V-Dem on Indian democracy appear curiously baffling to us in Bhārat.

In summary, universalist views of the West have been intellectually challenged by the Rest, and the challenge is now resonating in geopolitics. Some Western thinkers too painfully accept now that the West is not the exclusive source of modernity.[35] There are different ways of being modern. The West now needs to accept that countries that are very different from them in their ways of thinking can be just as prosperous and stable with a high degree of social satisfaction. Enlightenment and civilization are now interchangeable. Enlightenment may be equated to social evolution and not just individual evolution. In this sense, civilizational continuity means and includes change within continuity—*smriti* within *shruti*—a prized ideal in Bhārat over the ages.

Independence in thought and self-conception mirrors independence in action as well. One can trace this quite vividly in Bhārat's foreign policy as it has shifted from non-alignment to multi-alignment, being more confident in engaging with whichever country at that particular time suits its interests. Naturally, emotive but fundamentally meaningless or potentially lethal statements of unqualified friendship, such as the disastrous 'hindi-chini bhai bhai', have been replaced with cold transactionalism in favour of the nation. Bhārat favours the highest bidder. The confidence to do so arises from the acceptance of two things: one, that the West is not all powerful and two, that its views are not universally applicable. The Indian gameplan, thus, mirrors that of China under Deng Xiaoping: use fluctuations in international politics to enhance your own power, increase the wealth of your own population, augment your techno-industrial capabilities, and keep on building on your strategic autonomy to take the decisions you see fit. From being just one amongst many in a diffuse and West-imposed bundle, referred to as the comity of nations and bound by a so-called 'rules-based order', Bhārat is moving towards expressing itself as a one-of-a-kind, sui generis civilizational state.[36] Since the external mirrors the internal—*yathā brahmānde tathā pinde*—the politics of Bhārat itself is changing with its increasing self-expression and is aligning itself with the values that the nation cherishes, instead of the musings of select elite pockets.

Countries constantly experiment with their forms of governance, and no situation is really static. The meaning of democracy is also negotiable provided the people are always paramount. Constitutions change too depending on the conditions of the time, and many countries have seen multiple constitutions through the course of their history. Rome's political history is a good example and involved a republican period, followed by Julius Caesar, a dictator, who was succeeded by a triumvirate, giving way to an empire that lasted many centuries and one in which any full-fledged Roman citizen was equal to another. Post-independence India is still a stripling in its experiments with a written constitution. According to Aristotle, constitutions which aim at the common good are right and are in accord with absolute justice, the core of any democracy. Statistically speaking, India's seventy-five years of freedom pale in comparison to the 1,500 years of the Roman republic and empire in terms of experience.[37] We inherited a liberal democracy but are now termed an electoral autocracy by those who call themselves liberal. None of this is good or bad. It is merely a sign that we are evolving in our systems of governance. We are attempting to hardwire the basic democratic principle—rule by the people, of the people, and for the people—into our age-old civilizational matrix. Ideally, citizens and their government should coexist in harmony while maintaining their respective rights, obligations, and responsibilities.

Democracy is totally compatible and even inherent to *sanātani* thought. Democracy in India is a hybrid species as it is a mingling of a variety of thought streams. There is an element of liberalism, but this is tempered by a belief in a plural multicultural world order that is even accepting of closed autocracies like China. Mostly, the new Bhārat does not subscribe to the 'one size fits all' pre-2008 Western economic thinking with its accompanying unbridled liberalism. We are also moulded in part by our colonial experience and post-colonial identity. We have begun to appreciate that the full liberal democratic model of the West does not match with our present civilizational, dharmic awareness that comes along with an aspiration for regional leadership and its corresponding geopolitical identity. There is still an adherence to Westphalian ideas of sovereignty and a marked aversion to interference by others in our affairs, the latter possibly a consequence of our colonial background. All in all, the word 'hybrid' describes our democracy the best, and perhaps the term 'hybrid democracy' is more suited to us than 'electoral democracy'. In the end, free and fair elections are just one facet of democracy, and while we do have them, democracy in India is a lot richer.

CHAPTER 2

Are Today's State Demarcations Good Identity Markers?

'All discomfort comes from suppressing your true identity.'

—Bryant H. McGill

Bhārat is an ancient land, and India is a new country. The landmass covering both these mostly congruent (if not in terms of political geography then spiritually and ontologically congruent) entities is vast by all standards. The India of today is the seventh largest country in the world in terms of area and the largest in terms of population. Any domain this large will be divided into smaller units purely for the purposes of local administration, if nothing else. Independence brought with it the need to consider the subdivisions of the new country, and there was a widespread feeling that the demarcations that were in existence in 1947 had to be reworked. This was the origin of modern India's states.[1] There are currently twenty-eight states along with a curious addition in the form of eight union territories (UT).

Regional demarcations of any type imply that the larger unit is politically a single one and in a position to subdivide its territory into smaller units. This is definitely the case in India constitutionally too—the parliament, that is, the nation, can divide, unify, form, and change the boundaries of any state without being bound to the opinion of the said state in the matter. In this context, it may be mentioned that there was a thoughtful division into provinces in the larger empires in ancient and medieval India, based on a confluence of organic identities, economic design, and military compulsions. However, none of the demarcations of these old provinces find a meaningful correspondence with the states of modern India, which are recent political contrivances. The political entity we call India today is a creation of the British, and two landmark dates stand out in the consolidation of British power in the Indian subcontinent: 1757, signifying the Battle of Plassey and 1858, signifying the takeover of direct administrative authority of India by the British Crown from the East India Company.[2] The subdivision of India into provinces or presidencies by the British represents the beginning of India's states and not the previous divisions which had well-served Bhāratiyas for centuries.

A fascinating aspect of Indian history is the way in which some of the small kingdoms that had stabilized from the final days of the Mughal empire were accounted for by the British in the consolidation of their Indian empire. The British brought the most economically significant areas of India under their direct rule in the form of the three presidencies of Bengal, Bombay, and Madras, and provinces such as the United Provinces of Agra and Oudh, the Punjab, and the Central Provinces and Berar. The rest of the country (about a third in terms of land area) constituted what became known as the princely states.[3] These were administered by local kings, chieftains, and zamindars with varying shades of influence and financial power. While the princely states had considerable autonomy in local matters, they acknowledged overall British suzerainty in the matter of taxation, international relations, and long-distance communications.

This then was the situation in India in 1947. The primary role of Sardar Vallabhbhai Patel in incorporating the 546 princely states, which had fallen into India's share after Partition, into the Indian State, thus making no difference thereafter between what was originally British India and what were the princely states, is of outstanding importance. The contributions of Patel were truly monumental and have been written about and documented extensively.[4,5]

In the context of this book, what is important is that our lawmakers had the entire geographical area that we now call India as their canvas, on which they could paint the political map of independent India, on the basis of practically any sensible criterion that they might have chosen to employ: history, geography, language, religion, culture, ease of administration, and so on.[6] What they actually did was unsystematic. It was driven by political compulsions of the day, and whimsicalities and weaknesses of successive prime ministers. They were ad hoc actions.[7] All this has resulted in the crazy quilt of our present twenty-eight states and eight UTs, which do not have much rational nexus with the economic aspirations and cultural sensitivities of the people they ought to represent.

This chapter tries to briefly chronicle the causes and circumstances that led to large linguistic states becoming administrative units. An overview of administrative structures existing from the time of the *Arthashāstra* in the Iron Age onwards until the British era shows that units of administration were quite small and were organized on principles which did not exclusively include language. Thereafter, the British plundered their way through the country, immiserating even prosperous areas through inordinate revenue demands and destruction of indigenous trade and industry. Social systems which gave both livelihood and identity to entire communities were destroyed. For the first few batches of Western-educated Indians, keen to secure their socio-economic positions under British rule, the only viable answer was to join the bureaucracy. Since these bureaucrats necessarily had to read and write in the languages deemed 'official' by the British in an area, demanding 'official language' status became a strategy for securing the economic future for the first few generations of educated Indians. As we will come to see, these economic compulsions were then masqueraded as political demands, including those for provinces defined in terms of language, that is, linguistic states, by remoulding regional histories. After the embers of the rebellion of 1857 had cooled, the British were keen to find a way to instigate artificial divisions in the country by contorting histories—while they had already used caste to their favour, they needed something more racial and geographical to pit certain parts of the country against others. With linguistic states, they found the solution to their predicament—the country could be neatly divided in a way that neighbouring peoples were locked in antagonism, as official languages became a proxy for economic competition in a time of great scarcity.

Odisha sounded the bugle merely a decade or so after 1857 following a disastrous famine, which, as history conclusively shows, was more about jobs in the bureaucracy than anything else. However, the floodgates opened with that, and a race to the bottom began. The Congress, fresh from the experience of *Bongo-bhongo* (the division of Bengal), followed by Bengal's reunification, also needed issues to fight on and played into British hands by picking up provincial reorganization on linguistic lines as a political issue in the 1920s. Thus, buoyed by both British and the Congress's designs, political identity on linguistic lines was invented, articulated, and then instilled in the people. As a result, linguistic chauvinism and parochialism became political vectors post-Independence, underpinned by an economy of scarcity where *sarkāri naukri* was the best shot at life one could have. Though the Congress was reticent, perhaps recognizing the mistake it had made, it was too late. Bengal had already been made into a Bangla-speaking state by default with Orissa and Bihar becoming separate states. The separation of Andhra Pradesh from Madras province left the latter with an overwhelming Tamil-speaking majority. Consequently, these three states and their people adopted language as their primary identity, with Tamil Nadu presenting the most pernicious template for linguistic chauvinism based on the historical legitimization of a racial fiction where colonist-missionaries proliferated the falsehood of a separate Dravidian 'race'. The cycle continued until fresh sets of economic grievances became political, and control over natural resources spun into matters of identity,[8] leading to the emergence of states such as Uttarakhand, Chhattisgarh, and Jharkhand. Throughout this 150-odd-year saga, the common thread is that economic grievances stemming from bad governance were plastered over, by design, with reformulated identities rooted in rephrased histories for the sake of political legitimacy. Whether paucity of meaningful employment and overdependence on government jobs, extraction of resources without taking into account the aspirations of locals, or distant control by regions which cornered away revenue was the reason, the result was the same. We got a system which inevitably led each person to hate their neighbour as rational economics gave way to a more emotionally driven political sentiment predicated on othering Bhāratiyas who did not speak one's own language.

States before States

Prior to 1757, when with the battle of Plassey India's stormy and sordid tale of British dominance began, the country was home to a number of administrative divisions and what can be loosely termed as provinces. Largely under the nominal suzerainty of the Mughal empire, different parts of the country organized themselves in varying ways. However, what one may note is that hardly any of these older, arguably more organic, divisions reflect themselves in our modern state boundaries. Likewise, even within bigger states like Awadh and Bengal, the subdivisions remained quite small. While in some cases the reason one cannot find correspondence with current-day states and older units is due to administrative rationalization, the phenomenon in India is mostly a result of wanton British redrawing of boundaries—with which India has continued to persist even after independence. *Plus ça change, plus c'est la même chose.*[9]

The *Arthashāstra*, a manual of sorts designed to optimize a sprawling empire, goes in-depth into the ordering of its basic unit of administration, the *janapada*. Chapters 10, 11, and 12 of *Adhikarana 7* give a detailed analysis of how to approach different kinds of territories for setting up and governing a janapada, with factors related to land, forts, irrigation works, forests, mines, trade routes, and roads. The *Arthashāstra*'s conceived territory of control was as large (if not larger) than the extent of modern-day India.[10] Nonetheless, the biggest administrative division, a province headed by a *sthāniya*, was to be established only for around 800-odd villages.[11] Thus, provinces were kept consciously small.

The same system roughly continued with constant tinkering and was reformed by Sher Shah Suri. In his system, the largest unit of administration was a *shiqq*, and the whole empire was divided into sixty-six shiqqs. While in frontier regions such as Bengal a few shiqqs were grouped together under a *vilayat* or *khittā*, such grouping was generally limited to military and general supervision.[12] Terminology from those days pertaining to smaller divisions of land, such as *parganā* or *mandala*, remain in use even today. In essence, big states did not exist for the majority of India's history.

States, of the size we understand them to be today, came into being with Akbar's reign. The shiqqs of old were rebranded into being called sarkars, and sarkars were then placed under *subāhs*, of which twelve existed in the empire at the time of establishment and were then expanded to fifteen by the time Akbar died. Akbar, thus, attempted a process of centralization. Yet, as peripheries continued to rebel, and as the initial size became unwieldy to govern, successive emperors kept increasing the number of subāhs and carved out new ones from those already established. Jahangir commenced the process by carving Orissa out of Bengal. Shah Jahan excised Sindh from Multan, Kashmir and Kandahar from Kabul, and Bidar out of Ahmednagar. Aurangzeb's Deccan campaigns added a further four subāhs to the list, increasing the total number of subāhs established or carved out to twenty-seven. As one may notice, even though one may see that the number of subāhs in the Mughal era is close to the number of states in India today (that is, twenty-eight), there existed no subāhs as big as states of Uttar Pradesh or Rajasthan, nor ones as small as those of the Northeast. In essence, these subāhs were arbitrary divisions carved across India to secure different objectives in different parts of the country—in the south and northwest, the subāhs were essentially military arrangements, while those in the Ganga basin were for maximizing revenues. None of these divisions paid much credence or respect to the local culture, its peoples, or their aspirations as such; they were the divisions of a colonizer who intended to exploit different lands differently. Unsurprisingly, when subāhs such as Bengal and Awadh became all but independent, except in name, they embarked on wide-ranging decentralized administrative mechanisms within the borders they had inherited.

The rise of the British Raj saw a haphazard continuation of administrative units. These came to be due to conquest and conspiracy. British India's provincial organization was created with two goals in mind: first, to maintain the direct authority of the imperial power in crucial areas of economic and strategic importance and second, to replace the political void left by the fall or annihilation of the ancient princes. Of the two, the first was undoubtedly the main goal and necessitated the dismantling of the customary dynastic and regional allegiances. This was attempted by removing previous borders and dividing the country into new provinces without consideration for shared economic interests or natural affinities. The goal of these provinces' administrative structure was to guarantee their submission to British gauleiters. Before 1857, it would be somewhat inaccurate to say that a single British Raj existed—the presidencies of Bombay, Madras, and Bengal were effectively three independent colonies, which at times were even competing with each other. The three presidencies had their own armies, their own peculiar administrative machineries, and their own designs on Indian princes surrounding them.

As the Bengal presidency became too unwieldy, the North-West Provinces[13] were set up under a lieutenant governor in 1836 by detaching from Bengal all territories to the west of Bihar. When Punjab was annexed in 1849, it was also subsumed as a province stretching till its old boundaries into Pashtun territories. Punjab was later made a lieutenant governor's province when Delhi was transferred in 1859. Oudh, annexed in 1856, was placed under a chief commissioner until it was later attached to the North-West Provinces in 1877. Underneath this layer of presidencies, provinces, chief commissionerships, and various other arrangements, the older systems of administration remained as the basic systems on which the country ran. Thus, older offices of justice, law and order, and revenue remained in place; the fact that *patwaris* remain in place in the revenue departments across the northern parts of India today, or that every lawyer needs to file a *vakālatnāma* to appear on behalf of a client, is testament to the fact that the British were quite aloof from altering the basic administrative mechanisms of the country. However, this was not an act of benign neglect; it was simply unnecessary for the British to do so as long as systems of committing a subcontinental, intergenerational drain of wealth continued unimpeded.

The British system received a severe shock with the rebellion of 1857. Important administrative changes were put to motion, the very first of which was a freeze on the annexation of whatever remained of the princely states. More important to the discussion at hand, the British government began the process of centralizing and rationalizing the litany of systems which kept the haphazard company rule in place. Somewhat more 'organic' states began to be set up. The districts of Saugor and Nerbudda were removed from the North-West Provinces and combined with the former kingdom of Nagpur, which had been overthrown in 1854 by Lord Dalhousie, to establish the Central Provinces in 1861. Having been acquired in 1826 and joined to the Bengal presidency, Assam became its own province under the chief commissioner's office in 1874. The strategically significant northwest boundary areas were divided from Punjab in 1901 and established as a distinct chief commissioner's province. The North-West Provinces and Oudh were renamed as the United Provinces of Agra and Oudh. Likewise, the various Supreme Courts, Sadar Diwani Adalats, and Sadar Faujdari Adalats of the presidencies were replaced with a more uniform system of high courts in 1861, corresponding with a consolidation of other mechanisms of administration, including the police command system and a unified army.

The administrative integration of India also saw a flurry of important economic decisions. The princely states were made to open up to and integrate with railway lines, salt agreements, duty-free customs, and British laws. The nigh forgotten report of the Linguistic Provinces Commission, 1948, concurs with the observation by stating: '(Princely) states are closely identified with numerous branches of all-India activity, and that this process has already gone far before the emergence of the federal idea. To a great extent indeed railways, currency and coinage, posts and telegraphs and salt are already federal subjects.'[14] Devolution of powers and responsibilities to units of the presidencies, provinces, and chief commissariats were also undertaken, partly for British convenience and partly out of the increasing pressure from Indian nationalists who were successively getting greater representation in governance structures. One may track this increasing decentralization through a study of the successive Government of India Acts of 1909, 1919, and 1935. In some ways, India transitioned from imperial feudalism to imperial federalism. Nonetheless, the federal units themselves remained artificial creatures born from British design, disconnected with the people they ought to have been governing. None of these units were in any sense *federal* if one were to consider the meaning of this term in political science theory.

Clause 20, Chapter I, Part I of the States Reorganisation Committee Report of 1955 characterizes the motivations of the British provincial organisation: 'Thus far the formation of provinces had been mainly governed by considerations of administrative convenience and economy and by reasons of military strategy and security. To the extent, therefore, there was a conscious or deliberate design behind the demarcation of the territories of administrative units, it was grounded in imperial interests or the exigencies of a foreign government and not in the actual needs, wishes or affinities of the people. Administrative convenience itself required compact units with some measure of homogeneity. In some cases, therefore, various factors conducive to the growth of natural units operated in the backsound. They were, however, subordinate to the prime considerations of administrative and military exigencies.'[15]

Linguistic States: From a Colonial Project to a Hesitant Capitulation

The story of linguistic states commences in the post-1857 British era, when ancient cultural and trade linkages which held Bhārat together had been replaced with general destitution and an increasingly desolate life for the vast majority of Indians. India's traditional systems of education, cultural exchange, trade, industry, and justice and administration had been either eradicated or mutated by the British into hitherto unrecognizable forms. Indians themselves were not clear as to how they wished to proceed—the relationship between so-called 'modernists' or 'progressives' who wished to recast India in the image of the West, and 'traditionalists', 'conservatives', or 'extremists' who wanted to use Bhārat's own past as a blueprint for the future was one of unease and tension. There was also the problem of Indians not being sure as to whether the British were to be fully boycotted or whether their governance was to be used to engage in the betterment of the lives of Indians. These groups split, often violently, as one can see in the aftermath of the Surat Session of the Congress in 1907. Sensitive issues of identity, power, politics, and the future of the country did not have a consensus. While moderates welcomed British-enforced measures such as the prohibition of sati or the introduction of a minimum marriageable age, stalwarts such as Bal Gangadhar Tilak opposed the methodology of doing so via British diktat and wanted it to be an affair of social change purely by and between Indians. Tilak himself foresaw greater cultural interference by the British in the lives of Indians in the name of progress.[16] As history stands testament, it was the moderates who won out, largely on account of the British administration being ready to cut deals with them, and also because of the rampant Anglophilia inculcated in the nouveau elites of the country through Western education.[17] The unfortunate outcome was, as Dharampal puts it, that 'It is in such a context that, as time passed, the Indian elite began to look at India through British eyes.'[18]

This perspective has not only led to the formation of linguistic states but also to their continuance today. Let us begin this account, therefore, with Odisha, a very instructive case study for linguistic states.

Orissa and Bengal: Opening Pandora's Box

Despite being one of the peoples of India whose continuous history stretches back to the Kalingas of the Mahabharata, the Odias were hardly united in any political sense at the time the British began their takeover of India. The Bengal Sultanate, under its Afghan rulers, had invaded and ended Chalukya rule over a somewhat politically united Odisha in 1568. By 1593, Mughal forces, under Raja Man Singh of Amer, replaced Afghan rule completely. Initially made a part of Bengal Subāh, Orissa was made into a separate subāh by Shah Jahan. Nonetheless, large parts of southern and western Orissa remained with various principalities, prime amongst which were the Rajas of Khurda, who came to be recognized as successors to the Gajapatis of yore. The Rajas of Khurda, despite repeated defeats by Mughal forces, maintained his independence and extended protection to the Jagannatha Puri temple by sacrificing territory and daughters to the Mughals. Aurangzeb was constantly harassed by the rebelling Odia and tribal principalities. When Murshid Quli Khan established Bengal's independence from Mughal rule in all but name, he took Mughal-held Orissa with him (being the Governor of Orissa and Bengal Subāhs simultaneously) and allowed southern principalities to progressively reclaim lands. His successor, Shuja ud-Din, was less permissive and carried out invasions and built Islamic monuments across the land. With the commencement of Maratha raids, Odia territories began to be lost, and by 1751 the Marathas held what was once Orissa Subāh up till the Subarnarekha.[19] From 1568 till 1751, Odisha had seen little extended periods of peace; the Jagannatha Puri temple itself was witness to repeated tragedies, persecution, and mass violence. The murtis within the temple had to be whisked away into hiding multiple times as invaders came to desecrate and demolish the temple complex (as also sack cities).[20] Trade and prosperity was sapped away from the land throughout this extended period.

The Maratha interlude, which saw fresh investments and some revival as security returned to a part of Odia lands, was short-lived. The British viewed Orissa as a crucial separator between Madras and Bengal presidencies, which had come under British control swiftly after 1757. Thus, the British marched on Maratha-held Orissa during the Second Anglo-Maratha War and swiftly edged out the Marathas. Paralikhemundi rebelled the very next year, in 1758. Soon after, an incensed Khurda and a few Garhjat states rebelled in 1804; this could not be put to rest until 1806. Soon after, in 1817, the British dealt with an even more intense Paika rebellion, again spearheaded by Khurda, which was suppressed in 1818. Another rebellion broke out in Sambalpur in 1827. After 1857, partly as a result of centuries of incessant warfare and partly due to the British policies of revenue maximization, the *Na Anka Durvikhyan* (nine-figure famine) killed more than a million inhabitants in 1866.[21]

The British had successfully reorganized Odia-speaking lands to suit their economic and military needs, much to the detriment of the Odia-speaking peoples, who were spread across multiple administrative units. Northern Orissa, which had been first a part of the Bengal Sultanate and then a division of the Bengal presidency, was the smallest and most remote of its divisions, which naturally resulted in lackadaisical administration. The situation was similarly repeated with the parts of Orissa which were conjoined with Central Provinces and Berar; administrators there went as far as replacing Odia with Hindi as the official and court language in the province's

Odia-speaking parts in 1896. The British strategy was clear—divide Orissa into zones of control with the help of areas where they had a tighter grip. The region from Midnapore to Cuttack was one zone, which the British controlled directly as part of the Bengal presidency. The second zone consisted of fourteen feudatory states, including Khurda, which were also governed indirectly from Bengal. To keep a check on the tribal areas and the Garhjatis, the ever-rebellious Sambalpur was placed within Central Provinces and Berar as the third zone. Certain Odia-speaking tracts were retained in Madras as they could be easily accessed from the bilingual territories of Ganjam and Vizagapatnam, forming the fourth zone. The principal motivation was perhaps to rapidly deal with any further rebellious activity by the intractable Odias and their tribal feudatories.

The above historical overview is important to understand why Orissa was the first state to begin a sustained, and successful, campaign for a unified linguistic province. Centuries of brutal invasions and rebellions had broken the economy of the region, and as Bengal and the Deccan had begun to see warfare since the fall of Vijayanagara, trade had dried up. The *Na Anka Durvikhyan* further worsened the general state of the Odia-speaking peoples, devastating their economic life and social fabric. The loss of Oriya as the official language also disenfranchized ethnic Odias from official jobs and the bureaucracy. Simultaneously, as has been the case with British rule across Asia, the British imported officials and policemen from other areas to stymie any organized resistance—Tamils in Bombay, Indians in Singapore and Canton, Telugus in Madras, and in Odisha's case, Bengalis in the Mughalbandi north, and Telugus in the princely south. Being scarcely connected or sympathetic to the people they administered, the British themselves left copious documentary evidence and were horrified to witness the maladministration wrought by Bengali bureaucrats in particular; the then collector of Cuttack stated that 'a regular system of oppression and peculation appear to exist throughout and instead of proving a protection to the country and a preventive against improper conduct, these people (the Bengali personnel) are considered as the terror and the scourge of the district'.[22]

The economic hardships of the Odia people and the loss of their relative prestige as they lost representation in the bureaucracy (which was at one time the only interface with the state with which the vast majority of the population would ever come into contact with) was a direct result of the dispersal of Odia-speaking peoples into multiple provinces, in each of which they were a small minority. Naturally, the first organized demand from a rattled Odia populace, particularly from its educated segment, was the demand to make Odia an official language so that they could enter the bureaucracy. The *Utkal Deepika*, Odisha's first indigenous newspaper which was established during the 1866 famine, served as a platform and catalyst for the Odia intelligentsia to unite on the issue of language.

In 1870, a public meeting of Odia speakers in the Madras presidency was convened, and a resolution was passed demanding the revival of Odia as an official language. The resolution was readily carried by the *Utkal Deepika*.[23] The resolution catalysed Odias across the sundry jurisdictions in which they lay scattered across. Sambalpur, in particular, became a beacon of Odia officialization. Petitions to the British and scathing criticism of the princely states for their silence became the norm; the poet Gangadhar Meher criticized the kings, even his own, for their convenient quietude.[24]

The demand for linguistic parity quickly morphed into a demand for a separate Odia-speaking province itself.[25] Evidently, the same was also rooted in economic concerns; an exclusive Odia province would eliminate competition for government jobs from Bengali, Telugu, and Hindi speakers. Thus, in 1875, Raja Baikuntha Nath Dey of Balasore and Bichitrananda Pattnaik of Cuttack submitted a lengthy memorial for the unification of the scattered Odia-speaking tracts under a single administration. In 1882, the intelligentsia's views on the matter began to crystallize, and the Utkal Sabha was formed, which emerged as the preeminent platform to impress upon the British that the Odias exist as a separate society, and that its erstwhile rebellious temperament has given way to organized negotiation. The British began to take positive interest, and in July 1895, H.G. Cook, the commissioner of Orissa, supported the movement for the amalgamation of all Odia-speaking tracts.[26]

George Nathaniel Curzon,[27] the most pernicious of the British imperialists, outdone perhaps only by Robert Clive, was emblematic of the British dictum of divide and rule. It was fairly obvious to Lord Curzon that new divisions need to be sown between Indians to stifle the tide of nationalism which threatened the rise of a pan-Indian national consciousness. The Odias, who had been rebelling constantly, had been pacified—the princes were standing with the British empire to secure their own existence, while the people had been so thoroughly stripped of wealth that they were scrambling for the limited number of government jobs. Curzon's design was to use the Odias as a loyal people by providing them certain concessions, and with this, to breed antagonism between the Odias on one hand and the Bengalis and Telugus on the other. The Odias were culturally quite close to these two communities.

Bengali is partially intelligible to an Odia, and the two share deep religious bonds. Telugus and Odias had cohabited since centuries in areas such as Ganjam, with frequent familial bonds between the princes of Odisha and Telugu nobles (many of the Khurda Rajas were not only fluent in Telugu but were also ethnic Telugus themselves). Economic concerns could thus be transformed into lasting political stances, particularly when viewed in context of the illustrious history of the Odia peoples.

Curzon, thus, asked the chief commissioner of the Central Provinces to explore the transfer of Sambalpur to the Orissa division of Bengal, based on linguistic considerations. Chief Commissioner Frazer responded in 1901, taking into account the general discontent amongst Odias: 'What I am convinced of is this, that Oriya, not Hindi, ought to be the Court Language of Sambalpur, and that in this case, Sambalpur ought to be joined to Orissa, to which it really belongs.'[28]

What happened next, and how Odisha came to be the first linguistic province to be formed, is inextricably tied to what transpired in Bengal.

Joy Bangla: Ahead of India?

Curzon was simultaneously grappling with whirlwind nationalistic fervour in Bengal, which had become a hotbed for activities that were attempting to cause a cultural, religious, and economic rebirth of the nation. Bengal emerged as an epicentre for nationalistic Indians, who were also beginning to challenge the orientalist fictions passed off in the name of India's history by the British and were rediscovering the innate unity, glory, and scientific progress of Bhārat.[29] The challenge before the British was to invent new social divisions, politicize the same, and nip the nascent revival of a Bhāratiya identity capable of expressing its myriad diversities while retaining its sense of civilizational unity. The British were closely monitoring the situation and intended to split Bengal along religious lines such that each half was placed in perpetual opposition to each other. In 1904, the home secretary to the British Government of India wrote that 'Bengal united is a power. Bengal divided will pull in several different ways.[30] One of our main objects is to split up and thereby weaken a solid body of opponents to our rule'.[31]

The 1905 partition of Bengal, called *Bongo-bhongo*, was a turning point in modern Indian history for many reasons. The politics of the overwhelmingly Western-educated 'moderates' received a serious challenge from a broad upsurge of radical nationalism led by an elite inspired more from Indic value systems rather than the political climate of London. Swadeshi, swaraj, and boycott evolved as political ideas. Nationalist literature flourished, the formulation of national education systems was attempted, and fledgling Indian entrepreneurs began the process of setting up Indian-owned and -controlled businesses. This phenomenon was not restricted to Bengal; publications such as V.D. Savarkar's *Abhinav Bhārat* were established roughly in this time period, and all of India was swept with revolutionary fervour. The British were forced to fall back on parasitic princes such as the Nawab of Dhaka, whose political futures depended on identitarian conflicts and British patronage. The mood of the nation is captured by what the *Yugantar*, a Bengali periodical, wrote in 1906 in the wake of the clamorous Bengal Provincial Conference at Barisal (born from the tradition of the Hindu Mela in the month of Chaitra):[32] 'The remedy lies with the people themselves. The 30 crores of people living in India must raise their 60 crores of hands to stop this curse of oppression. Force must be stopped by force.'[33]

Much like the Pauranic account of *samudra manthan*—the great churning of the oceans—this was a time of much churn from which emerged the foundations of modern India and a crop of leaders who would lead it to independence and beyond. Nonetheless, much like how along with the elixir of immortality (*amrit)* came the poison of *halāhala*, the rejection of division along religious lines ended up morphing itself into an approval for the division of the country on linguistic lines. Language became the obvious rallying point for those trying to counter religious division. While rejecting the politicization of one kind of identity, Indians fell prey to another insidious kind of identitarian politics. Unsurprisingly, the views of the great many nationalists for whom Bengal's storms proved to be a political crucible took on the view that linguistic identity ought to be one's main identity marker, a concept that was hitherto alien to India. The fact that the Bengal division was a national affair meant that nationalists from various parts of the country swiftly transplanted and normalized the politicization of linguistic identity across India in an exceedingly short time frame. The primacy of linguistic identity came to be deeply ingrained in the zeitgeist of the nationalists, who were to construct the political bedrock of the Indian State and society. The political pressure to maintain (at least in public) the dictum of Hindu–Muslim unity further accelerated the process.

The Odia demand, as legitimate as it was, presented the British with an opportunity to cleave another deep social division through Indians' psyche while mollifying Bengal. Merely three days after announcing the division of Bengal, the officiating governor-general swiftly decided to transfer

Sambalpur and adjoining feudatory states to the Orissa division, commencing the consolidation of Odia-speaking areas; the stage was set to pit the speakers of one language against another. Around this time, the Risley circular of 1903, which contained Curzon's supposed plans to unify Odia-speaking territories, was revived in Britain's discussions with the Odia intelligentsia. The intention was quite clear: Orissa could be used as a counter to Bengal, and national politics could be fractured by characterizing linguistic groups as separate 'races' or 'nations'.[34] Indian nationalists, perhaps myopically, ended up accidentally endorsing these views when they argued that instead of dividing Bengal, a separation of Odia- and Bihari-speaking areas from Bengal would be preferable.[35] This too was driven by a zero-sum game between speakers of different languages: Bengalis were quite anxious that they would become a linguistic minority within West Bengal post-division, which eventuality could seriously imperil their hold over government jobs. In essence, a wholly novel intersection of language and politics was instituted in this country by British design.

The fate of the country was all but sealed when the British reunified Bengal in 1911. While nationalists counted this as their first major victory against imperial arrogance and insidiousness, the British plan of sowing divisions to weaken national unity had already found an alternative means of operation. In 1911, as Bengal was reunified, Bihar and Orissa were separated from Bengal on explicitly linguistic grounds. Simultaneously, Orissa received Odia-speaking districts from Madras presidency as well. Bengal had, since its earliest days, symbiotically included parts of today's Maithili-speaking parts of Bihar within its ambit; the Palas had ruled from Bhagalpur, while Munger had been Mir Qasim's capital for the Bengal Nawabate. A similar situation existed with respect to Odias. The rise of Bengali linguistic consciousness, originally as a response to the *Bongo-bhongo*, began to morph once Bihar and Orissa were separated from it. Post-division, Bengal was left with not just a new ethnography composed almost exclusively of Bengali speakers but a new supremacist political idea of itself. Bengal began to think in a far more inward-looking way, and linguistic and cultural chauvinism began to take root. The Bengalis, who were historically a people who dispersed themselves far and wide for trade and who had assimilated peoples from geographies as far away as Karnataka, Rajasthan, and Tibet within its fold, began to parochialize themselves. Even as Bengal continued to be at the forefront of the Indian national movement, the seeds of the cultural, moral, and economic decay which Bengal was to fall prey to were placed with this division.

The immediate motivation to keep Bihar and Orissa as a single province was to sandwich the princely states between the more connected plains of Bihar and coastal Odisha. The Odias' antagonism to Bengalis was well-cemented by now, and keeping Odias and Biharis under a common administration meant forcing these two communities to compete for government jobs: the British were repeating their strategy of dividing communities and crystallizing hard political identities from soft cultural affiliations. A provincial sense of identity which leads to a clientelist form of politics, in which language and caste groups corner away government benefits took root, instead of nationally oriented, development-centric political thinking. For all these retrograde developments we need to thank the British for their experiments in the political laboratories of Bengal, Odisha, and Bihar. Their actions severely dented national unity and delayed India's civilizational reemergence long after the British had left India's shores.

Bengal and Odisha had shown that in under fifty-odd years, one could manufacture a political identity out of language in India, position such nascent identities to be inimical to each other, and make sure they could be justified with out-of-context historical exegesis.[36] However, the formation of competing, oppositional, and nationally divisive linguistic politics had to be exported beyond eastern India. Regrettably, it was the Congress which became the conduit for these British designs that eventually (almost inevitably) became the blueprint for India's governance.

The Odias, stuck in an unhappy arranged marriage with the Biharis in the composite state of Bihar and Orissa, continued their agitation to achieve a separate Odisha. These attempts had only intensified with the transpirations of 1911, and by the 1916 Congress session at Lucknow, the demands for federalism were given formal approval—albeit without consensus on what exactly the term 'federalism' ought to mean or what the units in this federal set-up would look like. The loss of the Odia-speaking districts in 1911, as also the dominance of Tamil Brahmins in the bureaucracy of the Madras presidency, caused an almost spontaneous transference of linguistic politics to Telugu-speaking areas. This manifested itself in demands for a Telugu province. The decision of the All India Congress Committee to demand a Telugu-speaking state be carved out from the Madras presidency in 1917 resulted in the term 'federalism' to be characterized by and be even synonymous with linguistic states.

The floodgates opened with the single decision to separate Odisha and Bihar from Bengal in 1911. Demands for linguistic states began to spring up across the country, where the severe overdependence on government jobs and its connection with languages made it a scramble for *sarkari naukri* neatly hidden under a varnish of identity. This gave way to bigotry nonetheless. M.K. Gandhi entered into close correspondence with leaders of the Utkal Union Conference and wrote in 1920 that the movement for a unified Odia province 'raises the large question of redistribution on linguistic basis' and 'this fine (Oriya) race cannot possibly make the natural advance which is its due, if it is kept split up into four divisions for no sound reason'.[37] That same year, the Congress accepted the creation of linguistic states as a principle at its Nagpur session in 1920 and recast its provincial committees on linguistic lines—rejecting one kind of British borders only to adopt another. Linguistic states and their associated politics entered the corpus of what was to be India's constitutional history when linguistic statehood was included in the Nehru report of 1928. While a separate Orissa province was formed in 1936,[38] the economics of scarcity combined with *sarkari naukri* and the politics of a fabricated and fractious subnationalism was unleashed by Indians upon themselves as the nation fell into the strategic trap set up by the British.

The Tamil Language: Civilizational Amnesia

Tamil Nadu, the state having the greatest number of temples and once home to empires such as the Pandyas and Cholas who were the foremost patrons of dharma, has also been the state hit by the most severe storms arising from linguistic identitarianism. Tamil has become a clarion call for linguistic chauvinism. Unlike the demand for other linguistic states, the cry of the Tamils is that they are actually different from other Bhāratiyas *because of their language*. Tamil particularists question whether they are even Bhāratiyas, that is to say sanātanis, and have based their existence solely on negating the Bhāratiyatā of their history and people.[39] This way, Tamil Nadu represents the most successful execution of the British scheme of instituting linguistic identitarianism, an arrangement where each linguistic grouping views itself as a separate 'race', views fellow Indians who speak other languages with hostility, and rejects the notion of any innate civilizational unity of Bhāratiyas. As has been the case for both Odisha and Bengal, the excuse of identity was predicated upon extractive economics; over time, people fall for their own lies, and then commit atrocities upon others and eventually themselves.

The Tamil language is indeed ancient—as old, if not older, than Sanskrit. Unlike Hebrew, which was resuscitated only in recent times, and Sanskrit, which has been relegated to being a liturgical medium, Tamil is a living language with a vibrant cultural milieu. However, the origins of organized Tamil polities are lost in the mists of time. Tamil is not an Indo-European language. The three other main Dravidian languages of India are related to it. It is the furthest from Sanskrit among the four major Dravidian languages, although versions spoken by Brahmins today have many Sanskritized words. It has been written in different scripts; Brahmi is of northern origin. The alphabet structure is different. There are fewer consonants but also unusual ones that have no equivalent in other Indian languages. The numerals are based on letters rather than being proper numerals.

Yet, Tamil history and that of the rest of the country are inseparable. If one sticks to language alone, one only needs to see the Sanskrit titles which the imperial Cholas, the first (and arguably most illustrious) power to politically unite the Tamil people, adopted for themselves: *Shivapādashekhara*,

Janānāthamangalam, and *Rājarājādhirāja*.[40] Likewise, by no means was it that patronizing temples was the preserve of some small economic or ethnic elite—temple inscriptions of Tamil Nadu are replete with donation records from all castes and women.[41] The Tamil lands under the illustrious three dynasties (*Muvendar*) of Tamil lands contributed much to literature, philosophy, and the sciences, which percolated throughout India. By no means was the attention to sanātana, Sanskrit, and *sanskriti* by the Tamil emperors one-sided; the rest of Bhārat equated Tamil cities with the most sacred and resplendent *kshetrams* of the north. The *Arthashāstra* refers to Madurai as the Mathura of the south, for example. When Varanasi and its temples were ransacked by the marauding armies of the Delhi Sultanate in the 1440s, as it had been multiple times from the 12th to the 17th century, the pain experienced by the faithful was just as intense in Tamil Nadu as it was in the devastated lands of the north. The Pandya king Jatavarman Parakrama Pandyan commenced construction of the Shri Vishwanathan temple at Tenkasi[42] in 1426, leaving behind this temple inscription: 'As the shrine of Shiva Vishwanatha at Uttara Kashi was demolished, Shiva commanded our King, Perumal Arikesari Thevar alias Ponnin Perumal Parakrama Pandya Thevar, in his dream, to construct a temple for him at Thennari Nadu, on the banks of Chitra river and consider it as Dakshina Kashi...'[43] Thus, even as the Tamil language prospered, and Tamil customs made the law of the land, by no means were the Tamils viewing themselves as existing beyond the overarching Bhāratiya rubric.

The onset of British rule in Tamil lands was the result of extraneous circumstances and the vagaries of history. The British had originally set up their first agency on the east coast of India in Masulipatnam in today's Andhra Pradesh.

Soon after, the British faced a shortage of cotton in the area, and came to be harassed by the Sultan of Golconda, who kept imposing impediments on Britain's trade and tradesmen.[44] The British, thus, looked further southward—quite reluctantly, as the distance from their power centres in Surat and Calcutta would render the factories vulnerable to stronger powers. However, they found solace in the fact that south of the sultanates of the Deccan and the Hyderabad Nizamate, no strong local power existed, save for the Malayali kingdoms. The Carnatic Nawabate, which formally oversaw territories south of the Krishna, was in fact nothing more than a small principality centred around Arcot which claimed only nominal suzerainty over fragmented local feudatories established by former appointees of the long-lost Vijayanagara empire. Thus, after negotiations with the ruler of Chandragiri, the British established a factory in a village called Madraspatnam, which later came to be shortened to Madras, and was thereafter renamed Chennai in 1996.[45]

One must note the geographical distance of the Tamil lands from British areas of interest. Until 1796, when the Hyderabad Nizam ceded most of Rayalaseema to the British, there were no territories from where the British could march to Madras from Bengal, and neither could they march from Surat (or later Bombay) until much later. Thus, prior to becoming a presidency in its own right, the Madras agency was not even governed from India—it was subordinated to the presidency of Bantam in Java, which lies in today's Indonesia. The nonexistence of any regional power of note south of the Hyderabad Nizam and east of the Malayali kingdoms subjected the region to a large power vacuum, which the British could fill with relative ease, as the only opposition they had were from the severely fragmented Poligars. The political isolation of the Tamil lands, combined with the corresponding collapse of trade volumes owing to a lack of security, made the region an ideal place for the British to experiment social engineering prior to exporting it to other parts of the country. How a people which were intimately connected with faraway places such as Kashi, and who nurtured the Tamil and Sanskrit languages simultaneously, came to call for secession and identified themselves as separate from the rest of the country is but one sordid outcome of said social engineering.

Luckily for the British, some of the ground for them had already been prepared. In 1606, one Roberto de Nobili, a Jesuit from Tuscany, made landfall at Madurai. His journeys through South India had convinced him that the best way to spread the Christian faith throughout the heathen territories of the East Indies was to appropriate local sanātani traditions and symbology, and thereafter deceive sanātanis into including Jesus in their pantheon.[46] By christianizing sanātana, he intended to use the cultural lexicon of the country to subvert the underlying religious basis for said culture. The fraud was perfected to a frightening degree. He called himself a 'teacher of wisdom', dressed as an ascetic, wore a white dhoti and wooden sandals while carrying a *danda* and a *kamandalu*. He shaved his head and kept a *shikha*. He wore a three-stringed thread (appearing identical to a *yajnopavita*) across his chest, claiming it to be a representation of the Holy Trinity.[47] Claiming noble parentage, he approached high-caste people as an equal. De Nobili also wrote the Khristapurana, which used the style of the sanātani Puranas to retell Jesus's life.[48] His modus operandi was adopted by many missionaries, who began their anthropological study of the Tamil people to identify the social cleavages which could be used for conversion, as also the language which could be used for the same.[49]

The reason why the above introduction to de Nobili is necessary here is because the rise of the sociopolitical idea known as Dravidianism, which has lodged itself deep into Tamil politics and today's Tamil psyche, commenced with him. The fundamental tenet of Dravidianism is that the Dravidians, an 'indigenous' people as compared to an 'invading' colonizing force of the northern 'Aryans',[50] and who spoke Dravidian languages as opposed to Indo-European languages, must reject the 'Aryan' contamination (subsequently identified with Bhāratiyas from the north of the country, sanātana dharma, and Brahmins) and thereby assert their independent political existence. Walking in de Nobili's footsteps came another missionary by the name of Constantius Beschi, who, while adopting the de Nobili methodology, identified the Tamil language as a potential vector for causing civilizational division between Bhārat and the Tamil people. Thus, while being well-versed in Sanskrit, he published an anthology of poems in praise of St Joseph titled *Thembavani* (The Unfading Garland). In this piece of work, he consciously avoided the use of Sanskrit-origin words, in an attempt to emphasize the 'separateness' of Tamil from Sanskrit. Beschi went on to concoct a fictional linguistic history of Tamil, where he invented the concept of a 'chaste' Tamil, free from the 'adulteration' of Sanskrit and prakrit-derived languages.[51] This 'chaste' Tamil forms the bedrock of the Dravidian idea because the separateness of this language became the context to claim a social, political, and possibly even anthropological identity distinct and separate from that of the imaginary blond, blue-eyed, fair-complexioned horse-riding Aryans.[52]

A rejection of the historical relationship between Sanskrit and the Tamil people was zeroed in on successfully by both the missionaries and the British who supported them, and was deeply consequential. A defenestration of Sanskrit from Tamil lands provided enough space for Tamils to be taught that they were a separate 'race', and hence a separate 'nation'—suiting the political aim of the British to negate the existence of a unified India sans British power. Secondly, the intimate relationship between Sanskrit and the Brahmins provided the dominant non-Brahmin castes of Tamil Nadu, who already enjoyed access to land and wealth, to also have a political narrative justifying their opposition to and replacement of the Brahmins who dominated the bureaucracy and intelligentsia, apart from their control over temple finances. Thirdly, a simultaneous assault on sanātana dharma and Brahmins enabled the ecclesiastical project of the church along with the political objective of the British to have a loyal base in India bound to the British by faith.[53] Thus, the interests of the British, the church, and the dominant non-Brahmin castes came to align with respect to Tamil society.

The de-Sanskritization of Tamil to fuel and propel the above political agenda reached its zenith in the 19th century under the stewardship of two missionaries, Robert Caldwell and George Uglow Pope, who continued Beschi's work with gusto. Caldwell, in particular, presented a systematic falsification of Tamil linguistics named *A Comparative Grammar of the Dravidian or South-Indian Family of Languages* in 1875, to cement the idea that the Tamils formed a distinct linguistic (and thus social and political) community vis-à-vis Bhāratiyas. Caldwell also understood that caste tensions and grievances could be leveraged to cause social discord; in 1849, he published a spurious pamphlet titled

The Tinnevelly Shanars, which imputed a 'non-Aryan' origin to the Nadars so as to pit castes against each other by according to them Aryan and non-Aryan origins. An alternate history of Tamil lands was fabricated. Basically, history was reduced to a counterfeit conflict between Aryan powers such as the Mauryans and the 'indigenous' Dravidians.[54] De Nobili and Beschi's projects received their crowning glory with mistranslations of the *Thirukkural* by Pope, which became a ruse for many to argue that Dravidian religion is separate from sanātana dharma.[55] In line with Thomas Macaulay's views in 1836 that 'No Hindoo, who has received an English education, ever remains sincerely attached to his religion', both De Nobili and Beschi operated schools and expended vast energies in 'educating' Indians.

One need not dig through furtive correspondence to establish British support for these racial, fissiparous ideas; the governor-general of Madras, Mountstuart Elphinstone Grant-Duff, spewed bile flagrantly in 1886 within the Madras University, declaring that 'the Brahmins are the real usurpers of social and literary superiority... You are of pure Dravidian race... I should like to see the pre-Sanskrit element amongst you asserting itself rather more... Ruffianly Europeans have sometimes been known to speak of natives of India as "Niggers", but they do not, like the proud speakers or writers of Sanskrit, speak of the people of the South as legions of monkeys. It was these Sanskrit speakers, not Europeans, who lumped up the Southern races as Rakshusas—demons. It was they who deliberately grounded all social distinctions on Varna, Colour'.[56]

The Tamil and Telugu peoples had coexisted and cohabited in each others' lands owing to the ascendancy of Telugu professionals and bureaucrats in the Vijayanagara empire. Telugu had come to be the language of high culture along with Sanskrit in much of Tamil lands, and ethnic Telugus had greatly come to enrich Tamil culture.[57] However, the unwieldy and geographically scattered structure of the Madras presidency which included Tamil, Telugu, Kannada, Malayalam, and Odia languages along with a host of small languages like Tulu, Kodava, and Beary made a clash of peoples for economic control all but inevitable. In particular, the dominant caste groupings of Tamil lands, who had enough economic and political standing to host an English-educated elite, faced two major challenges: first, from the dominance of Telugu speakers, and second from the Brahmins (both Telugu and Tamil) who dominated entrances to the bureaucracy and were in pole position with respect to temple economies. Unsurprisingly, Dravidianism's first targets were Telugu people and Brahmins, which intensified in the 1820s onwards. As we have seen before in the case of Odisha and Bengal, economics of conflict rapidly took on a political colour.

The British looked at the transpirations of the Madras presidency very carefully, and so did its neighbours. Mysore, a princely state which was an emblem of prosperity in all of southern India, came under the crosshairs of British conspiracies; while the blow was inflicted on Mysore, the target was undoubtedly Madras. The British consistently appointed Brahmins from Madras, not Mysore, as officers and dewans of the Mysore state; naturally, this shutting-out of Mysore Brahmins from the princely state's government jobs (a British doing) had fomented grievances within the influential Mysore Brahmins. The British sensed an opportunity to set a precedent and abruptly stopped the practice in 1912 by appointing the formidable M. Visvesvaraya as dewan.[58] This move convinced various castes that Madras Brahmins had lost British protection and could be edged out of government jobs. Within Mysore, the Vokkaligas and Lingayats began to correspond and agitate for government jobs, and while commencing with a narrative of meritocracy, quickly began to use caste (actually class) representation as an argument. Visvesvaraya opposed caste representation in administration and advocated for meritocracy sans caste, and went on to establish dedicated educational institutions for non-Brahmins for them to advance in life and for them to join administration as well. This was in line with Madras's own decision in 1895 to set up dedicated educational institutions for everyone but Brahmins. Disparate communities were grouped under the name 'Backward Classes' so as to catalyse a sense of caste unity against Brahmins.[59] However, the British had tasted blood; the Mysore maharaja, Krishnaraja Wodeyar, was forced to set up a committee under the British chief justice of Mysore, Leslie Miller, to fix a timeline for proportionate representation of Backward Classes in all departments of the state in 1918. The Bombay presidency followed suit in 1921 and defined 'Backward Classes' simply as all non-Brahmins not represented in administrative services. Instead of going to a bureaucracy which was meritocratic, as Visvesvaraya had wanted, administration went from being a caste monopoly of Brahmins to an arena for political contestation between castes and an avenue to enhance communal power. Clearly, the British plan of using existing fractures to carve out divisive cleavages against any unified sense of identity was playing out neatly.

The above British decisions to consciously reject educational support followed by a meritocratic system of appointment in favour of caste representation in administration rendered agitation and made caste animosity an inevitability. This economic mismanagement had direct political outcomes, the deleterious effects of which ail India to this day.

This was the time around when certain sections of the dominant non-Brahmin castes fully adopted Dravidianism as a political platform, for it allowed them to not only dislodge the Brahmins from administration but also permitted the marginalization of Brahmins in social and economic life itself, conveniently augmenting their own dominance.[60] The Justice Party, as it came to be called when it outgrew the modalities of the so-called Self Respect Movement, rode to power as a coalition of dominant non-Brahmin castes and imposed Dravidianism throughout the Madras presidency, resulting in lasting cultural corrosion, calls for secession, hostility towards Indians from the north of the country, and ethnic cleansing of Brahmins. Dravidianism's impetus to sever all civilizational links with Bhārat completely reframe history into a racial conflict between 'Aryans' and 'Dravidians', and concomitantly calls to eradicate Brahmins and sanātana dharma reached incredible heights under E.V. Ramaswamy Naicker, who was the de facto ideologue-in-chief of the Justice Party.

Naicker would garland Lord Rāma with chappals, go around with brigands and hoodlums to shut gurukuls, and would publicly burn sanātani scriptures. While many court chroniclers, who pass off as historians, have attempted to reinvent Naicker as a 'social reformer', his works and speeches can only be interpreted as that of a genocidal, bigoted instrument of the British desecration of Bhārat's civilization. Rather than engaging in historical analysis, it is far more useful to simply quote him and leave judgement to the reader.

> That legal offence and all is humbug. We can't be bothered that it is legally wrong. We have to come to this conclusion. Wherever we see a temple, we must go inside and break all the idols inside. Wherever we find a Paapaan [pejorative for Tamil Brahmins], we must kill and destroy him… If one non-Brahmin Tamil dies while trying to kill one Tamil Brahmin, only three of us will die out of every hundred. Ninety-four per cent of us will still remain but Tamil Brahmins will be eliminated. We will definitely go to this level.
>
> —Speech in 1973 at Karaikudi,
> *Collected Works of Periyar E.V.R*, compiled by K. Veeramani

> I went and told the British that it was not British honesty to hand over the power to them while we are the ones who have always supported you. The British smiled and said that they now knew only Hindu–Muslim difference and not Brahmin non-Brahmin difference. Then I went and saw Jinnah and asked for his help. He said that your bed (plan) looks good but it lacks the legs to stand on. And he told that only I had to look after my problem. The media wrote that Jinnah had tar-brushed the face of EVR.
>
> —From an interview in *Anantha Vikatan* in 1965

> The idols, the Vedas which breed ignorance, Upanishads, Manu code, Baratham and other literature which make the people foolish would be driven out of our Tamil Nadu borders.
>
> —Quote from *The Golden Sayings of Periyar*,
> a booklet published in 1949

The Justice Party, now headed by Naicker, was unfazed by the massacre at Jallianwala Bagh in 1919. Justice Party leaders T.M. Nair and P. Theagaraya Chetty, in fact, approved of

British actions in the wake of the Jallianwala Bagh massacre, including the Rowlatt Act. The public reason for why the Justice Party held these opinions was that Tilak was a Brahmin. In Chetty's own words, 'To what community belong most of the persons who find a bad eminence in that report (i.e., the Rowlatt Report)? Who is the central figure among them? He is none other than the Brahmin gentleman (i.e., Tilak) who has been elected to the presidential chair of the next session of the Indian National Congress.'[61] The real reason, however, was the Justice Party's policy of being hand-in-glove with the British. The proposed Montagu-Chelmsford 'reforms' were offering a formula which would have greatly expanded the Justice Party's representation to legislative councils. Clearly, the Justice Party was the British answer to the Home Rule movement and the rise of a nationalist Congress, whereby the possibility of splitting all of the south of India and forming a friendly regime there would have been an attractive proposition to the British.

There were no significant changes to the Justice Party's outlook post-Independence, by which time the stress on linguistic and implied racial separateness of the south of India was reflected in its new name, Dravidar Kazhagam (DK). Any idea of an independent South India that the DK might have had fell apart soon after Andhra Pradesh was created in 1953. The hold of the Justice Party had never percolated into the Andhra regions, possibly because the British did not want to disturb the crucial land tract connecting Madras to Calcutta that was independent of the Hyderabad Nizam. The Justice Party's ethos was inherited by its splinter organization, the Dravida Munnetra Kazhagam (DMK), which also inaugurated the trend of Tamil show-business figures becoming political giants. The DMK, however, was much more politically savvy as it refocused on linguistic concerns more than open assaults on sanātana dharma. The founder of the DMK, C.N. Annadurai said, 'I do not break coconuts for Pillaiyar, (a form of worship to Ganesha) neither do I break his idols.'[62] The DMK stole the DK's thunder in the 1965 Madras anti-Hindi agitation, in which it pedalled the hallucinogen of Hindi imposition, as also the anxieties of the Tamil people in losing government jobs due to unclear demands as to the position of Hindi in administration. As the DMK, unlike the DK, had dropped demands for secession in 1963, the then central government probably found it to be a lesser evil, and there are speculations concerning a behind-the-doors compact as well.[63] The focus on a concocted sense of linguistic identity, underpinned by economic apprehensions of being swamped by Hindi speakers, have ensured that the political and economic policies of the state have been crammed into a narrow compass; while industry, including Brahmin-owned sections, have prospered under a principled laissez-faire, the long-lasting benign neglect and electorally induced fiscal profligacy has been showing signs of fatigue. Since roughly 1967, when the anti-Hindi agitation came to a close after Tamil Nadu had successfully pushed itself into a cavern of its own making, the Tamil language has been reduced to a totem of Dravidian politics. Maintaining the 1967 boundaries of the state, notwithstanding its irrationalities, has become a political imperative to continue corralling state politics solely on the lines of language and 'race'.

Andhra: Après Moi

An interesting fact is that the Telugu-speaking populace is much greater than that of Tamils in India, and yet it was the larger of the two communities who demanded a separate space.[64]

A big reason why the Justice Party could not get adequate pushback from dissenting Telugu-speaking peoples, who had no history of Brahmin hatred, was simply because large parts of the Telugu populace were under the rule of the Nizam of Hyderabad. Madras itself was on the linguistic border between Tamil- and Telugu-speaking parts of the presidency; Madras itself had Telugu and Tamil localities. Being the cynosure of the entire presidency, Madras hosted Telugu professionals, bureaucrats, and businessmen. This compact between the Telugus and Tamils was an uneasy one, where linguistic competition for government jobs and over sectors of the economy was palpable. Demands for a separate Telugu state had existed since the 1910s, and as the Justice Party turned increasingly Tamil-centric, these demands intensified. The bone of contention was the city of Madras, over which both peoples claimed ownership.

After the Report of the Linguistic Provinces Commission, 1948, rejected demands for linguistic states and went against the Congress's own direction taken since at least 1920, the central government was in a fix. Legislators from Telugu-speaking areas of the Madras Vidhan Sabha unanimously were already committed to a demand for a separate Telugu state right after Independence. Thus, to 'review' the 1948 report, the Congress appointed a committee comprising Jawaharlal Nehru, Vallabhbhai Patel, and Pattabhi Sitaramayya, which came to be known as the JVP committee. Sensing that the linguistic state genie had long been let out of the bottle, the committee reported that the Congress's stance on linguistic states needed to factor in practicalities, and a case-by-case approach was warranted. Relying on the findings of the 1948 report, the JVP committee stated apprehensions due to the possibility of the emergence of language as a secessionist force, mutual conflict, administrative dislocation, and threat to the security, unity, and economic prosperity of the country.[65] Knowing that the traction to have a linguistic state had intensified in the Telugu-speaking regions of the country owing to differences with Tamils and the integration of Hyderabad following the terrors of the Nizam, the JVP committee wanted to nip the trouble in the bud. Thus, the JVP committee threw a googly—they said that the Telugus could have an Andhra state, but only if they gave up Madras to the Tamils. Feeling that the proposal would be deemed preposterous, they expected the Telugus to simply continue with the present arrangement, albeit in a disgruntled manner.

Things took an unexpected turn when Potti Sriramulu, a freedom fighter, went on a fast-unto-death for a Telugu state in 1952. Agitations, strikes, and violent demonstrations on linguistic lines (with underlying economic drivers, as discussed above) took on a frenzied pitch. C. Rajagopalachari, a stalwart of India's freedom movement and the then chief minister of Madras, took an anti-division line; his standing with the people vaporized because of this decision; trains coming into Madras from the Andhra regions were scribbled with graffiti reading *Rajaji chāvāli*, that is, Rajaji has to die. As Potti's fast entered its eighth day and the threat of mass violence loomed, Jawaharlal Nehru wrote to Rajaji, attempting to induce the latter to relent.[66] Yet, before the latter could accord his decision, Potti passed away. Telugu-speaking areas erupted in arson and uncontrollable public outbursts. Recourseless, the very next day, Nehru declared that there would be an Andhra state.

Knowing that the war had been lost, the 1948 report was given a silent burial, and a new States Reorganization Commission was instituted, which gave its report in 1955, written so that further violence and agitations for linguistic states could be pre-empted. Essentially, all linguistic demands were conceded. The motivations for the same emerged from the basic fact of India's finances: only a government job offered any meaningful employment for most of India's semi-educated and educated, and a *sarkari naukri* was the acme of what an Indian could aspire to. The easiest way to secure one community's claim to jobs would be to set up an exclusionary barrier in the form of official languages; this tool of the British to sow discord between Indians had become all but standard politics in independent India too. Upon this foundation, each community erected grotesque towers of cyclopean identitarian politics, replete with linguistic chauvinism, cultural rigidities, and tortured retellings of their own histories divorced from their civilizational embedding in Bhārat and sanātana dharma.

Andhra Pradesh inflicted a coup de grâce on the views of Rajagopalachari and B.R. Ambedkar, who whilst not opposed to language being a factor to decide statehood, wished to take a more measured and composite view of identity and economics. This model of statehood was exported pan-India with the States Reorganization Act, 1956, and forms the principal benchmark for what a state ought to be to this day. Nehru probably understood that what he had unleashed would come to consume most of the country. He thus wrote soon after his decision to allow Andhra Pradesh to come into existence that '... we have disturbed the hornet's nest and I believe all of us are likely to be stung'.[67] Stung he was, when the bilingual Bombay state collapsed soon after in 1960, and Punjab began to simmer.

Of Accidents and Misfortune

The early days of independent India saw a strange situation where an independent country attempted to continue administrative divisions by and large as left behind by the British, regardless of their remoteness to both the identities and economic concerns of Indians.

Table 1. Part A, Part B, and Part C states of India from 1947 to 1956

Part A States	Part B States	Part C States
Andhra	Hyderabad	Ajmer
Assam	Jammu and Kashmir	Bhopal
Bihar	Madhya Bhārat	Coorg
Bombay	Mysore	Delhi
Madhya Pradesh	Patiala	Himachal Pradesh
Madras	Rajasthan	Kutch
Orissa	Saurashtra	Manipur
Punjab	Travancore-Cochin	Tripura
Uttar Pradesh		Vindhya Pradesh

The erstwhile scheme of Part A, B, C, and D states was a repetition simpliciter of the British scheme of administration; the Part A states were the erstwhile governors' provinces, Part B states were erstwhile princely states, Part C states were the erstwhile chief commissioners' provinces along with a few smaller princely states, and the category of Part D states had to be conjured to accommodate Andaman and Nicobar. There was no rationale for this arrangement, which was a map of the British scaffolding of the country based on colonial convenience and apathy. The Constitution carried forward not only the boundaries carved by the British on India's map but also, by implication, the British rationale for such divisions. Naturally, this state of affairs was wholly incompatible, even insulting, to India's independence. Clause 14, Chapter I,

Part I of States Reorganization Committee (SRC) Report of 1955 summarizes the position pithily: 'The existing structure of the States of the Indian Union is partly the result of accident and the circumstances attending the growth of the British power in India and partly a by-product of the historic process of the integration of former Indian States. The division of India during the British period into British provinces and Indian States was itself fortuitous and had no basis in Indian history.'

The recommendations of the 1955 SRC are given below. It may be noted that these recommendations were not followed completely even as the linguistic formula was by and large applied, namely that of 'One Language One State'. Keeping Uttar Pradesh as a single large state was the biggest drawback in these recommendations.

Table 2. Recommendations of the SRC 1955 with respect to India's states. We note that Hyderabad and Andhra were included in one state called Andhra Pradesh and that was essentially reverted to the two states recommended here in 2014. We note also that Vidarbha was not carved out as a separate state but included in the mixed language Bombay state

State	Area (Sq. Km.)	Population (cr.)	Language
Madras	1,29,940	3.00	Tamil
Kerala	38,798	1.36	Malayalam
Mysore	1,88,371	1.90	Kannada
Hyderabad	1,17,327	1.13	Telugu
Andhra	1,68,221	2.09	Telugu
Bombay	3,92,022	4.02	Mixed
Vidarbha	95,519	0.76	Marathi
Madhya Pradesh	4,43,408	2.61	Hindi
Rajasthan	3,42,657	1.60	Hindi
Punjab	1,50,583	1.72	Punjabi

State	Area (Sq. Km.)	Population (cr.)	Language
Uttar Pradesh	2,93,732	6.32	Hindi
Bihar	1,72,287	3.82	Hindi
West Bengal	89,588	2.65	Bangla
Assam	2,30,614	0.97	Assamese
Orissa	1,55,762	1.46	Odia
Jammu and Kashmir	2,40,300	0.14	Kashmiri

An adjustment of sorts took place in the early 1950s. The system of Part A, B, C, and D states was done away with, and a two-tier system of states and union territories (UTs) was instituted through the Constitution (Seventh Amendment) Act, 1956. However, closer inspection of this Act shows that the changes it sought to bring about were arguably cosmetic and superficial. The deep dysfunctionalities which the British had systematized within the country by crystallizing religious and caste identities were cleverly evaded. Independent India simply fell into another British-constructed identitarian cul-de-sac.

Language was historically, at best, a very weak source of identity in India. Illustrious dynasties would speak multiple languages, and patronize multiple languages at once. Even in the histories of the four states which had the greatest impact on the idea of linguistic identitarianism, examples are found aplenty. One notes the prevalence of Telugu in southern Odisha and northern Tamil Nadu; the originally Kannadiga Senas of Bengal patronized proto-Bengali, and the Satavahanas, whose Pauranic name gave Andhra Pradesh its name, claimed descent from the Andhra tribe of the Aitareya Brahman of the *Rigveda*, which called the banks of the Yamuna its home.[68] Bhāratiya identities, which were at once highly localized and civilizational, were morphed into a dyspeptic imitation of 19th-century nations as the British sought to dismiss the notion of the existence of any Indian 'nation'. So strongly had the British shaped the way Indians looked at themselves that an otherwise alien concept of linguistic xenophobia gripped the country in its founding years and forced a full-fledged reordering of the country's administration. Ambedkar was trenchant in his criticism of linguistic states that were created on the basis of One Language One State—in other words, all those who spoke a particular language being included in just one state. He said the SRC recommendations were 'full of poison'. Very sagely he commented that the Union of India 'expresses only an idea' and that 'it does not indicate an achievement'. How far away are these wise words from the cacophony of today's political leaders who call our Constitution a holy book.

The wide difference in the populations of the SRC-recommended states is also worthy of comment (Table 2). It seems incredible that no one thought fit to comment that the ratio of population in the largest (UP) and smallest (J&K) state was as high as 45.14, a number that has the most unhealthy of implications for the entire electoral exercise in the sense that smaller states would get completely snuffed out of the national discourse. Again, Ambedkar was scathing in his criticism of the SRC when he said that 'the Commission evidently thinks that the size of a state is a matter of no consequence and that the equality in the size of the states constituting a federation is a matter of no moment. This is the first and most terrible error cost of which the commission has committed. If not rectified in time, it will indeed be a great deal'.

It is a fashionable exercise among politicians today, across party lines, to pay lip service to Ambedkar. The high and mighty move flashily to his statues on 14 April and garland them in full view of the press and the TV cameras. He has been reduced to a token figure limited to protecting the lower castes and the scheduled caste (SC) communities to the extent that anyone criticizing him in any way is pounced upon by various outfits and threatened legally and physically. Yet, many of his critical constitutional and political ideas have been given a silent burial by those who ostensibly advocate for his views. Would any of these so-called admirers of Ambedkar bother to read his comments on the SRC and try to understand his far-seeing comments on linguistic states and population disparities among our states? Would they care to follow that his arguments accurately predict the present north–south divide in our polity? A true tribute to this great son of Bhārat would be to attempt to comprehend his statements and undo the 'terrible' damage that linguistic states and super large states have wreaked on the country.

The above-described four states—Odisha, West Bengal, Tamil Nadu, and Andhra Pradesh—are the most consequential in our discussion owing to the fact that their collective experience forms the template and informs the methodology of linguistic statehood adopted countrywide.[69] However, each state in India has its own additional chest of absurdities. Uttar Pradesh and Madhya Pradesh have no rational reason to exist with their present boundaries, and both are amalgamations of various regions with their own cultures, which came into being simply due to British policies at the time. Mithila and Magadh have been clubbed together despite stark differences between the people in the two regions. Punjab in its present shape came into being as a result of language being a thinly veiled proxy for religion and due to which India lost thousands to bloodshed in a separatist movement. The relative prosperity of the nine districts of the princely Mysore state, which were quite advanced in multiple ways, has largely vanished after their merger with what constitutes north Karnataka today, thanks to a caste competition to capture state largesse.[70] Jammu and Kashmir, even in its present UT form, defies logic considering the polar opposites of its two constituent divisions. Maharashtra's various regions do not look eye to eye and have separate identities (and economics), leading to constant regional tussles. Even Tamil Nadu, the pole star and cheer leader of the linguistic statehood, had historically never seen itself as one political entity even during the Chola era—the Chola kings would symbolically wear three crowns,[71] representing the separate homelands of the Cholas, Cheras, and Pandyas—regions which to this day host peoples having vastly different approaches to life and other differences, including in their dialects, which were relentlessly suppressed by Dravidianists so as to impose a uniform identity.[72] It is indeed quite a damning indictment of events that some of the old princedom boundaries, such as those in erstwhile Rajputana, were perhaps more representative of the original identities and economies than the current framework of twenty-eight states and eight union territories.

All administration is an ongoing experiment and changes as the values which it ought to animate undergo flux. Simultaneously, the benchmark against which administration ought to be evaluated is whether, at the time of its operation, it is able to efficiently operationalize the principles espoused by the political community responsible for the country's governance. In India's case, this would mean last-mile governance which is accessible, approachable, and affordable, and which advances the economic interests of the people while permitting them adequate space to express their culture and ways of life. The consequences of linguistic states have, in multiple essential respects, caused unbridled harm to both the nation as a whole as well as the constituents of respective states.

Large linguistic states have had lopsided developmental trajectories. Karnataka, Maharashtra, Tamil Nadu, and West Bengal, each with a huge metro city, are grossly overdependent on the same. Take, for example, Karnataka—the state's gross state domestic product (GSDP) of ₹ 16.1 lakh crore would drop to ₹ 10.2 lakh crore if only one district, Bengaluru Urban, is removed from the number, that is, more than a third of the entire state's GSDP comes from just that one district.[73] All of politics, talks about the economy, and the interests of powerful lobbies are concentrated in Bengaluru, much to the detriment of the northern districts, which have lagged behind. Such oversized dependence takes more gnarly forms, such as how Bengaluru ruthlessly extracts water from areas near the Cauvery and about 100 kilometres away from the city—out of sight and silently, with little regard to the health of the ecosystem there. Maharashtra, too, remains preoccupied with the transpirations of Mumbai, with the little remaining political and economic attention going to the Pune region. Vidarbha, meanwhile, has a per capita income which is barely a fourth that of Maharashtra and suffers from acute poverty.[74] West Bengal, likewise, suffers from singular dependence on Kolkata, with Asansol coming a distant second—similar problems have resulted. Even Odisha, which heralded the idea of linguistic states, is preoccupied with the happenings in and around Bhubaneswar and Puri—the severe economic backwardness of Odisha's inland districts is appalling, and there have been demands to place them with the peoples of central India instead of with the coastal Odiyas.

Concerns of those who live beyond the shadows of the states' primary cities are eclipsed. This greatly fuels inequalities within the state. How democratic and representative is it when politics, economics, and state finances of vast territories are canned within singular cities? This needs no exposition. Unfortunately, the general rule of thumb in India is that the worth of a citizen is inversely proportional to their distance from the state capital.[75]

The above phenomenon is also responsible for keeping the vast economic potential of large parts of the country untapped. When the political elite is preoccupied with a city or a specific region where identities of their political interests reside, the top-down decision-making system of our state administration does not provide adequate policy and fiscal support to regions which are being politically sidelined due to their identity. This cripples broad-based economic growth for the entire nation and reflects in low standards of living and vast income disparities between regions within the same state. An egregious example of the same was how in the erstwhile state of Jammu and Kashmir, the Kashmir-centric politics of the state ensured that Ladakhi apple farmers were systematically denied access to the broader Indian market so as to prevent competition with Kashmiri apples. Transportation and horticultural support by the state was systematically denied to Ladakh. It was only in 2021, after Ladakh was separated from Jammu and Kashmir, that the first consignment of Ladakhi apples could be shipped to the rest of the country.[76] There are countless such economically neglected regions, which could be economic dynamos but are the victims of being placed in a large state and out of sync with the electoral calculus of dominant identity groupings.

At both national and state levels, economic growth is closely related to the number of 'second cities', that is, where there is a prevalence of cities which have at least a third of the population of the biggest set of cities in a region. A departure from this rule results in long-term political instability driven by regional grievances and conflicts, mostly driven by stunted growth beyond the big cities.[77] We have seen countries such as Thailand and Chile, which have lost decades many times over due to the concentration of political and economic power in singular centres. One must note that between 1985 and 2015, an era when the economic chasm between China and India reached stratospheric heights, China developed nineteen second cities, while India could manage just two, Malappuram and Kollam. Even this is misleading since these satellite cities arose only due to a redrawing of administrative maps. A large reason why this disparity came into being was because of capital-centric state administration and interests that neglected the state beyond its capital's suburbs; each state capital has developed an ivory tower replica of what was once Lutyens's Delhi. Beyond the limits where media attention dries up, state presence evaporates. This was both a factor as well as a symptom of a political system which has failed to deliver robust and equitable economic growth in India and is in urgent need of correction.

Likewise, the current model of One Language One State, which for the sake of convenience may be called the Nehru–Prakasam model, has critical cultural drawbacks.[78] The first, which is actually a reality, is that the larger a state, the more is the diversity contained within it. Bhārat being as diverse as it is, castes, languages, dialects, faiths, and other such identity markers increase rapidly with state size. The minority population, especially Muslims, can become sizable in larger states. Inevitably, this leads to long-term conflict. The inclusion of minorities, whether by caste, linguistic, religious, or any other facet of identity with a large enough dominant population, causes politics to devolve into a race between smaller identity groupings to ally with or against the dominant grouping to capture power.[79] This underlying social fragmentation is the principal driver behind clientelistic politics. Identity groups compete to capture state resources and then use the same to dispense favours to themselves. Naturally, this leads to bad economic outcomes for all as the economic discourse shifts from public infrastructure, governance, and services to aggrandizement of one's own identity grouping by emptying the state's coffers. This was perhaps why the British maintained large provinces; the higher the social fragmentation in a place, the less was the access to public goods.[80] Not much has changed today. These very debilitating factors also suit the electoral calculations of the political parties today because these parties have emerged as a product of this very same semi-feudal and extractive system. Thus, the Congress did not further divide Uttar Pradesh and Maharashtra, going against specific recommendations of the 1956 SRC Report.

Similarly, the only way for identities to survive, negotiate, and ultimately capture power in the state depends on their numbers within a state—the larger the state, the more the pressure for similar groups to give up their cultural differences and present a united front. This, unfortunately, leads to a loss of cultural diversity over time. As we saw above, the Tamils lost a lot of their unique linguistic and cultural differences owing to the drive to 'standardize' what it meant to be Tamil.[81] Large states, thus, cause an artificial homogenization—differences within distinct groupings in a state are erased so that dissimilarities between states may be accentuated. Cultural nuances and gradations are smothered by the singular blanket of linguistic uniformity. And regions with markedly different identities (Garhwal and Kumaon, Jammu and Kashmir, Rayalaseema and Andhra) are disturbingly homogenized. The diversities within a state are, therefore, suppressed while differences between states are exacerbated for purely political reasons. Politics ceases to represent diversity but becomes a tool of social engineering to infuse pathological mutations in the social, political, and economic make-up of the country. This leads to divisive politics marked by clientelism, casteism, and secessionist subnationalism.

The rise of social media, instant communication, and digital public infrastructure has rattled political outfits which are identitarian. This is because the economic bedrock of identitarian politics in linguistic states is clientelism, as described above. One cannot dispense too many exclusive benefits to their identity grouping (usually particular castes) if benefits are linked to universal identification like Aadhaar, or delivered straight to their bank accounts without conveniently placed middlemen diverting flows. Likewise, with grievances having the potential to become national from local overnight thanks to social media, the systematic neglect of regions which would otherwise be electorally manageable is a difficult task. These changes to India's political economy, infused by technology, makes certain kinds of technological solutions natural targets of the political losers in this scenario; unsurprisingly, reforms which would be gladly welcomed on grounds of increased efficiency and citizen access are challenged in courts and made subject to disinformation campaigns.[82] Thus, the kind of identitarianism wrought by having linguistic states in their present shape is fundamentally opposed to citizen-centric reform, particularly those leveraging technology. Considering the gains which digital public infrastructure has already delivered to India and the future possibilities which such technological solutions hold in unlocking India's economic potential, linguistic states and their contingent politics are particularly incompatible with tech-driven governance and economy, particularly welfare.

The Constitution's Strictures and Silences

The subject of whether India is federal or not has been a matter of constant judicial and political squabbling. In fact, the debate predates the Constitution itself, with lively debates on what the term 'Union' and 'state' ought to mean when Ambedkar presented the draft constitution to the Constituent Assembly. Defending the choice to not include the term 'federation' in the Constitution, Ambedkar clarified, 'The Drafting Committee wanted to make it clear that though India was to be a federation, the federation was not the result of an agreement by the states to join in a federation and that the federation not being the result of an agreement, no state has the right to secede from it. The federation is a union because it is indestructible. *Although the country and the people may be divided into different states for convenience of administration, the country is one integral whole, its people a single people living under a single imperium derived from a single source* (emphasis added).'[83]

Three important takeaways may be derived from Ambedkar's statement. First, the Constituent Assembly ascribed no shred of sovereignty or independent existence to states. Their choice of terminology for the term 'state' was merely a convenient continuity from the Government of India Act, 1935. Second, the purpose of a state is to accord administrative convenience, which, in modern parlance, corresponds to the broader concept of effective governance and accurate representation, not just efficient regulation. The third, and perhaps most important expression, is that the country is one indestructible whole which derives legitimacy from one single authority, the Union of India, while states are what the Union chooses the country to be subdivided into to achieve the aforementioned expansive understanding of administrative convenience.[84] To summarize, states in India are just administrative arrangements in which diverse Indians can express and secure their particular iterations of Indian identity, while advancing their economic interests through differential regulation.

All politics essentially boils down, therefore, to only a combination of two priorities—identity and economics. In many instances, it is attempted to define one of these two factors in terms of the other, and this often offers only imperfect explanations. The Constitution of India contains one such conundrum, the vagaries of which have caused considerable damage to both the economy and the sense of identity of Indian citizens. The Constitution defines, in a fairly comprehensive manner, how a constituent state of the Union works and what it is supposed to do, through a clear division of powers and responsibilities. Rather irregularly called 'federal', the scheme is fundamentally economic and financial in nature; it is a division of finances and of developmental responsibilities. However, what factors ought to be considered to constitute a state, and thus a significant portion of what being a state ought to mean, have been left to the wisdom of the legislature.

The reason, as one may glean from the Constituent Assembly Debates (CAD) as well as the views of successive statesmen, was to stress political integration, maintaining the unity of the country, and to accord flexibility to a country arising from a traumatic partition arising from questions of identity. As time has progressed, these priorities have lessened in their importance, and the unity and integrity of the country is no longer in doubt. Partition, too, has largely receded from public memory.[85] In such a context it may be suggested that in omitting to more clearly specify the identity of a state, the Constituent Assembly was remiss; this omission was, in hindsight, counterproductive. Today's attempts at igniting a north–south divide in India are but one such consequence of the lack of a rational, uniformly applicable metric of state (re)organization. As Bhārat is reengineering itself to be more in line with a future-facing economy which is rooted in its layered yet robust identity, the reorganization of states into more cogent and representative units is an imperative.

One realizes somewhat regretfully that the determination of the basis on which a state has been constituted in India post 1947 is as much an exercise in history as it is one in schizophrenic ad-hocism. A question as important as how Bhāratiyas are to be governed cannot be relegated to the vagaries of *jugaad* and *chalta hai* attitudes. Primarily, there was a conscious or unconscious neglect of the fact that smaller political units are easier to administer. That Bhārat is a land that is made beautiful by its micro diversities and that the smallness of these naturally present territories would match well with the smallness required for effective administration was given the go by. The dominance of Uttar Pradesh in any political calculus to gain power at the Centre has been a most unfortunate reality in the political panorama of the country.[86] The Congress in its time and the BJP at the present time have crafted very skilful caste- and religion-based arrangements so as to capture a bulk of the parliamentary seats from this key state, literally the electoral crucible of the nation. While this might be applauded from an electoral point of view, given we have the system we have, what has been completely forgotten is that when one has states of wildly uneven sizes, any pretence of decentralized rule[87] vanishes. Finally, since one reaps as one sows, the effects of the short-sighted delimitation freezes of 1976 and 2001 have now come back with a vengeance so that the basic principle of One Man One Vote, the fundamental idea in an electoral democracy, has been compromised.

A look at the history of ancient India is useful. In any larger political entity, issues of federalism, that is centralization versus decentralization, are bound to crop up. The discourse between unitary and peripheral units is an old story in India. The establishment of small republics in ancient India as opposed to large kingdoms arose from the administrative convenience in managing more compact areas. There are limits to operating a centralized imperial system in a large domain, and this was accentuated in former times (before the industrial revolution) when communication systems were poor. The roads in the Roman and Mughal empires had a lot to do with the efficiency of unitary governance. However, practical issues of connections, conveyance, and coordination became insurmountable in the end. There is indeed an absolute limit to imperialism that is placed by territorial size, nature, and geography, what one might term imperial overstretch. Even the best of arrangements cannot permanently withstand the tendencies of centrifugal disruption. British India was probably too large by the end to hold together, and the British were constantly fiddling with new stratagems to divide groups of people artificially, including the well-known divide-and-rule methodology. Language, of course, was the most lethal of these methodologies. The tendency to disintegrate is not particularly Indian or even Asian. It is perhaps the primary reason why ancient and mediaeval empires worldwide effectively remained collections of small states, conglomerations of loose almost independent nationalities that paid nominal tribute to a distant suzerain.[88] A fusion of nationalism as exemplified by democracy and federalism as symbolized by republicanism has always been the most stable combination in India and will continue to be so.

That all the redrawings of state boundaries post Independence happened due to short-term political exigencies tell us there is nothing fixed about them. They can be changed based on longer term calculations in the more mature democracy we have today. Playing into the hands of the British and then regional parties like the DMK, the Shiv Sena, and the All India Trinamool Congress (AITC), Indians have clung to language as an identity marker because we seem to perceive some real or mostly imagined injustice. These insecurities have been stoked by political parties. Rich countries like Italy and Switzerland manage to be multilingual easily. Poorer countries like the ones in the Balkans have used language to separate from one another. As India becomes richer, will there be less linguistic friction? As we have explained, the British were able to use language as a divider because it could be coupled with economic betterment in an abysmally poor country. Economics always plays a primary role in inducing social, psychological, and cultural divides.

Recalling ancient India, we observe that a map is more than just the lines that are drawn on it and the labels that are placed next to them. A map narrates the history of a country and its citizens. It is evident that a significant portion of our narrative has been lost when we look at a map of the Indian subcontinent, or Bhāratavarsha as it were. Is it possible for us to redraw the map and restore the links between the ancient and the modern? Could we combine our civilizational ideals with our government, specifically the existing system outlined in our Constitution, to bring out the best in India in terms of modernization, development, and economic growth? The matter has come to haunt us with urgency because 2026 is not far off, and we will be obliged to go in for a nationwide delimitation exercise. Or will we cop out again and introduce another twenty-five-year freeze?

Every form of government in India must allow for the best possible representation of the vast diversity that exists within our country. Our governing frameworks need to accommodate this diversity more strongly. States can be made smaller to achieve this. The next chapter goes into detail on a previously suggested division of India into seventy-five states with population distributions that are evenly balanced. This division is necessary if One Person One Vote is to be associated with states that have an equal relationship with the Centre. When suitable in each situation, such demarcation can be made based on geographical, historical, linguistic, religious, and cultural grounds. Why do we persist with states that have such large populations? Around twelve of them have populations well over 5 crore each—only thirty countries in the world are so highly populated.

The potential of our nation's diversity is considerably more than what our states' existing sizes can convey. We can realize this potential by using an ideal structure consisting of smaller governing units. Such reorganization may also result in more profound psychological effects. It will establish the prerequisites for every citizen's mental decolonization. It will inspire each of us to embrace our identity as members of a civilization without apology and to utilize it as a powerful tool to further our social and economic objectives. Therefore, state delimitation and Bhārat's psychological regeneration are related.

CHAPTER 3

Why Does Bhārat Need Delimitation of Electoral Constituencies Today?

'People often say that, in a democracy, decisions are made by a majority of the people. Of course, that is not true. Decisions are made by a majority of those who make themselves heard and who vote—a very different thing.'

—Walter Judd

India is the most populous country in the world as also its largest democracy. The logistics of our general elections have, therefore, been truly staggering and beyond the comprehension of many people in smaller democracies (many of which are comparable in size to India's individual states, even constituencies). In this sphere, India has an advantage of scale, and with this size factor in play, the likelihood of systematic rigging, extensive booth capturing, and other types of widespread foul play are greatly reduced (and diluted). Around 64.2 crore (roughly 36 crore being women) of a possible 96.88 crore eligible voters cast their ballots from 19 April through 1 June in seven phases and have sent 543 members to the Lok Sabha in 2024. This feat was undertaken through the 11 lakh booths overseen by 1.5 crore election officials across the 28 states and 9 Union Territories in a seven-phase election supervised by the Election Commission of India (ECI), its officers on the ground, and more than 3.5 lakh security personnel from various agencies. Electronic Voting Machines (EVM), along with Voter-Verified Paper Audit Trail (VVPAT) have been universally deployed to deliver dependable results, notwithstanding accusations which are yet to be buttressed by any evidence worth its salt. As soon as the elections were scheduled in March 2024, the ECI promptly transferred key senior bureaucrats in several high population states to prevent any perceived conflict of interest and to ensure a level playing field for all political parties, big and small. Throughout the process the ECI has been ever vigilant and has lived up to its charge as an impartial constitutional body, censuring leaders across political lines when required. It has given its decisions without fear or favour. Our elections stand testimony to our maturity as a democracy and stand in contrast to other liberal democracies, even the venerable US where elections have had a chequered and colourful (of recent, even acrimonious) history.

The essence of democracy rests on the concept of citizenship. Citizenship is a particular kind of political membership in which a nominal sense of equality is provided to all citizens in terms of some key rights, duties, and relations with the state. Citizenship in a democracy mandates that each vote has an equal value in determining the outcome of any election anywhere in or throughout the country, since each citizen ought to have an equal say. In a large country following the first-past-the-post system, effectuating equal citizenship would require constituencies to be roughly equal to each other in terms of population (since one constituency has just one representative). A constituency which is more populous than others would dilute the value of a vote in the constituency, since a larger number of people are electing one representative. Similarly, 'rotten boroughs',[1] or constituencies which have very small populations, provide their voters an unequal privilege through over-representation, as a smaller body of people get to appoint a representative who is equal in power with one elected by a greater number of people. Thus, one needs to 'delimit' constituencies in such a way that each constituency has roughly equal number of people, and thus, each voter will have a roughly equal vote.

Delimitation refers to the procedure of fixing the boundary or limits of an item. In the context of Indian politics, it means determining the number of constituencies, their size in each state, and their boundaries. Delimitation is the process by which the Indian State ensures that each constituency has nearly the same number of voters so that the value of any vote in electing a member of the Lok Sabha is the same anywhere in India. Any citizen of India should have the same say in deciding who is to represent him or her in the lower house of parliament. Since the population density is quite varied across different regions of the country, the geographical size of a Lok Sabha constituency can vary a lot. Such a phenomenon is normal since democratic franchise is about citizens and not territories. This creates, in itself, logistical problems for the ECI because voters in sparsely populated areas might have issues in even getting to a polling booth near their homes. The number of booths will also vary widely, and one needs more booths in low density population constituencies. In extreme cases, the constituencies may be made artificially small for these logistical reasons, and in these situations the value of an individual vote goes up.

Delimitation essentially creates a relationship between an increase in a state's population and an increase in the number of elected representatives that the state sends to its legislature and parliament. It guarantees that there is no over-representation or under-representation of an elected representative by the electorate. To guarantee that the electorate's votes are distributed equally, delimitation balances the constituencies according to the strength of the electorate. A uniform Population Seat Ratio (PSR) between states in the Union (macro level) and between multiple constituencies within each state (micro level) is the goal of delimitation. When delimitation at the constituency level is carried out appropriately within states and between states, no state can have a political weight that is not commensurate with its population. The micro and the macro thus converge if citizens are made equal in terms of their vote. The 'One Person One Vote' notion serves as the philosophical ideal throughout this entire exercise.

Delimitation is not a continuous procedure, for obvious logistical reasons. It is carried out at discrete time intervals. Although the population of a country grows continuously, its effects become apparent only over time in terms of the disproportionate population growth across several states and constituencies due to differential fertility rates as well as migration flows. Accordingly, the sizes (and number) of constituencies are reset at fixed time periods. In the majority of nations, delimitation is a clear democratic process that is carried out on a regular basis. This period is ten years in the US, Canada and (ought to be in) India. It is eight to twelve years in the UK due to their Redistribution of Seats Act, 1992. It is seven years in Australia and six years in New Zealand. There is no fixed interval for delimitation in France.

Election delimitation is a critical process in liberal democracies to ensure fair and representative elections. The US undergoes redistricting every ten years following the national census. This process has been marred by controversies due to gerrymandering, when political parties (who get to draw district boundaries when in power) manipulate boundaries to gain electoral advantages. Recent efforts have focused on introducing nonpartisan or bipartisan commissions to oversee redistricting. In the UK, boundary commissions regularly review parliamentary constituencies to ensure fairness and equality in representation. The most recent review aimed to reduce the number of MPs to 600 and equalize constituency sizes. This must be done continuously to ensure fairness. However, political disagreements and public consultations have delayed the process. In Canada, electoral boundaries are redrawn periodically by independent commissions. The Australian Electoral Commission manages redistributions of electoral boundaries for federal elections. This process follows specific criteria to ensure fairness and representation. Challenges include addressing population shifts between states and territories. The process aims to reflect population changes and maintain fair representation. Other challenges include accommodating diverse geographical and demographic factors while upholding democratic principles. Some of these issues are pertinent to India.

Delimitation in Germany occurs at both federal and state levels. Boundaries are redrawn to reflect population changes and maintain proportional representation. However, controversies arise regarding the weighting of rural versus urban areas in the process. Following the reunification of Germany in 1990, significant changes were made to the electoral constituency delimitation process to accommodate the new political landscape. The delimitation of electoral constituencies in Germany is governed by specific rules outlined in the Federal Electoral Act, 1993. The principle of equal representation was paramount in the delimitation process. The goal was to ensure that each electoral district had a roughly equal number of inhabitants, thus preserving the democratic principle of One Person One Vote. Delimitation took into account geographical factors such as natural borders, administrative boundaries, and population density to create coherent and manageable electoral districts. Historical considerations were also taken into account, particularly in regions formerly divided by the Iron Curtain. Efforts were made to reconcile historical and administrative divisions with the new political reality.[2]

These delimitation exercises highlight the ongoing challenges in balancing representation, population shifts, and political interests in liberal democracies, emphasizing the importance of transparent and fair processes to uphold democratic values.

Ideally, the delimitation exercise in India would need to be done after each census, which till recently has been held in every year that ends with the numerical 1, for example, 1991, 2001, 2011. The decennial census has, however, not been held in 2021, and no reason has been given for this omission by the government, though the exigencies of the coronavirus pandemic is a convincing imputation.

Following the distortionary and wholly deleterious freeze on delimitation in 1976, despite the partial (and nonetheless deeply flawed) relaxation in 2003,[3] India remains the only large liberal democracy where delimitation has been frozen for a time period as long as fifty years.[4] Before we describe the reasons for this, a brief survey of the eighteen general elections, especially the earlier ones, is useful to trace the contours of delimitation in India.

Summary of the General Elections with Respect to Delimitation

Let us go back to the years when India was making the transition to a Republic. The Constituent Assembly notified the establishment of an Election Commission in November 1949. However, the problems in conducting elections were onerous. There were nearly 18 crore eligible voters but 85 per cent of these could neither read nor write. The sheer logistics of the operation were daunting to say the least. Perhaps even more challenging was to democratize a nation that had been shackled by colonization and the resulting degradation of their culture—for instance, Sukumar Sen, India's first chief election commissioner, had electoral rolls corrected to include names of women who had registered themselves as someone's wife or someone's mother without using their own names, an action which granted thousands of women an opportunity to view themselves as individuals having a political existence of their own.[5] We began with 'One Nation One Election'; in other words elections were held for parliament and the state assemblies simultaneously. Nobody objected to this very sensible procedure, unlike certain sections of the commentariat today.[6] Voting for the first general election took place in 1951–1952, and there were 489 seats for the Lok Sabha, curiously, for 401 constituencies because some constituencies sent more than one member—one from the general category and one or more from the reserved categories. Possibly such an arrangement could be reviewed again in the present context.[7] Using simple arithmetic, this delimitation worked out to 3.7 lakh voters sending a representative to the Lok Sabha on average, an entirely reasonable figure, and one that compares with the numbers in other Western democracies.

The second general election was held in 1957. There were 494 seats for the Lok Sabha, a marginal increase from the first election. There were some small rearrangements in the constituencies after 1957, mostly in the Northeast region. Goa was liberated in 1961, and members of Parliament (MPs) were needed from there. There were still some nominated members from Lakshadweep, the Andaman and Nicobar Islands, and Nagaland. The third and fourth general elections in 1962 and 1967 saw other changes, notably the end of One Nation One Election because the tenure of some of the state assemblies ended before the stipulated five years, with the imposition of president's rule with Article 356 of the Constitution becoming progressively prevalent. In the context of delimitation, we note that there were 494 seats in the 1962 election with 2 crore eligible voters, maintaining a still respectable ratio of 4.5 lakh voters per each member of the Lok Sabha. In 1967 the strength of the Lok Sabha was 523 and this small increase from 1962 was mostly on account of the regularization of boundaries of certain states, redrawing of the Punjab, Haryana, and Himachal Pradesh borders, and elections in some places where there were only nominated members previously. There were now nearly 41 crore eligible voters, meaning that the potential number of people sending a member to the Lok Sabha had now crawled up to nearly 8 lakh, more than double the number with which we had started the process.

The fifth Lok Sabha election was held in 1971 and because Indira Gandhi decided to go for a snap poll, the full five-year cycle of parliamentary elections was broken. At issue was the prime minister herself and her interpretation of the Constitution. It was the first of our 'presidential' type elections where the person became more important than the party. She appealed to voters to ratify her decisions concerning bank nationalization and the abolition of privy purses. One Nation One Poll was effectively given a go by but now at the all-India level. This period saw the rise of regional parties, largely hereditary and sometimes linguistically based. Parties such as the DMK in Tamil Nadu and the Akali Dal in Punjab received large numbers of votes, and regional concerns came to the forefront of national politics.

Most significantly, the prime minister took a significant decision and froze the parliamentary constituencies based on the 1971 census for twenty-five years till 2001. This decision was implemented during the Emergency period through the controversial 42nd Constitutional Amendment. Another twenty-five-year freeze was put in place with the 84th Amendment in the coalition regime of Atal Bihari Vajpayee. The boundaries of constituencies were altered in 2001 to balance populations among parliamentary and assembly seats. However, state-wise Lok Sabha seats and the seats in legislative assemblies have remained unaltered since the 1971 census. Hence, the One Man One Vote principle deteriorated rapidly, and all of the imbalances which we have outlined in the current system began to infect India's polity. A piecemeal concession came in the form of Constitution (87th Amendment) Act, 2003, when assembly constituencies in states were readjusted to reflect 2001 census numbers, but without altering the number of seats reserved for scheduled castes and scheduled tribes.

A significant change, perhaps, might only be observed after 2026, as the 84th Amendment's freeze on seats operates only until the first census after 2026. Since the first census after 2026 will be in 2031 (if not brought forward), we will perhaps see no movement on delimitation till then. In any case, we cannot have the next delimitation until we have a census. To summarize, general elections after 1975 did not have much bearing on delimitation because the constituencies were frozen then and again in 2001 for a total of fifty years. Meanwhile, the population of the country increased while the number of Lok Sabha seats was levelled off at 543, and consequently the average number of persons electing a single member of the lower house has skyrocketed to nearly 17.9 lakh today, an unwieldy number with massive variance hidden behind this average.[8]

It is pertinent to examine why Indira Gandhi froze the parliamentary constituencies in 1975. Her decision resulted in the consolidation of her political power. The ostensible reason of preventing the south from being economically 'punished' for 'successfully' implementing family planning has been all but debunked—an increase in income leads to a fall in fertility, and not vice versa—implying that the very justification given for such a grave representational distortion was based on spurious considerations.[9] During that time, her government faced significant opposition from various political parties. She also faced opposition within her own party. By freezing delimitation, she ensured that the existing electoral boundaries remained unchanged. This move was advantageous for her party because it preserved the political status quo that favoured the Congress party at that time, which had historically dominated Indian politics. The move aimed to undercut the regional parties, which were beginning to credibly challenge the Congress.

Put another way, freezing delimitation helped Indira Gandhi maintain control over the distribution of political power and resources. It prevented potential challenges from emerging political forces that could have arisen from redrawn electoral boundaries. Additionally, it allowed her government to retain a certain level of control over the electoral process itself, ensuring favourable conditions for her party in future elections. Already, there was a demographic shift with the population of the northern states increasing somewhat faster than those of the southern ones. It is hard to make out if these shifts arose from a generally and historically higher standard of education and a better economy south of the Vindhyas.[10] Some numbers are useful: the population of Bihar was 4.2 and 10.4 crore in 1971 and 2011, respectively, an increase of 247 per cent. The corresponding figures for Karnataka are 2.9 and 6.1 crore, respectively, an increase of 210 per cent. The corresponding number for Uttar Pradesh is 227 per cent, and for Tamil Nadu 175 per cent.[11] Since the population of Bihar and Uttar Pradesh is larger than that of Karnataka and Tamil Nadu, these numbers show that the overall population increase of India in this time period (210 per cent) has a disproportionate contribution from large northern states. This means that a strict population-based delimitation would have led to more seats from the north as compared to the south. Whether this is in itself good or bad is open to debate.

The north–south political divide itself was a result of the States Reorganization Act, 1956. In the words of Ambedkar, the States Reorganization Commission consolidated the north and balkanized the south, creating not only a linguistic but also a political problem;[12] resultantly, the north's relatively larger states had better bargaining terms than the smaller states of the south by virtue of their Lok Sabha representation. K.M. Panikkar, in his dissenting note appended to the commission's report, voiced a similar grievance by flagging the disproportionate influence Uttar Pradesh had vis-à-vis the Centre. The north–south divide itself would have been non-existent if states were roughly equally sized, as no one state would have disproportionate electoral heft, and nor would a clear dividing line exist between north and south, as none of the large northern states would exist in identifiable (and hence, targetable) forms.

If one sticks to the principle that each vote should have the same electoral value, Bihar and Uttar Pradesh would have ended up with more seats than Karnataka and Tamil Nadu, if population delimitation based on the latest census was employed. The problem really is that with our pseudo-federal understanding of the Constitution, we tend to think of our states as units that should parley on equal terms with the Union government.[13] In the present situation, however, a state with a larger representation in the Lok Sabha is more likely to dominate in the national discourse.[14] Since many smaller states are also governed by regional parties, one may begin to identify the bone of contention.

The crux of the matter, and this has been alluded to in Chapter 2, is the following: Are our present state boundaries the best possible delimiters of identity in our efforts to preserve our precious micro-diversities? The incompatibility between 'Each Vote Same Value' and 'Each State Same Heft' is the conundrum, and Indira Gandhi chose the easy way out—by freezing delimitation. Atal Bihari Vajpayee was either unwilling or unable to change the situation in 2001 when he extended this freeze for another twenty-five years, that is, till 2026. Both missed the essential point—there is no avoiding this incompatibility between achieving equality of electoral voice while maintaining parity in socio-cultural character and economic significance unless the states themselves are redefined so that electoral equality, the basis of our parliamentary democracy, is encoded in their very scaffolding. In other words, all states should be of roughly similar population. Freezing delimitation for a full fifty years is no solution.

The present condition of our parliamentary and assembly constituency limits is not healthy. While the population of India has been growing, this growth is not being reflected in her representative institutions. The freeze on the number of elected representatives has been on the basis of allocations and delimitations made by the previous Delimitation Commission (1972) which used the 1971 census figures. Delimitations due in 1981 and 1991, and following the 84th Constitutional Amendment, 2003, the one following the 2011 census, had to be postponed. Since the 2021 census has not been held, we now await the 2031 census—unless a census is called before that. The 42nd and the 84th Amendments of the Constitution have together had a far reaching and disturbing effect on our electoral democracy. Each vote no longer has the same value in elections to the Lok Sabha and Legislative Assemblies.

The Present Delimitation Scenario: In Abeyance for Fifty Years

Let us examine this matter further. A number of inconsistencies have been brought about by freezing the Legislative Assemblies and the Lok Sabha strength without simultaneously taking into account the population changes in the respective constituencies.

1. Our parliamentarians and legislative assembly members are now overstretched. Each of them now speaks for a sizable and disproportionately large segment of the

electorate, resulting in a number of issues that are important for a relatively smaller section of the electorate getting drowned out, diluting the representative efficiency of the system. If the size of an electoral constituency is sufficiently small, local issues will be electorally relevant for representatives—an impossibility under the present state of affairs. This might also be a contributing factor in the rise of absentee or rentier elected representatives who are mostly aloof from their constituencies and the general lack of effective communication with the electorate.

2. The inability of parliamentarians from different states to represent the same proportion of the population is in violation of the constitutional provision enshrined in Art. 81(2)(a) that 'there shall be allotted to each State a number of seats in the House of the People in such manner that the ratio between the number and the population of the State is, so far as practicable, the same for all States'. This is because throughout the past fifty years, the population growth rates in Indian states have varied. The Constituent Assembly had drafted this provision to precisely prevent a situation like today, where one ends up with constitutional gerrymandering based on scientifically rejected reasons.
3. Not every MP or member of the Legislative Assembly (MLA) in a state represents the same proportion of the population in their respective constituency. This is due to the different population growth rates in different regions of any given state and flies against the face of the principle enshrined in Art. 14 which says, 'The State shall not deny to any person equality before the law or the equal protection of the laws within the territory of India.' While many states have carried out state-wide delimitation

> exercises, there is no uniform system or time frame for an institutional arrangement which directly impinges on the value of a citizen's vote.[15] These anomalies have also harmed the principle of the equality of votes as the value of the votes of voters in thickly populated states or the constituencies becomes less than that of the voters of the thinly populated states and constituencies. It is true that in some cases of small states the requirement of Art. 81(2)(a) has been waived so that every state, however small and thinly populated, gets at least one seat in the Lok Sabha. But the bigger states get no such advantage, again going against the principle of Art. 14. The matter is not the north gaining or losing at the expense of the south or Bengaluru Urban pitted against Mysore; the principal problem is that one citizen has been rendered unequal vis-à-vis the other in terms of the single most important political right under democratic citizenship, that is, their vote.

Let us examine some further incongruities. As per the ECI, the largest five parliamentary constituencies of the country in terms of number of electors constitute 1,16,51,249 electors taken together, while the smallest five together have just 7,56,820.[16] The total electorate size in the largest five constituencies is thus 15.4 times that in the smallest five constituencies. We may term this as a 'skew ratio'. These skewed numbers clearly show that the electoral significance of a vote can differ significantly from one constituency to another. Let us also remember that the 1950 constitution capped the number of Lok Sabha seats at 500 and allowed a maximum of one MP for a population size of 7.5 lakh. We are now close to exceeding the 1950 limit by a factor of three.

Additionally, if one takes the voting population of India as roughly 97 crore, there are currently on average 17.9 lakh voters represented by each Lok Sabha member. This number is way too large, and it means that an individual voter has, for all practical purposes, lost direct contact with the person he or she has elected to the Lok Sabha. A lone representative in the Lok Sabha cannot possibly represent a constituency which is more populous than, say, all of Sweden. We have already seen how this average itself hides more than it reveals since the very small and the very large are shrouded by this number and are responsible for vast inequalities in the value of a vote.[17]

The original constitutional scheme envisaged a perfectly apportioned parliament, in which both Lok Sabha and Rajya Sabha members for each state were in proportion to the population of the given state, although they were elected through direct and indirect processes. This was because Article 80 capped the maximum number of Rajya Sabha members from states at 238, with an additional 12 members designated for functional representation or nomination. However, the most interesting aspect of Indian bicameralism is that the original constitution allowed for no erroneous apportioning in either house of parliament. It required that Rajya Sabha members from states also be chosen by the state legislature 'in accordance with the system of proportional representation by means of the single transferable vote'. So, whatever was true for the Lok Sabha was paralleled with fidelity in the Rajya Sabha. Further, since populations grow, and not evenly across all constituencies, Article 82 provided for delimitation based on the numbers from each decennial census. This was a self-adjusting, self-balancing system.

This system worked well till the fifth general election in 1971. Census data was used for redrawing constituency boundaries, and Delimitation Commissions were set up to allow seats to states as well as to draw boundaries. The Constitution (Seventh Amendment) Act, 1956 increased the seats to 520, and the Constitution (Thirty-first Amendment) Act, 1973 brought it to a maximum of 545 seats. Currently, the Lok Sabha strength is capped at 552 seats. The Constitution (Forty-second Amendment) Act, 1976 put an end to this balanced and self-adjusting system of proportional representation.[18] The ostensible reason given was uneven population growth. The politicians from the southern states of India claimed that they more strictly and successfully had followed the central government's population control mandate compared to the northern states. As a consequence, they alleged, they were electorally and politically being penalized for complying with the government mandate. As we have repeatedly stated, the idea that government policy and not rise in incomes can lead to lower fertility rates has been rejected and empirically so in India.[19] Thus, such claims only point towards political rent-seeking by then incumbents by manipulating the value of citizens' votes.

However, the original Indian Constitution was crafted to address this very issue. The job of allocating seats to states under direct and indirect proportional representation, respectively, fell to the Lok Sabha and Rajya Sabha. Uneven population growth was, therefore, not a problem, since the seat share in both Houses would adjust based on population, and any malapportionment would be eliminated after every census. Likewise, Parliament has been granted the unilateral right to change the boundaries of states, carve out new ones, or merge existing states, with the view that changes in both outlook and demographics must reflect in the way the states are organized. The actual cause for the freeze was that

India under Indira Gandhi's centrally planned economy in the 1970s lacked fiscal and political federalism, with some unique political conditions in the country overriding the quasi-federal features in the Constitution. Citizens of the richer southern states made larger contributions to the overall Indian income stream as they had a greater share of industry. The poorer northern states, with higher fertility rates and hence higher population and population growth, received a considerably larger proportion of the revenue than what they earned within the state when the Union government dispersed resources based on need. The political consolidation of the north following the States Reorganization Act, 1956 only worsened matters. The north was thus forced to depend on government handouts as private industry got decimated under the pressures of socialist dogmas, becoming politically and economically shackled to the then ruling elite cutting across party lines. The south was under the constant threat of the licence-permit raj and outright nationalization, forcing them to generally align with the diktats of the said ruling elite. The main problem was always money and power, not population or people.[20]

With the 42nd Amendment freezing delimitation, the reverse problem then began to set in. Tamil Nadu had five seats more than its population share while Uttar Pradesh had eight seats less by 2001 as a result of changes in India's demography and fiscal centralization. As was to be expected, Kerala and Andhra Pradesh gained seats while poorer states like Rajasthan, Madhya Pradesh, and Bihar suffered disadvantages and lost seats in relation to their population proportion. Because of a drop in reproduction rates, Maharashtra keeps losing in terms of seat share; yet it receives the most inward migration from other states, and the votes of these incoming citizens is often in their states of origin. The issue needed to be revisited in 2001 when the twenty-five-year freeze ended, but the Vajpayee government was in a politically delicate situation then with coalition compulsions deciding important policy issues, and a further twenty-five-year freeze was imposed, making existing problems worse.[21]

When the delimitation freeze expires in 2031, the issue will only get worse. Tamil Nadu is expected to have eleven seats more than its population percentage, while Uttar Pradesh and Bihar are expected to fall between twelve and thirteen seats short of their respective population proportions. The remaining states are expected to lie in the middle. It is also worth considering that except Bihar, all of North India is also now below replacement in terms of fertility rates, that is, their populations are also shrinking. Uttar Pradesh was at the precipice in terms of fertility rates in 2011 and by now may also be below replacement. Further, economic activity in North India has been consistently rising, especially in Uttar Pradesh (which has recently surpassed Tamil Nadu to become the second largest state in economic terms).[22] Thus, propaganda that a highly fertile northern India will, if delimitation takes place, feast upon the prosperity of the south is all but a red herring. These new realities can be gleaned simply by looking at economic and population growth rates; the fact that the south depends on markets, raw material, and talent from the north in the supply chains of many of its key industries responsible for its prosperity is only an additional point to highlight the futility of the argument which paints northern India as parasites for narrow political benefits. Politics ought to be based on issues and aspirations, not engineering conflicts between

Bhāratiyas to deflect attention from failing to deliver on their ambitions.

Effectively, we need to wait till 2026, and depending on when the next census is held, delimitation could be taken up. However, we currently have no real clarity as to how the inconsistencies of demography, economy, and federal impulses can be resolved.[23] There is the further question of whether or not the next census will include a proper and authentic enumeration of caste due to both political and constitutional factors. This aspect cannot and should not affect the principle of One Man One Vote, but given the present polarized atmosphere in the country, it is difficult to imagine how these several contentious issues can be delinked. It would almost appear that a reboot of our entire constitutional apparatus is required even though political parties today strenuously maintain that there is no question of rewriting the Constitution.[24] Apparently it is a holy book that cannot be altered or dispensed with, instead of being a work-in-progress record of institutional arrangements provided by the nation to itself. Like the freeze on delimitation, politicians have found much virtue in proclaiming their commitment to turning the Constitution into a relic even as time marches on. When a problem appears too contentious to handle, simply declare that you will not handle it. This seems to be the easy way out, the *chalta hai* attitude which has come to haunt us time and again.

The delimitation of seats in Indian elections from 1976 to 2026 has been a complex and contentious process, fraught with numerous challenges and implications for the country's electoral landscape. Over this period, several issues have emerged, ranging from political controversies to demographic disparities. We may summarize the problems that have arisen:

1. Population Growth and Redistribution: One of the primary challenges is the uneven population growth across states and regions within states, leading to the need for frequent redistribution of parliamentary seats to ensure fair representation. Delimitation exercises aim to address this by adjusting constituency boundaries, but this often sparks debates over the allocation of seats among states and regions. The freeze has clamped down on such discussions but the long-term consequences (such as the north–south divide and unequal allocation of central funds) are disturbing because pent up grievances might erupt with greater vigour in the future.
2. Political Manipulation: Delimitation processes have been accused of political manipulation and gerrymandering, with ruling parties sometimes attempting to redraw boundaries in their favour to secure electoral advantages. This has led to accusations of unfair electoral practices, undermining the principle of equal representation. While this has always been an issue in electoral democracies, accusations of manipulating constituency boundaries are surely going to be levelled against the ruling coalition, as has been observed in the aftermath of the delimitation exercises carried out recently in Jammu and Kashmir and Assam. The pre-election run-up saw the opposition parties accusing the BJP of wanting to change the Constitution if they won and the BJP maintaining stoically that the Constitution was immutable.[25] Both positions are quixotic because no Constitution is forever—in any country. Now that the NDA has a comfortable majority, it remains to be seen what it will do.

3. Caste and Community Dynamics: India's diverse social fabric, characterized by caste and community dynamics, adds another layer of complexity to delimitation. Changes in constituency boundaries can disrupt existing caste-based political equations, leading to tensions and conflicts within communities. Unknown surprises might await us in an all-India caste and denominational census, and these could cause further disruptions in any future delimitation process.
4. Geographical Challenges: India's vast and varied geographical terrain presents logistical challenges in the delimitation process. Remote and inaccessible areas may be underrepresented or face difficulties in accessing electoral resources and infrastructure, exacerbating disparities in political participation. To some extent, these difficulties have always been there, but the fifty-year freeze might well reveal hidden problems.
5. Legal and Constitutional Issues: Delimitation exercises must adhere to constitutional principles and legal frameworks, which sometimes clash with political interests and regional demands. Legal challenges and disputes often arise, further complicating the process and delaying its implementation. Does the present Constitution, straitjacketed as it is by the capricious 'basic structure' doctrine, have enough flexibility to accommodate new and troublesome issues that were not known seventy-five years ago?
6. Data Accuracy and Integrity: Accurate demographic data forms the basis of delimitation, but issues such as incomplete census coverage and inaccuracies in population estimates can undermine the integrity of the process. Inadequate data can lead to erroneous boundary adjustments, affecting the fairness of elections.

7. Impact on Minority Representation: Delimitation can have significant implications for the representation of minority communities. Changes in constituency boundaries may dilute the electoral influence of minority groups, raising concerns about inclusivity and minority rights in the democratic process.
8. Technological Challenges: With advancing technology, there is a growing emphasis on leveraging GIS (Geographic Information System) and other digital tools for delimitation. However, technological challenges such as data privacy concerns and digital divide issues need to be addressed to ensure the integrity and accessibility of the process.

In summary, delimitation of seats has led to a multitude of challenges, encompassing political, demographic, legal, and technological dimensions. Addressing these issues is of urgent priority so that a greater element of fairness, transparency, and inclusivity enters the electoral process.

Jammu and Kashmir

Jammu and Kashmir is a special case, since multiple historical oddities converge there at once. Whether it is the communities which call it home, population densities, histories, narratives, and aspirations, the erstwhile state of Jammu and Kashmir was an unnatural creation which was allowed to continue by the British for their own convenience. Post-1947, these idiosyncrasies festered into a deep, multi-decadal polycrisis. The revocation of Article 370[26] removed a self-inflicted ambiguity as to the status of the state and its relationship with the rest of the Union, which was the final chapter in India's political integration. Since Article 370 was revoked in 2019, what was originally a state has now been redesignated as two Union Territories: (1) Jammu and Kashmir, and (2) Ladakh. Article 370 had granted special autonomous status to the region, including provisions related to its representation in the Indian parliament. With its abrogation, the process of delimitation became inevitable to ensure equitable representation in the Lok Sabha. Accordingly, the constituencies were delimited recently owing to the urgency of the matter. This exercise was a contentious issue, fraught with political, demographic, and legal challenges. The Delimitation Commission visited the area twice. During the first visit, the Commission interacted with approximately 242 delegations at four locations, that is, Srinagar, Pahalgam, Kishtwar, and Jammu. Approximately 1,600 people attended and expressed their views at public sittings during the second visit held at Jammu and Srinagar in April 2022.

One of the primary issues in the delimitation process pertains to the region's unique demographic composition. Jammu and Kashmir was characterized by its diverse religious and ethnic make-up, with significant populations of Muslims, Hindus, and Buddhists in Kashmir, Jammu, and Ladakh, respectively. Even in Ladakh, Leh has a Buddhist majority, while Kargil has a Muslim majority. Coreligionists in each region have vastly different cultures and ways of life as also their own sense of history and belonging. Ensuring fair representation for all communities while maintaining the integrity of geographical boundaries posed a significant challenge. The peculiar geo-cultural landscape of the (now) Union Territory presented unique issues arising due to factors like competing political aspirations of the geographically and culturally distinctive Jammu and the Kashmir regions; vast differences in population density between districts ranging from 3,436 per sq. km in districts in the valley-plains on one side to 29 per sq. km in the predominantly hilly and difficult districts on the other; existence of sub-regions within certain districts having extremely difficult intra-district connectivity due to extraordinary geographical barriers with some remaining totally cut off on account of the snow blocking the mountain passes for months during winter; and uncertainty of life and inadequate availability of connectivity and public conveniences in villages along the international border that are prone to unprovoked intermittent firing or shelling in the adjoining districts.

Another critical aspect involves the political implications of redrawing constituencies. Historically, the Kashmir Valley within Jammu and Kashmir enjoyed disproportionate political influence, leading to concerns over gerrymandering and unfair electoral practices. In particular, the limits of the constituencies had been drawn in the 1950s so that only a Kashmiri Muslim, for all practical purposes, could ever become chief minister of the erstwhile state. Delimitation provided an opportunity to address these disparities and promote more inclusive and equitable representation. The legal framework surrounding the delimitation process added more complexity. The Delimitation Commission, responsible for redrawing boundaries, navigated intricate constitutional provisions and legal precedents to ensure adherence to democratic principles and constitutional norms.

As per the final Delimitation Order, out of the ninety assembly constituencies (AC) in the Jammu and Kashmir regions, forty-three are a part of the Jammu region, and forty-seven are in the Kashmir region, keeping in view the provisions of Section 9(1)(a) of the Delimitation Act, 2002 and Section 60(2)(b) of Jammu and Kashmir Reorganization Act, 2019.[27] This is far less disproportionate than in the previous dispensation where there were thirty-seven ACs in the Jammu region and forty-six in the Kashmir region.[28] After wide consultation, nine assembly constituencies have been reserved for scheduled tribes (STs), out of which six are in the Jammu region and three are in the Kashmir Valley. There are five parliamentary constituencies now in the Union Territory. One of them was newly carved out by combining the Anantnag region in the Valley with the Rajouri and Poonch regions in Jammu.[29] Through this reorganization, each parliamentary constituency will have an equal number of eighteen assembly constituencies each.

A number of representations to the Delimitation Commission were made from the Kashmiri migrants and the displaced persons from Pakistan-occupied Kashmir (PoK). The delegations of Kashmiri migrants represented before the Commission that they had been persecuted and forced to live in exile as refugees in their own country for the last three decades. It was urged that in order to preserve their political rights, seats should be reserved for them in the Jammu and Kashmir assembly and parliament. The displaced persons from PoK also requested the Commission to reserve a few seats for them in the Legislative Assembly. Accordingly, the Delimitation Commission also recommended that there be at least two members (one of them mandatorily a female) from the community of Kashmiri migrants in the Legislative Assembly. With representation being given to peoples whose territories are under foreign occupation, Bhārat has further cemented its right over these lands and has given its displaced citizens proper political representation. One of the authors of this book has been an ardent and longstanding advocate for the same and had drafted a constitutional amendment bill as an example to evolve a corresponding legal roadmap for adequate representation.[30]

In the context of upcoming Lok Sabha elections, the delimitation exercise will have far-reaching implications. Redrawing constituency boundaries alters the political landscape by redistributing seats based on population shifts and demographic changes.[31] This will impact the electoral prospects of various political parties and individuals in the future, leading to realignments and new power dynamics within the region. Most importantly, Valley-centric politics has greatly reduced, and the diverse peoples inhabiting the Union Territories which have succeeded the erstwhile state have found proper representation and attention. To summarize, the delimitation of constituencies in Jammu and Kashmir after the revocation of Article 370 involved navigating through a maze of demographic, political, and legal complexities. The outcome of this process will significantly influence the representation and electoral dynamics in the region for years to come.

What Next?

Two independent issues are of concern in any future delimitation exercise. The first is that the size of our parliamentary and assembly constituencies is way too large, and any contact between an individual and his or her elected representative is, for all practical purposes, lost. Table 3 gives the sizes of the electorate and the number of elected representatives to the lower legislative house in important democracies. A casual inspection of these numbers shows that India is very much an outlier. The population is too large, and the number of seats in the lower house is too small.

Table 3. Some voter statistics in major democracies. The figures are current. We need a Parliament much larger than we have at present if voter representation is to be meaningful. Ideally, there should be around 1,500 members in the Lok Sabha

Country	**Population in crores**	**Eligible voters in crores**	**Ratio of voters to population**	**Seats in lower house**	**Number of voters per seat in lakhs**
US	33.4	25.5	0.76	435	5.86
Japan	12.5	10.6	0.85	465	2.28
Germany	8.4	6.1	0.73	735	0.83
France	6.8	4.9	0.72	577	0.85
UK	6.7	4.6	0.69	650	0.71
Canada	3.9	2.8	0.72	338	0.83
Australia	2.6	1.8	0.69	151	1.19
India	141.8	97.1	0.68	543	17.86

The second issue of concern is that even in our 543 Lok Sabha constituencies, the number of voters per constituency, that is, the skew ratio, is too lopsided. Based on the number of seats in the new Parliament building, one might assume that there will be 888 Lok Sabha members in a lower house constituted after a nationwide delimitation exercise; one arrives then at an average figure of 10.9 lakh voters per constituency, which appears to be much more reasonable than the present figure of 17.9 lakh. However, if this exercise is merely done proportionately (one constituency today becomes 1.63 constituencies after delimitation), the skew ratio[32] still stays high, meaning that the value of an individual vote will still remain widely different in different parts of the country. Alternatively, if the exercise is carried out population wise, there will be a marked decrease in the representation of the southern states, as explained earlier. Both methods are, therefore, unsatisfactory.[33] Any increase in the number of constituencies must, therefore, be accompanied by a complete redrawing of limits so that there are just around 10.9 lakh voters *in each and every* new constituency with the skew ratio approaching 1.00.[34] These limits, however, do not necessarily pertain just to intrastate boundaries. They must be applied to interstate boundaries as well so that the heft of each state is more or less the same. Any meaningful delimitation exercise must, therefore, be nationwide with a complete redrawing of state boundaries so that one achieves several, say seventy-five, small states with roughly two crore inhabitants in each state. This and only this will solve the north–south divide and other related problems.

This brings up the connection between any future parliamentary delimitation exercise and the manner and way in which states of the Indian Union have been defined by parliament till now. The present twenty-eight states and eight UTs are shockingly different in size.[35] These differences are partly on account of former historical events and partly on account of a reluctance by some, mostly in the larger (linguistic) states, to consider division of their states into smaller, more governable units, blocking such moves and using language as a convenient excuse. A comprehensive reorganization of states is, however, almost mandatory today, and unless this exercise is done *ab initio* it will lack objectivity and rationality. It cannot be done incrementally. Delimitation and states' reorganization are two sides of the same coin; one cannot have balanced constituencies with skew ratios approaching 1.00 if states themselves are of wildly differing sizes and vice versa.

CHAPTER 4

Identities, Small States, and Delimitation

'What's in a name? That which we call a rose by any other name would smell as sweet.'

—William Shakespeare

The ad hoc nature of the boundary lines between India's states began on the platform of our Constitution that imagined India in the model of the post-Westphalian nation state. The redrawing of the map of Europe after World War I was in many ways the template for drawing boundaries between and within countries. Countries in Europe are the archetypes of a nation state. Each country has its own culture, language, ethnicity, and, in many cases, history; the norm, especially after World War I, was to reshape the continent along the lines of One People One Country.[1] This idea was taken to an extreme in Nazi Germany, which based itself on the credo of *Ein Volk Ein Reich Ein Führer*.[2] There are very few multilingual countries in Europe, and those that do exist are the result of recent political experiments between other countries in need of buffer zones (Italy, Belgium) or ancient entities that were geographically insulated (Switzerland). Other multilingual experiments (Czechoslovakia, Yugoslavia) have failed.

When we adopted the nation state model in 1950, it was perhaps unsurprising that we fell into the trap of linguistic states—after all, they had been set up and institutionalized by the same British who had imposed the idea of nation states on areas of the world which did not go through the historical context responsible for Westphalian thinking.[3] This model also served the British political goal of denying the existence of any shared sense of Indian-ness, and instead characterized India as a purely geographical entity housing distinct 'races', each worthy of having a nation state of its own. This is exemplified by Winston Churchill's statement that 'India is a geographical term. It is no more a united nation than the equator',[4] a political lie which was subsequently embellished and institutionalized by orientalist and Marxist historiography. These political lies have been converted into ex-post facto half-truths by subsequent actions of political outfits in their race to the bottom, carving out vote banks for themselves, to the political and economic detriment of citizens across the country.

Since Bhārat is very definitely not a nation state but rather unequivocally identified as a thriving civilizational state with a tradition going back at least 5,000 years, it is perhaps no surprise that our present hotchpotch arrangement of twenty-eight states and eight UTs is totally ill-suited to our civilizational character—one that does not even recognize language as a major parameter in its construct. The history of Bhārat is that of a unified, assimilative people finding shared expression of the higher truths of human existence in the environment and circumstances they find themselves in.[5] The seventh and tenth mandalas of the *Rigveda* with their retellings of the conflicts which came to define the political structure of the Sapta-Sindhu peoples display a unified sense of being and a common methodology in the pursuit of objectives even during these conflicts. The Bharatas, the ancestors of today's Bhāratiyas, while being the victors of the cataclysmic war of the ten kings in the *Rigveda*, came to institute a system of tribal intermarriages to forge a common identity following their victory. This is very emblematic of the Indian way of assimilating diversity. Instead of viewing unity as being a negotiated settlement between hitherto irreconcilable peoples, Bhāratiyas have historically viewed the existence of diverse peoples as varied expressions of a singular truth. It is thus not surprising that the Western notion of federalism, which is rooted in the Roman idea of varied peoples pooling together select political powers as *fœderatis*, makes little sense in the Indian context—our model is of the singular all-pervading Brahman manifesting itself in many forms by declaring 'May I be many, may I grow forth'[6] instead of preexisting bits and pieces agglomerating together.

It is of importance for us, therefore, to recognize the basic incorrectness of our present state boundaries. It would be a waste of time to tinker with the present boundaries in an attempt to smoothen out short-term local tensions and grievances because these boundaries are, at a fundamental level, false. Many of the conflicts which have characterized inter-state relations in India are a direct result of this falsehood and can only be put to an end if this false conceptual framework is done away with. What we need is a complete reconsideration of our diversity markers so that we may correctly identify borders between new, small states that correctly encapsulate identities and economic realities that go back several millennia and are yet dynamic and forward-looking.

The much-maligned report of the SRC, 1955, is strangely at odds with many of the decisions taken by the then political executive in the name of implementing its recommendations. The very first divergence is in the conceptual understanding of identity itself, with the report unequivocally taking a composite understanding of identity as opposed to the narrow emphasis on language taken by the politicians. The report had summarized the same thus: 'After a full consideration of the problem in all its aspects, we have come to the conclusion that it is neither possible nor desirable to reorganize states on the basis of the single test of either language or culture, but that a balanced approach to the whole problem is necessary in the interests of our national unity.'[7]

The single most important point of departure between the report and what followed it was the idea of linguistic states as we understand it: One Language One State. A brief perusal of the current political map of India, save for anachronistic units such as Uttar Pradesh and recent experiments such as Chhattisgarh and Telangana, would show that particular linguistic groupings have been organized within singular states. One can easily correspond West Bengal with Bangla, Tamil Nadu with Tamil, Karnataka with Kannada, and so on. Yet, the report was explicit, to the point of being tactless, regarding its opposition to the idea of One Language One State. Two passages warrant quotation in full, which will be sufficient to exorcise any ambiguities:

> [T]o reject the theory of 'one language one state', which is neither justified on grounds of linguistic homogeneity, because there can be more than one state speaking the same language without offending the linguistic principle, nor practicable, since different language groups, including, the vast Hindi-speaking population of the Indian Union, cannot always be consolidated to form distinct linguistic units.

And equally clearly the report cautions:[8]

> [F]inally, to the extent that the realisation of unilinguism at state level would tend to breed a particularist feeling, to counter-balance that feeling by positive measures calculated to give a deeper content to Indian nationalism; to promote greater interplay of different regional cultures, and interstate cooperation and accord; and to reinforce the links between the centre and the state in order to secure a greater coordinated working of national policies and programmes.

The above opinions, as a matter of fact, did reflect in the report's operational recommendations, which included the formation of a separate Vidarbha state, distinct from Maharashtra. K.M. Panikkar's note of dissent which also wished for the division of Uttar Pradesh was appended to the report. His note advocated for a uniform system of states as opposed to Part A to Part D states which existed until 1956. In reality, many of the commission's recommendations were disregarded for electoral purposes. The commission itself was subject to these pressures—the Uttar Pradesh Congress was vehemently opposed to any subdivision of the state and made corresponding representations to the commission. Likewise, the commission had to grapple with competing demands from states with respect to territory. States had already begun to think territorially and were viewing their neighbours with resentment over territorial concerns.[9] Likewise, even though the commission recommended the separation of Bombay city and its surroundings, the government decided against the same and retained it within a mixed bilingual state. Having big states suited the Congress of the day, as it could maintain power over large areas and finances by stitching together selective caste alliances. The very first Lok Sabha already had representation from outfits which were demanding selective states which, if granted, would have meant the Congress potentially losing hold over such states; the Jharkhand Party, Shiromani Akali Dal, and three separate units from Tamil Nadu had already found their way into the first Lok Sabha.

Why Small States? Ambedkar's Ideas

The States Reorganization Commission, while recommending some sweeping changes, maintained a stifling sense of incrementalism on other points. The same can perhaps be justified by the fact that India had just been subjected to the harrowing violence of Partition, and at that time, parallels to the violence in the erstwhile Madras presidency for linguistic states would have been evident. At the same time, the integration of the princely states and colonial outposts was still a work in progress—while they had acceded to the Union, how to administer them while maintaining the privileges and navigating the continued political heft of the princes would have been a challenge. Many of the industrial houses of the Bombay Plan pedigree were also averse to any big changes to state boundaries as it could have led to new state taxes on the sources of their raw materials and supply chains. While all of these points are speculative to some degree, the takeaway remains that the States Reorganization Act, 1956, which shaped the country's internal contours, should perhaps have been taken only as an interim measure. Instead, it has been frozen in time and lingers on like an ill-fitting shroud. There seems to be no evidence that there was any thinking along the lines of a totally new *ab initio* pattern for our states at the dawn of Independence, even considering the wide powers given to the Union by Article 3 with respect to the drawing and redrawing of state boundaries.

For the sake of convenience, one may call the kind of states which emerged from the 1956 Act as states of the Nehru-Prakasam type, with their essence being One Language One State. This model of statehood is responsible for many ills, as we have outlined already. Linguistic subnationalism has stoked political and economic disputes in an otherwise united country. Instead of identities shaping the way our states are, these state boundaries have ended up shaping the way we identify ourselves—an artificial process which is fundamentally divisive in nature. The limits of the Nehru–Prakasam model were exposed when states of the Vajpayee model began to take shape: Uttarakhand, Chhattisgarh, and Jharkhand are prime examples. The formation of these states was based on a canvas of identity that was far broader than just language; the demands of these places were fundamentally economic and cultural rather than linguistic and revolved around the claims to local resources. Many of these states, particularly Uttarakhand, showed significant economic improvement after their formation, which does lend credence to the economic impetus behind smaller states.[10] Nonetheless, while being a significant improvement, the Vajpayee model suffers from the same conceptual poverty which plagued the Nehru–Prakasam model, in the sense that it does not articulate any clear metrics for *what* a state ought to be. It is still a function of local electoral politics rather than any thoughtful national policy. A state of the Union of India should ideally be based on a clear sense of purpose and be functionally optimal in the objectives which it is to serve. Reactive politics cannot be the basis for long-term economic and sociopolitical organization of the country.

In this context, there is a need to revisit both the Nehru–Prakasam and Vajpayee models and seek an alternative that embodies conscious, intelligent design. Such an alternative was actually presented by Ambedkar in 1955 in a short note entitled 'Thoughts on Linguistic States'. While politically sidelined by then, owing to the political whimsicalities of the day, Ambedkar critiqued the States Reorganization Commission's report and proposed a model far more cogent than what was ultimately put into operation. Revisiting the Ambedkar model for states is a meaningful exercise not just to highlight that alternative views on linguistic states existed back in the 1950s but also because his model is far more in sync with the political and economic requirements of a competitive and self-confident Bhārat today in the 2020s. In his preface to the short collection of essays that constitutes his note, he wrote, 'The formation of Linguistic States, although essential, cannot be decided by any sort of hooliganism. Nor must it be solved in a manner that will serve party interest. It must be solved by cold blooded reasoning. This is what I have done and this is what I appeal to my readers to do.'[11]

Ambedkar's views on how a state ought to be constituted offers a clear, considered, and far more harmonious model compared to the Nehru–Prakasam and Vajpayee models. A summary of his key recommendations, which remain just as applicable today as an alternative foundation of Indian political organization, is in order.

1. States should generally be overwhelmingly unilingual to minimize social conflict and prevent linguistic politics within the state; One State One Language.
2. The idea of One State One Language should not be confused with One Language One State. States should be equally sized to prevent any one state from exercising outsized influence on national politics. There can be multiple states which speak the same language.

3. As the area of a state increases, the proportion of the minority to the majority decreases,[12] and the position of the minority becomes precarious so that the opportunities for the majority to practise tyranny over the minority become greater. The states must, therefore, be small. Ambedkar's original estimate for the approximate population of a state was around 2 crore, which optimizes both administrative efficiency and keeps individual votes relevant.

In addition to the above, there are additional economic reasons for why states should be small. As seen by the recent governmental push of One District One Product, both history and experience shows that sub-regions of this country can specialize in different products or services to maximize their incomes. This requires tailor-made economic policymaking, which is best done when the state is small and its capital is not too far-flung from its districts, and thus the energies of the state can be focussed only on select industries. Examples of this will follow later in the chapter.

Ambedkar's views have stood the test of time, both in terms of causes as well as effects. Sunil Bhandare of the Tata Strategic Management Group has observed that smaller states have been more sensitive to local aspirations and have done better in terms of social and economic development, administration, and popular outreach. He goes on to succinctly recognize the political perversions which are responsible for larger states irrationally persisting, 'One, it reduces the sphere of influence of politicians. Two, in a large state there are some regions that do very well in terms of economic development and other parameters. The state politicians exploit this in order to disguise their incompetence in other regions. Three, the larger states have a stronger influence on national politics. And four, no one wants to take unpopular decisions. There are political considerations to be met. It's a question of both mindset and political will.'[13]

A Rational Reorganization

One ought to understand that the current quasi-federal set-up as also the manner in which states are demarcated are stamped with the indelible imprimatur of Partition. Despite successive reorganization, one can still see some of the princely states' irrational boundaries surviving notwithstanding ground realities. Likewise, the threat of territorial disintegration which had reigned supreme in the minds of Indians well into the 1960s also led to political resistance to diversity lest it degenerate into the kind of divisiveness which led to Partition. Simultaneously, the freeze put on delimitation in 1971 for reasons which do not hold up to scrutiny has introduced a systemic deficiency which has only served to inflame disputes between the south and the north of the country. These factors are anachronistic residues from factors which have been rendered irrelevant with the passage of time.

Any constitutional set-up which derives its legitimacy from a democratic process has an inherent responsibility to stay true to its representative character. Such a constitution ought to be shaped by the demands and aspirations of its people instead of being an end in and of itself. In a *lokatantra* or *prajātantra*, that is, democracy (literally, a system of the people), the *rājatantra*, that is, governance mechanism, ought to be an operationalization of the former. What is thus warranted is a constitutional acceptance of Bhārat's civilizational character. A necessary implication would be that the units in which the country is organized ought to be a representative reflection of the realities which shape the lives and identities of its citizens. The organization of states thus should be an optimization between history, geography, economics, religion, language, and preventing the disproportionate concentration of power in individual states, while in accordance with the overall dictum that there will be better administration.

For administrative simplicity and efficiency, we propose that Bhārat should be divided into seventy-five states, each with a population of around 2 crore each,[14] rather than purely according to resources, language, race, or religion. Geography, economics, and communication logistics are better markers of state identity because they are more long-term, both running into the past as well as the future, being non-emotional in nature.[15] To an extent, however, the boundaries of the states could be drawn using historical factors such as the former princely state borders and the ongoing desire for smaller states to be split off from larger ones.[16] Smaller states would lead to stronger economics, genuine decentralization, better administration, and fewer linguistic and religious disputes. However, as one may see, there are a few key deviations from this approximate rule. Such deviation is necessary owing to the extreme diversity in the states (particularly hilly states) coupled with low population sizes. On the flip side, a few states such as Mithila are so homogenous that any further division would be wholly artificial, although the present Mithila has a population of nearly 7 crore.

An indicative map is in order.[17] Table 4 gives the names of the states, the state capitals, and populations based on data from the 2011 census. The reader may extrapolate to today's populations.

Figure 1. Map of Bhārat with seventy-five proposed states of around 2 crore population each

Certain clarifications are necessary when referring to the map and the table. The state demarcations generally follow the present district-level boundaries. In most cases, all the districts in our new states were contained completely within only one of our present twenty-eight states. Only in a few cases are the new state lines defined with taluks or sub-districts in today's districts lying in two different new states. All present UTs except Delhi, Lakshadweep, and Andaman and Nicobar Islands have been merged with the nearest state; for example, Puducherry with Thondai Mandalam, Yanam with Andhra Pradesh,

Daman with Virakshetra, and Diu with Saurashtra. As far as possible, local names are used with local spellings, for example, Nagalim, Baltiyul, Kongu and Chola Nadu.

Certain new states are formed by combining districts from two different states in the present dispensation. For example, Mewat is formed by combining Dhaulpur, Bharatpur, and Alwar districts of present-day Rajasthan and Mewat district of present-day Haryana. Its capital is designated as Alwar. Similarly, Sahibganj, Godda, Pakur, Damka, Deogar, and Jamtara districts of present-day Jharkhand are clubbed with twenty-two districts of present-day Bihar[18] to form a new state, Mithila, with capital Darbhanga, which incidentally will be the largest of our seventy-five new states with a population of nearly 7 crore, well over the national average of 2 crore. Again, Saran, Siwan, Kaimur, Rohtas, Bhojpur, Gopalganj, and Buxar in present-day Bihar are clubbed with fifteen districts from present-day eastern UP.[19] to form the new state of Kashi with a population of 6,49,57,250. Kashi would be the second largest of our new states. Bundelkhand and Baghelkhand are defined by clubbing proximate districts from Uttar Pradesh and Madhya Pradesh that are geographically, culturally, and economically homogeneous, and it is our view that separating these ancient domains artificially between UP and MP was an ill-conceived move. This aspect, including the importance of the ancient kingdom of Rewa, has been described in the earlier book, *Bhārat: India 2.0*.

Similarly, Mahakoshal, centred around Jabalpur, contains a sizeable tribal population and has historically housed Gond polities. The waters of the Narmada and the rocky lands dominating the state lead to a distinct economic profile which is a mix of agriculture, forestry, marble products, and some minor minerals works. Mahamayagarh, which corresponds to the northern districts of Chhattisgarh, forms a separate belt in terms of identity; while sharing ethnic relations with the rest of the south, linguistic, cultural, and economic interests differ, warranting a separate state. Kosal has been beset by longstanding demands for a separate state on grounds of both identity and economics, considering ethnic and linguistic differences and sustained underdevelopment. Gondwana, which borders all of the foregoing states in Chhattisgarh described here, has its roots in shared cultural and economic priorities, and its formation vis-à-vis Mahamayagarh separates the coastal and river basin areas from hilly regions and plateaus, fostering specialization.

All the states of the Northeast, except for Assam, are retained with their present boundaries as we are confident that the Union government has accurately identified ethnic, linguistic, and cultural fault lines in delimiting Meghalaya, Arunachal Pradesh, Mizoram, Manipur, Nagalim (presently Nagaland), and Tripura. As for Assam we have separated the districts of Kokrajhar, Chirang, Baksa, Udalguri, and Tamulpur (undivided) and defined a new state, Bodopur, in keeping with the long-standing demand for a Bodo homeland. As in the greater J&K region, the cultural diversities in the Northeast are bewildering, and it is important that this diversity is respected in creating new, viable states.

The five states configured out of the domains of Maharaja Hari Singh as they stood in August 1947 also require explanation. We affirm that the entire area (plus Chitral) is an integral part of the Union of India. The districts in the Jammu and Kashmir divisions (including also Pakistan-controlled Mirpur and Poonch in Jammu and Muzaffarabad in Kashmir) constitute the two new states of Jammu and Kashmir. Gilgit[20] includes Chitral, illegally occupied by Pakistan and incorrectly assigned from British times to the North West Frontier Province, now Khyber Pakhtunkhwa,[21] while the

Kargil district of the present-day Ladakh UT[22] is merged with today's Baltistan to arrive at the new state Baltiyul,[23] leading to a unification of the Balti peoples and reduction of ethnic tensions in today's Ladakh. The Astore and Kharmang districts of Diamer division (created by Pakistan) are assigned to Baltiyul, while Diamer, Darel, and Tangir have been assigned to Gilgit. The new Ladakh, in turn, incorporates the Lahaul-Spiti and Kinnaur districts of present-day Himachal Pradesh, leading to a consolidation of ethnic, cultural, social, economic, and environmental interests of its denizens. The whole arrangement is respectful of cultural differences which are pronounced in this region.

Sikkim's statehood is due to the fact that it joined the Union only in 1975. In its time, the kingdom of Sikkim contained within itself vast stretches of today's Darjeeling, and with Kalimpong district, all these districts have ethnic Nepalese majorities. Darjeeling itself was wrested from Sikkim by the British through war. Naturally, a merged state having Sikkim, the hill subdivisions of Darjeeling (Kurseong, Mirik, Jorebunglow Sukiapokhri, Rangli Rangliot, and Darjeeling Pulazaar) and Kalimpong makes both identitarian and economic sense.[24] The name 'Sikkim', however, is a remnant of the Lepcha–Bhutia minority rule and may not be palatable to the rest of this consolidated state. Likewise, the ethnically loaded name of Gorkhaland may cause grievances to the sizable non-Nepalese indigenous minorities present there. The Pauranic era name of 'Indrakil' should be acceptable to the biggest ethnic and religious groupings there as it relates culturally to the vast majority of the populace. Finally, it may be noted that the small area between Naxalbari and Kurseong which does not fall under any sub-district has been awarded to the new state Indrakil. Likewise, the plains subdivisions of Darjeeling district, namely, Naxalbari, Matigara, Phansidewa, and Kharibari, are apportioned to Kamtapur. This way, the two distinct areas of the district are merged into states with which they have the greatest cultural and geographical similarity. Siliguri municipality, which is surrounded by Matigara, naturally goes to Kamtapur, which now contains the vital chicken's neck between the country and its Northeast states. Similarly, Kishanganj in present-day Bihar goes to Kamtapur as the people there, although largely Muslim, are mostly culturally Rajbongshis like in Cooch Behar.

Delhi also warrants a mention. The present boundaries of Delhi were arbitrarily carved out by the British from erstwhile Punjab province in 1911 and have remained the same since. The small city has since then become a leviathan metropolis, having a population of a whopping 1.68 crore. To accommodate the same, Article 239AA was inserted into the Constitution in 1991, leading to a semi-dysfunctional and rancorous governance system in which the municipal council, the state government, and the Union government acting through a lieutenant governor are often at odds. The singular solution to the conundrum is to limit the national capital to only the area occupied by buildings of national importance and official institutions of the Union government, and to transfer the remaining areas to the adjoining states, Hastinapur and Haryana, where they may be represented properly. Our concept is that the UT should be restricted to the central area with the ceremonial buildings and a small surrounding region, including parts of old Delhi.[25] Thus, the national capital territory, which will revert to becoming a union territory simpliciter, will comprise Chanakya Puri, Connaught Place, Parliament Street, Kotwali, Delhi Cantonment, and Darya Ganj subdivisions. Some historical places of Delhi, such as civil lines, do not have much officialdom remaining in them and may be ideally separated from the national capital. Thus, the population of the capital will shrink to around 10 lakh, with a large proportion being government employees and their dependents. The East and North East districts, which correspond to Jamnā-pār Dilli, will naturally be transferred to Hastinapur state. The remaining subdivisions are transferred to Haryana, considering the south and southwest districts are economically intertwined with Gurgaon, and northern Delhi is generally aligned with the rest of Haryana.

By looking at the map of around seventy-five small states, one immediately appreciates that the concept is based not just on administrative convenience and historical antecedents but naturally falls into a template that seeks its origins in sanātana dharma, India's ongoing civilizational legacy spanning over 5,000 years and the singular ontological source of the diversities pervading the country. Here is a modern-day image of what our ancient civilization might have been, including concepts of democracy and republicanism, rules of administration, upholding order, statecraft and diplomacy, and so forth. Naturally, the topic of definitions of Hindu, Hinduism, and Hindutva arises, and one may draw upon Savarkar's statements to argue that these identities are more civilizational and inclusive than starkly religious ones. The broad canvas of modern constitutional governance, economic progress, religious tolerance, and communal togetherness are painted with strokes of sanātana dharma.

The concepts underlying the choice and demarcation of the seventy-five states above are embedded so deeply in the *grundnorm* of the nation that it has been expressed almost identically in the political organization of the country in the past and was diluted only when the suffocating stench of foreign occupation descended upon the land. Not just in the ancient kingdoms but even in the historical annals of contemporary India, our map of seventy-five states finds a rough approximation. The principles from which such a map is derived are indelibly etched into the cultural make-up that animates the nation. For example, striking similarities can be noted with a map which was proposed by Rasheeduddin Khan in 1973, which is replicated below.[26] Various other similar schemes have been proposed, while demands for states like Harit Pradesh, North Karnataka, Kongu, and Vidarbha have been in the political and public discourse for decades in some cases.

Figure 2. Rasheeduddin Khan's proposed states, 1978 (reproduced from 1973, Seminar Issue 164)

Table 4. Proposed seventy-five states of Bhārat with an approximate average population of 2 crore each[#27]

State	State Capital	Population
Gilgit	Gilgit	8,14,156*
Baltiyul	Skardu	6,74,881*
Jammu	Jammu	85,23,241*
Kashmir	Srinagar	79,70,070*
Ladakh	Leh	2,49,172
Himachal Pradesh	Shimla	68,64,602
Garhwal	Dehradun	58,57,297
Kumaon	Nainital	42,28,998
Punjab	Ludhiana	2,87,98,788
Haryana	Jind	3,51,13,978
Mewat	Alwar	85,18,420
Hastinapur	Meerut	2,61,36,532
Braj	Mathura	1,79,13,933
Panchal	Bareilly	2,57,98,559
Awadh	Lucknow	5,32,04,778
Kashi	Varanasi	6,49,57,250
Doab	Kanpur	2,49,35,876
Bundelkhand	Jhansi	1,47,57,150
Baghelkhand	Rewa	1,26,93,350
Gwalior	Gwalior	1,09,88,266
Avanti	Ujjain	1,80,18,436
Nimar	Maheshwar	58,97,300
Vindhya Pradesh	Bhopal	1,34,72,353
Mahakoshal	Jabalpur	93,17,003
Vidarbha	Nagpur	1,17,54,434
Mahamayagarh	Ambikapur	1,08,54,432
Gondwana	Raipur	1,76,08,874
Bikaner	Bikaner	81,47,344
Ajmer	Ajmer	25,83,052
Dhundhar	Jaipur	1,24,75,712
Hadoti	Bundi	56,95,894
Shekhawati	Jhunjhunu	48,14,378
Mewar	Udaipur	1,22,31,763

State	State Capital	Population
Saurashtra	Rajkot	1,53,25,649
Kachchh	Bhuj	52,13,251
Virakshetra	Vadodara	3,86,30,723
Konkan	Mumbai	2,86,01,441
Goa	Panaji	14,58,545
Pune	Pune	2,34,49,049
Nashik	Nashik	1,85,79,420
Marathwada	Sambhaji Nagar	1,87,31,872
Amravati	Amravati	1,12,58,117
Assam	Guwahati	2,80,54,529
Bodopur	Kokrajhar	31,51,047
Arunachal Pradesh	Itanagar	13,83,727
Manipur	Imphal	28,55,794
Meghalaya	Shillong	29,66,889
Mizoram	Aizawl	10,97,206
Nagalim	Kohima	19,78,502
Tripura	Agartala	29,66,889
Mithila	Darbhanga	6,91,82,585
Magadha	Patna	2,13,30,165
Jharkhand	Ranchi	2,60,19,037
Odisha	Bhubaneshwar	3,29,33,212
Kosal	Sambalpur	53,00,382
Mallabhum	Kharagpur	1,88,24,687
Gauda	Kolkata	5,52,40,424
Kamtapur	Cooch Behar	1,80,47,147
Indrakil	Gangtok	12,64,673
Telangana	Bhagyanagar	3,51,93,978
Andhra Pradesh	Vijayawada	3,41,95,655
Rayalaseema	Kadapa	1,51,91,144
Bayaluseeme	Bengaluru	2,48,20,811
Mysuru	Mysuru	76,04,108
Karunadu	Belagavi	2,05,20,966
Karavali	Karwar	14,57,169
Malenadu	Shivamogga	28,90,714
Tulunadu	Mangaluru	46,57,904

State	State Capital	Population
Kodagu	Madikere	5,54,519
Kongu Nadu	Kovai	2,07,43,812
Pandya Nadu	Madurai	1,38,66,592
Chola Nadu	Thanjai	1,09,67,369
Thondai Mandalam	Kanchipuram	2,60,87,034
Padmanabha Kshetram	Thiruvananthapuram	92,62,005
Cochi	Ernakulam	1,22,97,047
Malabar	Kozhikode	1,05,39,636
Delhi	Official area (UT)	10,79,638
Andaman and Nicobar	Port Blair (UT)	3,80,581
Lakshadweep	Kavaratti (UT)	64,000

 # While the numerical average of states is around 1.57 crore based on 2011 numbers, the average currently would stand to be roughly 1.89 crore. We have chosen not to extrapolate differential population growth rates for individual states in our calculations, since having around seventy-five states may lead to a major reorganization of supply chains and hence migration flows.

** Data for Pakistan-occupied territories has been garnered from the 1998 Pakistan census,[28] which was the last proper census carried out in those territories and has been extrapolated at an annual estimated growth rate of 2.76 per cent to arrive at 2011 population estimates for such areas.*

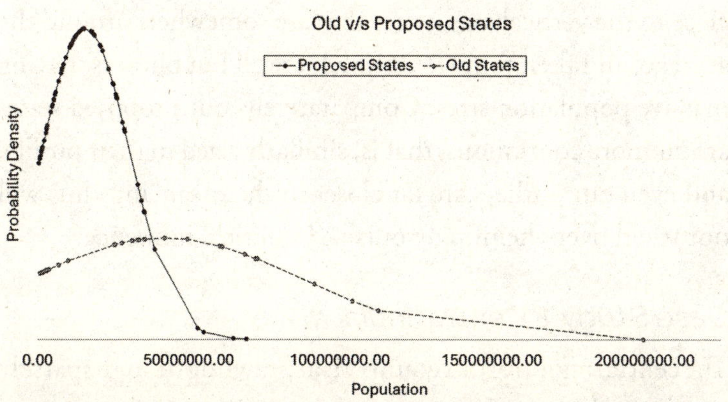

Figure 3. Distribution graphs of old and proposed states

Figure 3 compares the distribution of populations of states as they currently are and those of our proposed states (with populations given in the preceding table). The X-axis shows population. Each curve represents the populations of individual states, and they peak at their respective averages. The Y-axis shows the density of the probability function, that is, the higher the point in a curve, the more is the probability for an individual state to have that corresponding population. For reference, dots on the curves represent states as proposed or existing, as may be the case. Firstly, the distribution of our proposed seventy-five states is much tighter around its peak, which means that our proposed states are much more equal in size than in the current scheme. Secondly, all but four[29] of our seventy-five states are smaller than the average size of states as they are now (that is, 4.21 crore). This implies that our states are much smaller than the present states, and even the biggest states in our proposed scheme are smaller than present-day West Bengal, Bihar, Maharashtra, Madhya Pradesh, Tamil Nadu, and, of course, the elephant in the room, Uttar Pradesh. Thirdly, one can identify three discrete clusters of states as they stand currently—states that are very small and close to the vertical axis, states that are somewhere around the average, and then four states which are all but outliers, having massive population sizes. Comparatively, our proposed states are far more continuous, that is, similarly sized in their profile, and even our outliers are far closer to the mean and thus will not wield overwhelmingly outsized political influence.

Case Study 1: Central India

The central region of our country is a sprawling though sparsely populated hilly landmass in the heart of Bhārat, criss-crossed by the Vindhya and Satpura ranges and by rivers and ravines.

It corresponds broadly to today's Madhya Pradesh, Chhattisgarh, and parts of Uttar Pradesh, and is an example of how an ancient land that contains some of the first inhabitants of the subcontinent dating from the Neolithic era and with a rich history, cultural diversity, and economics has been artificially compartmentalized into a single large state and an appendix of a small state, the criteria for the formation of both of which are mostly undefined and largely meaningless.

Let us consider the British period first. The colonial government preferred to define an area which they held under direct rule as the so-called Central Provinces. As mentioned in Chapter Two, this was formed in 1861 by the merger of the Saugor and Nerbudda Territories and Nagpur Province. The district of Nimar, which was administered by the Central India Agency, was added in 1864. The Central India Agency itself was created in 1854 by amalgamating the Western Malwa Agency with other smaller political offices which formerly reported to the governor-general of India. The agency was overseen by a political agent who maintained relations of the Government of India with the princely states and who would exert an influence over them on behalf of the governor-general. The headquarters of the agent were at Indore. In general, this was a loose arrangement that satisfied the interests of both the British and the small and large princely states in the area, notably Indore, Bhopal, and Gwalior.

Inspection of Table 1 shows that Independence found itself with three states called Madhya Pradesh, Madhya Bhārat, and Vindhya Pradesh in this region. Madhya Bhārat, also known as Malwa Union, was created in 1948 and largely corresponded to twenty-five princely states in the Central India Agency. Vindhya Pradesh was created in 1948 from the Baghelkhand and Bundelkhand princely states in the eastern portion of the former Central India Agency. Madhya Pradesh was the old Central Provinces as it was in British India, including the Vidarbha area, and Nagpur, which was actually the capital.

The fashioning of the post-1956 Madhya Pradesh was, in many ways, as arbitrary and irrational as the demarcation during the British period and in the 1947–1955 interregnum. In some ways, the state was conceived of as a residual entity—something which exists only because no one wanted to organize its territories in any meaningful way. Chhattisgarh was detached from the state in 2001, indicating the completely artificial nature of the 1956 borders of Madhya Pradesh.

In our present structure of seventy-five states, the new suggestions are defined through old pre-British entities, which reflect in the ways of life of their inhabitants even today, and the reader will find that Gwalior, Avanti, Nimar, Vindhya Pradesh, and Mahakoshal find a ready correspondence with these former states that have real civilizational, economic, and cultural value addition. Bundelkhand and Baghelkhand, both being neglected areas with unique geographical challenges have been needlessly split across two states and warrant a separate and distinct existence. Gwalior had been, and continues to be, an industrial zone as well as a market connecting routes to northern cities such as Delhi to routes going to and from Maharashtra and Gujarat. Avanti, another ancient population centre, also has industrial areas and trade connectivity with Maharashtra, apart from robust religious tourism centred around the Mahakaleshwar temple. One may similarly deduce the reasoning for the proposed new states, which can be arrived at through a confluence of history, economics, geography, and culture.

Vidarbha is thus also formed as a state, with demands for a separate state persisting since Independence; the States Reorganization Commission had recommended a separate Vidarbha state as well, but this was not acquiesced to by the government of the day. This region is quite distant from Mumbai with many cultural, social, and geographical differences. Despite being a Marathi-speaking region, Vidarbha has always had a separate identity.[30] It has mineral and forest wealth, but it still remains a gravely backward region. It should develop itself as a separate unit, a kind of intrastate *atmanirbhar* that capitalizes on its unique distinctive character. Amravati, which is also in eastern Maharashtra, is designated as a state separate from Vidarbha as it formed a part of the former Hyderabad state, unlike Vidarbha; it is important to respect older cultural fault lines.

Case Study 2: Gauda

The ancient Vanga region was encompassed between the Padma-Meghna river system in the east and Bhagirathi-Hooghly system in the west. This ancient region became the core for a multi-millennial cultural efflorescence which not only shaped the Bengal region as we know it today but has also contributed immensely to Bhāratavarsha's culture and beyond. Bengal gave Sri Lanka its first dynasty and rejuvenated Vajrayana in Tibet. Bengal, apart from being the epicentre of Shakti worship and tantric practices, has seen Vaishnavas, Shaivas, Buddhists, and Jainas prosper throughout its history.[31]

Even in the later ancient and mediaeval eras, Bengal was not considered a single unit. Northern Bengal, that is, the region north of the main branch of the Ganga, preceded other parts of Bengal in human habitation and retained a distinct identity as Pundravardhana due to its geography. Vanga, the central region, was defined by the rivers Bhagirathi (Hooghly), Padma, the lower reaches of the Brahmaputra, and Meghna. Much of this central region now lies in Bangladesh. Within Vanga was a division known as Upa Vanga, which was centred around Jessore and adjoining areas of the Sundarbans. Until the Palas unified Bengal, the west between the Padma river and modern Bardhaman was a separate area known as Gauda or Radha, while the east retained its name of Vanga. The Palas, much like the Cholas, symbolically maintained this division between east and west, by adopting the dual titles of Vangapati and Gaudeshvara.[32] Only under stable Pala rule in the 8th and 9th centuries did the term Gauda and Vanga become interchangeable for all of what we today call Bengal.[33 34]

It is the historical Gauda region which can be the future basis for a Gauda state. The historical strength of Gauda had been trade and agriculture, but most importantly as an *entrepôt*. The area sits between the mineral-rich lands of central India and the massive population centres of Bengal, with overland trade routes to the Northeast, Bhutan, and Tibet via north Bengal, Nepal via Mithila and Bihar, and all of the Eastern Ghats. By sea, its influence across trade routes, old and new, extend across all of the eastern Indian ocean and beyond. A smaller, more integrated state of Gauda centred around Kolkata can focus solely on export-facing industries, sustainable agriculture, and trade, with convenient financial possibilities to connect all of India eastwards with ports such as Chittagong, Singapore, and Shanghai. Recognition of the name Gauda for this smaller, more economically focused state, will also acknowledge that much of what was Vanga is no longer a part of India.

The one critical, persistent failure since the Company Raj days was the inability to set up a network of modern ports and docks in and around Calcutta; it was not for want of trying, but it met repeated bouts of failures and apathy. Even after Independence, despite the setting up of Haldia, the overall performance of the area's ports has remained far behind its requirements. The politics behind the tragic deindustrialization of Bengal notwithstanding, the basic advantages for setting up industrial units in the area remain intact. While areas far from Kolkata will be able to step out from the shadow of the megapolis and overcome their neglect, a separate Gauda state will be able to focus on logistics, trade, and export-driven industry. Further, if trade picks up with some focussed economic policymaking and support, two outcomes will follow. Firstly, all of eastern India's economy will pick up through virtuous cycles of growth centred around the state. Secondly, the state can emerge as a financial centre, which can attract foreign investment and emerge as a Singapore-like entity, with a potential international financial services centre (IFSC) catering to investments from southeast and east Asia. A strategic outcome may also lead to increased Indian economic influence across southeast Asia which will further accelerate Indian growth as supply chains in the region will have an incentive to diversify away from China.

Case Study 3: Padmanabha Kshetram

Modern Kerala, while geographically compact, is densely populated and would have an estimated population just short of around 4 crore people. Unsurprisingly,[35] its make-up is quite diverse. The north of the state has close cultural similarities with the Tulu peoples of Karnataka and have similar economic interests. Central Kerala hosts the Palakkad gap, which cuts through the rugged Eastern Ghats and connects Tamil Nadu and Kerala, leading to a long history of cultural and economic exchanges between the denizens of the two areas. Simultaneously, the port of Kochi is a longstanding trade hub connecting the people to the sea and has been a gateway to foreign trade. Southern Kerala, contrastingly, has a maritime tradition which has developed due to the relative isolation between itself and other parts of the country and has led to the unique culture that characterizes it today. Culturally, it has traditions that are clearly distinct from the rest of the country, and it is a region which has been marked by a high exposure to foreign trade.[36] This exposition is necessary to underline that on both metrics, identity as well as economics, the three rough regions of Kerala are distinct.

If one concentrates only on southern Kerala, this region roughly corresponds to the area of the princely state of Travancore. Travancore is one the few royal houses that is remembered to this day with reverence by the people they once ruled. The illustrious Raja Ravi Varma, a scion of this royal house, refreshed the depictions of sanātani mythology and thus played a part in the revival of national consciousness. Swathi Thirunal Rama Varma, apart from establishing himself as a worthy successor of the musical trinity in Carnatic music,[37] made great strides in bringing modern engineering, medicine, and education to his kingdom. Moolam Thirunal Rama Varma introduced the first popularly elected legislative council in India. The imprimatur of the kings of Travancore have greatly shaped the economic and social conditions of the areas they ruled. Along with the erstwhile rulers of Mysore, the kings of Travancore have made their mark in history with the welfare of their subjects in mind.

At the same time, some of the problems which have caused much discord and degeneration in the rest of the nation had taken on a particularly hideous hue in Travancore, leading to instances such as Swami Vivekananda finding the region to be a 'lunatic asylum' owing to the incredulous institutionalization of caste oppression in India.[38] From the same churn has emerged many self-corrective movements; the region stands out for its intellectual and social dynamism. Of what we today know largely as Kerala, the erstwhile Travancore kingdom occupied the southern half, along with some of the southernmost areas of today's Tamil Nadu. Its cultural and social evolution is a one-of-a-kind phenomenon.

Economically, the south of Kerala has been more conducive to handling foreign trade than the rest of the country. Not surprisingly, Thiruvananthapuram has quietly blossomed as an information technology and start-up destination, which is on its way to becoming a major global information technology hub if it maintains its momentum.[39] Likewise, its links with both the West and the Middle East position it uniquely with respect to its economic and cultural influence abroad. The region, if turned into a state, can allow for a focus on international goods and services trade on the western seaboard and augment Bhārat's economic, cultural, and military influence across the Middle East and Africa's eastern coast.

One question which deserves a brief explanation is why the authors have chosen to not propose the name Travancore despite the historical region being known as such. The name Travancore is an anglicized corruption of Thiruvithamcode, also known as Thiruvithamkoor. The village, which lent its name to the kingdom, currently lies in the Kanyakumari district of Tamil Nadu. The history of how it came to be so is tortuous and involved violence and political disputation between Tamil Nadu and Kerala. No state ought to carry out irredentism as it defeats one of the purposes of the proposed reorganization. At the same time, a connection with the past is necessary to maintain a sense of continuity amongst the people. Thus, existing state names are to be generally eschewed when inappropriate as also historical names, which may lead to claims and counterclaims between states in the future. In 1750, Raja Marthanda Varma, embodying the highest principles of *rājadharma* and realizing authority to be a sacred compact, had symbolically offered his kingdom to Lord Padmanābhaswami, and ruled in his stead as a servant, becoming Padmanābhadasa.[40] To reinstill the idea of good governance as a mode of worship and as a holy duty, the name Padmanabha Kshetram is, to our minds, fitting.

Case Study 4: Mithila

Known as Videha since the Vedic period, Mithila has a special place in all of Bhārat as well as in Nepal, since it is the home of Mā Sitā. Mithila came to house Vaishali, a city of great commercial and political weight in ancient India. Mithila maintained its political existence throughout the mediaeval era, which culminated in the Darbhanga Raj, a principality which continued as a zamindari until India's independence.[41] Much like the kings of Mysore, the Darbhanga rajas have left behind a lasting legacy of public works with their donations and charitable works, underpinning a number of important infrastructural complexes in the region. Mithila, in some shape or form, had maintained both cultural and political existence for extended periods of time. The Maithili language, too, has maintained an independent, vibrant literary and media efflorescence.

Mithila's separate language, culture, cuisine, and history is one note of dissonance with respect to the rest of Bihar. However, two important additional points warrant mention. First, the region opens with the Terai to its north, and its boundaries are bound with the Ganga, Mahananda, and Gandaki. Resultantly, the lands of Mithila are particularly prone to flooding, and the grievances which follow due to inadequate relief. Secondly, the vast majority of Mithila was deindustrialized by the systematic destruction of the region by the British through repeated famines, followed by the stresses from the dominance of western Bihar and the separation of Jharkhand. Maharaja Kameshwar Singh of the Raj Darbhanga had started a number of industrial ventures ranging from steel to publishing.[42] The fertile region has, however, been reduced to engaging in subsistence agriculture, and the contemporary economic history of the region is of government apathy, leading to a wipeout of sugar mills in the area.[43] It is only with the recent central government's push for ethanol blending and associated changes in policy that green shoots have arrived of late in the form of ethanol production from sugarcane.[44]

The demands for a separate Mithila are not new and were based on grounds of both identity and economics. The first known demand was made far back in 1912 when Bihar was separated from Bengal. Before this, the Darbhanga Raj had patronized and formed the Maithil Mahasabha on the lines of the Utkal Union, which ultimately succeeded in convincing the British to form Orissa. Similarly, much like the *Utkal Deepika* for Odiyas, the magazine *Maithil Mihir* began to articulate economic and cultural concerns of Mithila 1909 onwards. The Darbhanga Raj did not abandon spearheading the movement for Mithila for decades on end—the maharaja petitioned the British in 1921[45] and then advocated for a separate Mithila state in the Constituent Assembly in 1947.[46] The demands for a separate Mithila stubbornly persist as the underlying causes remain unaddressed.[47] The non-manifestation of a separate Mithila had a strong underlying political undertone, as is evident from the fact that important markers of political attention such as the existence of a university remained absent, and funds allotted to the region remained disproportionately lower. The dominance of the Brahmin and Kayastha peoples in Mithila further led to a disadvantage for Mithila, as caste politics in the region was unfavourable for these groupings.[48]

Mithila's location provides it with a number of advantages for the reestablishment of food processing and heavy industry. From the south, it has access to the mineral-rich areas of Jharkhand and inner Bengal. In the east, it has ready access to what is north Bengal, providing it easy access to the Northeast (including Sikkim) via Siliguri and the ports of Bengal to the south.[49] At its north lies Nepal, and Nepal's adjoining Madhesi areas have been ethnically and economically integrated with Mithila for centuries. At its west lies the rest of Bihar and Uttar Pradesh, which host important markets and population centres. A separate Mithila will enable a greater channelization of funds and augur industrial growth through focussed economic policymaking. A reindustrialized Mithila can have a massive impact on the whole region; from the Northeast to eastern Uttar Pradesh, positive economic spillovers emanating from Mithila can raise incomes across this wide and populous region. Further, its old and continuing links with Nepal would enable an economically rising Mithila to be an important lever of economic diplomacy with a difficult neighbour.

In our present scheme of seventy-five states, Mithila will be the largest in terms of population with 6,91,82,585 inhabitants.

Case Study 5: Rayalaseema

The Rayalaseema region comprising Kurnool, Anantapur, Kadapa, Chittoor, Sri Sathya Sai, Nandyal, Annamayya, and Tirupati districts is marked by a difference in geography, climate, culture, and dialect with the rest of Andhra Pradesh. Unlike the water-rich and fertile areas of coastal Andhra Pradesh, Rayalaseema suffers from perennial water scarcity and complaints of political neglect. So much so, there have even been demands for Rayalaseema to be included in Telangana, as the issues faced by both regions have been similar.[50]

Once known derogatorily as the 'ceded districts', simply because the Hyderabad Nizam had ceded the same to the British in 1800,[51] the region received its current name when a high-level meeting of Andhra leaders under the banner of Andhra Mahasabha and Andhra Provincial Conference or Ceded Districts Conference, held at Nandyal on 17 and 18 November 1928, passed a resolution to that effect.[52] The name itself harkened back to the Vijayanagara empire—the territory corresponded roughly with those of the Aravidu dynasty, an ember from the mighty empire after its cataclysmic destruction following the battle of Talikota in 1565. Unsurprisingly, the region's history is connected with that of northern Tamil Nadu and southern Karnataka more than the rest of Andhra Pradesh. Its rocky geography, devoid of any major rivers, and its history of hosting a string of fortresses overlooking trade routes skirting the Eastern Ghats, has shaped its identity and economics in a unique way.

Attributing Rayalaseema's backwardness and lack of critical infrastructural support to state politics is not surprising. Coastal Andhra (also known as Seemandhra) and Rayalaseema were competing with each other for the favours of Madras prior to Independence. Differences came to a head when Andhra University was inaugurated in 1926, with its headquarters in Vijayawada. The people of Rayalaseema, being educationally backward compared to coastal Andhra, demanded the headquarters be shifted to Rayalaseema. The Andhra Mahasabha, dominated by people from Telangana, pitched in and passed a resolution that the university's headquarters be shifted to Anantapur in Rayalaseema. The Madras government stepped in and chose to render Andhra University a university of coastal Andhra only—the headquarters of Andhra University were shifted to Visakhapatnam, and all of Rayalaseema's colleges were affiliated with Madras University.

The Congress of the time took a stance against any of Rayalaseema's demands which could dilute the linguistic principle. This provided leaders of coastal Andhra ample space to outmanoeuvre Rayalaseema's political leaders and their influence. When C. Rajagopalachari (from coastal Andhra) won the Madras elections, not a single leader from Rayalaseema was included in his cabinet. Soon after, realizing that a brooding Rayalaseema could seriously upend the demand for a separate Telugu-speaking state, an olive leaf was extended to Rayalaseema. In 1937, at the residence of Kashinathuni Nageshwara Rao Pantulu,[53] leaders from Rayalaseema entered into an agreement with those of coastal Andhra Pradesh. This came to be known as the Sribagh agreement, and it informs us of the conditions based on which Rayalaseema chose to enter into a compact along with coastal Andhra.[54]

The Sribagh agreement had a set of concrete conditions which were to be fulfilled by coastal Andhra. Of the key terms, a few warrant recollection: irrigation up to the level which coastal Andhra enjoys, equal representation in the Andhra Pradesh legislature, and preference for Rayalaseema to have a capital and a high court.[55]

The Sribagh agreement was sidelined soon after Andhra Pradesh was formed, with no recourse left for Rayalaseema. Andhra Pradesh's capital, which was earlier in Kurnool, was shifted to Hyderabad in 1956. Of the 175 seats in Andhra Pradesh's current assembly, Rayalaseema gets only 56, which is lower than the half which were promised. The high court is currently in Amaravati in coastal Andhra Pradesh. Less than a quarter of the Rayalaseema region has been provided irrigation, making the remainder reliant on increasingly capricious monsoons—leading to repeated droughts and the resultant immiseration of the agricultural economy.[56] On critical metrics such as poverty rates, literacy rates, serious crime, and unemployment, the gap between coastal Andhra Pradesh and Rayalaseema is yawning.[57] The underlying reason for the union of Rayalaseema and coastal Andhra, that is, the idea of a single Telugu-speaking state, has ceased to exist with the departure of Telangana from the compact.

Industry associations have been candid in attributing the lack of industrial attention to Rayalaseema to political factors.[58] If clubbed with adjoining Telugu-majority areas in present-day Karnataka and Tamil Nadu and spun-off as a state in and of itself, it can emerge as an industrial powerhouse. Its small coastline is well-placed to develop a sizable port at Dugarajapatnam—a project which remains in limbo for extraneous reasons.[59] Heavy industries, particularly those related to smelting, cement, metallurgy, and steel production, are particularly well-suited for the region. The region is also mineral-rich, having sources of asbestos, barytes, China clay, calcite, dolomite, diamonds, green quartz, iron ore, limestone, silica sand, and gold.[60] The state would also have exclusive control over large endemic forests of red sandalwood, enabling proper attention to sustainable industrial forestry which can have a positive effect on the environment. The state would also host the Tirupati Balaji temple, which brings with it immense cultural might apart from proceeds from tourism. The region has silently emerged as an automotive manufacturing destination, which builds on its geographical advantages.[61] The state's prosperity would positively impact northern Tamil Nadu, southern Karnataka, and coastal Andhra as well.[62]

Seventy-five Economic Powerhouses

The above case studies show that a big reason behind the nation's underdevelopment is the lack of attention from distant capitals, geographically or otherwise. The problem of glueing together peoples who have fundamentally different identities and economic incentives is that the winner takes all—unless an area can consistently emerge as an electoral kingmaker, it is destined to be neglected by the electorally dominant area. The social fragmentation wrought by artificially glueing peoples overwhelmingly leads to competition rather than to cooperation. In each of the examples discussed above, we can see that the political, social, and geographical structure of a state becomes increasingly unfavourable as one moves further from the capital and the population centres of the communities which dominate state politics. This phenomenon is not unique to India, but can be seen in operation across multiple countries. One need not go far; the ongoing civil war in Myanmar has to do fundamentally with the grievances of the peoples which lie beyond the Bamar-dominated valleys of the country. Smaller states thus are a developmental imperative and can go far in maintaining social cohesion across the country.

The economic unlocking of potential in vast swathes of India, while important in and of itself, also holds the key to a pressing social challenge. Major centres of trade and industry have seen massive migrant flows over generations, which have led to indelible demographic shifts. When combined with the canker of linguistic states, the norm after 1956, economic anxieties of Indians about migrants took an ugly identitarian turn.[63] South Indians were relentlessly harassed, mocked, and even subjected to pogroms in the Maharashtra of 1960s.[64] 'Outsiders', in particular Bengalis, were persecuted and repeatedly subject to riots and grisly atrocities in Meghalaya well into the early 2000s,[65] and Bengalis faced an all-out pogrom in Assam on similar lines.[66] Likewise, properties owned by Bengalis who had otherwise spent generations in areas of Chhattisgarh, Bihar, and eastern Uttar Pradesh were targeted and forcefully occupied in the decades after 1956. Karnataka has seen repeated mob violence against Tamils, with 1991 being a particularly violent year.[67] Even today, the scorn against migrants from Bihar, Uttar Pradesh, Odisha, and adjoining areas remains manifest from Punjab to Tamil Nadu. Unlocking the economic potential of regions which are labour surplus can, over time, stem migrant flows and reduce economic competition. This has led to much conflict and sorrow already. Effective economic management in smaller states can result in lower permanent out-migration, as seen in Uttarakhand's case.[68] Considering that matters of identity and demographics are valid concerns for any people, the current model of migration-intensive development which depends on importing migrants into concentrated clusters from faraway places is a recipe for social fragmentation and conflict. Seventy-five states, each an economic powerhouse, presents a far more balanced, socially viable developmental trajectory which can enhance national integration while delivering broad-based, geographically dispersed economic growth.

Further, the identification of a person as 'Bihari', or the targeting of a Tamil-speaking person as a 'Madrasi' or 'Tamil' is predicated on an us-versus-them paradigm where it is assumed that all peoples speaking a single language should be in one state. This turns a somewhat amorphous and vague cultural attribute of language into a discrete political identity, rendering anyone who has inherited these cultural attributes to be a target for political reasons. Bigger states make the differences between the people of each state seem sharp and defined, instead of approximating gradual continuums which exist in real life, leading to a much easier identification of who ought to be the 'other'. While today it is easy for supremacists in Tamil Nadu to heap abuses on Uttar Pradesh, the scope for a denizen of Kongu Nadu to have major political and economic grievances against Bundelkhand becomes a difficult undertaking. The occasional lashing out in Bengaluru against 'outsiders', likewise, rests on a strong identification with linguistic identity, to the detriment of all other aspects of identity; if there were multiple Kannada-speaking states, tempers would undoubtedly cool, and disputes would be handled by the people who are impacted most by it, instead of distant capitals which are capitalizing on opportunities to spin sub-nationalist narratives for short-term electoral gains.

To illustrate, let us see how having smaller states can affect an intractable inter-state problem. The Kaveri water dispute has caused much strife for over a century. Currently, the dispute, which is purely economic in nature, has become an ethnic conflict. Every few years, anti-Tamil and anti-Kannadiga sentiments are aroused in Karnataka and Tamil Nadu, respectively, and manifest themselves in violence. This is because an economic dispute between two states can be conflated with an ethnic conflict since the two states themselves are defined in terms of linguistic groupings. Varied cultural identities have been sequestered into the narrow identity of politics, based on which artificial political units have been provided legitimacy as states in their current form; under such circumstances, economic negotiation between states inevitably becomes a battle of egos between peoples. In a paradigm where there are multiple Kannada- and Tamil-speaking states, the whole dispute becomes immediately localized between the Mysuru and Kongu states instead of being a quarrel between Tamils and Kannadigas at large. Large swathes of both these linguistic groupings become delinked from hostilities, at least directly. Upper and lower riparian states thus will have fewer political opportunities to give an emotive identitarian spin to economic issues, leading to a more fruitful engagement for a solution. So far, good politics has made for bad economics. Tomorrow, smaller states can align incentives and make sure that good economics translates to good politics.

The principal reason why smaller states tend to perform better economically is simply due to the gains of specialization. A very basic concept in economics is that in a world where the relative ability of different people to do particular things varies, everyone is better off if each person focuses on the particular things which he or she can do best.[69] This interplay between comparative advantage and specialization gains has been the secret to prosperity for countries ranging from mercantilist Britain of yore to the Asian tigers. This simple intuitive idea has underpinned trade for millennia; thus, particular regions in the world would specialize in a particular good or service and trade their offerings for those of others.[70] Thus, Kannauj came to specialize in perfume production, Khambat in agate jewellery, Idukki in growing cardamom, and the Dibang valley in weaving textiles from nettle fibres.[71]

In the current set-up, the economic policymaking of states has to simultaneously expend its finite resources on the infinitely long list of demands and grievances arising from different regions specializing in particular regions. Uttar Pradesh, for example, is expected to modernize and environmentally upgrade tanneries in Kanpur, address the use of banned fertilizers for mangoes and sugarcane in its western reaches, build a sustainable ecosystem and supply chain network for its defence corridor, regulate metallurgy in Moradabad, and devise sufficient technical support for electronics manufacturers in Gautam Buddh Nagar. Even with its emphatic endorsement of the One District One Product scheme, it is simply beyond the means of a single state to simultaneously nurture so many industries in an adequate and equitable manner. As if individual industries were not enough, the state also has to keep in mind the follow-on social and political consequences of supporting particular sectors: which political lobbies will gain or lose power, the terms of trade between industries, which regions need particular patronization due to electoral reasons, which industries are controlled by particular communities, and so on. In short, attempting systematic industrial development and buttressing it with requisite state support is a futile attempt if the state is a sprawling entity. The result is growth which is muted for all and unequal at the same time.

The alternative is to carve states so that no more than three or four major industries dominate, so that each state can focus on products or services which can enable it to increase income in the fastest possible way.

- **Kashmir**, for example, can focus on floriculture and industrial forestry, building on its natural strengths. While everyone knows about Kashmir's saffron and perhaps its timberworks, fewer people know that Kashmir has immense underutilized potential with respect to roses and lavender. Kashmir rose oil, for example, comes very close in both smell and chemical constituents to the current global monopolist, Bulgarian rose oil. The region's produce, which can be produced at a lower cost than Bulgaria, can enable the region to tap into a lucrative market.[72] Nonetheless, due to lack of sufficient supply chain support by the state despite the brave attempts of some scientists to work on the subject with limited resources, the industry has suffered from muted returns and farmers having to part with their produce at throwaway prices. Likewise, Kashmiri woodworking and horticulture remain local affairs and require sustained attention. If Kashmir is spun off as its own state, it will have to expend less energy on intrigues with Jammu and will be forced to contend with its own revenue deficits. It will also have fewer people on whom it can blame its woes. Finally, a parasitic class of middlemen that has emerged due to rampant clientelism will be cut off from their filthy lucre, which largely comes from mismanagement of the tax proceeds of Jammuites. Fiscal pressure and the demands of the people will lead to a focus on revenue buoyancy through serious economic policymaking. Maintaining the economic momentum, which has reflected in increased economic growth rate since 2014–2015, requires steady local attention.[73]

- **Kachchh**, a land which has engaged in international trade since the days when the Indus Valley Civilization was still thriving, has now been relegated to a backward region within Gujarat. Its inhospitable geography and the severance of trade networks post-Partition has had a deleterious effect on the region, which has reoriented itself with the commissioning of export-oriented ports at Mundra and Kandla. Lesser-known focus areas, however, include minerals such as lignite, bauxite, and gypsum. Most importantly, however, Kachchh's harsh climate can be turned into an asset if the region focusses on solar energy. Kachchh district is already home to a number of massive solar parks, yet its potential remains vastly untapped.[74] With the requisite infrastructural support, Kachchh can focus on becoming a solar and wind power; the region receives considerable solar irradiation, has a sparse population, and due to a low monsoon effect can provide year-round production.[75] Having established ports can also enable the region to set up industries for assembling and manufacturing renewable energy technologies, with a market for renewable energy production. Access to cheap and dependable electricity along with the presence of bauxite may also allow Kachchh to emerge as an aluminium refining and smelting centre, supplying automotive, aerospace, and other industries through its ports.

- **Kongu Nadu**, which has been conceptualized as comprising Coimbatore, Tiruppur, Erode, Karur, Nilgiris, Salem, Namakkal, Krishnagiri, Dindigul, and Dharmapuri, is an economically formidable region since time immemorial. The region had enriched itself through the Chola era Rajakesari Peruvazhi, a trade route which connected what is today Kerala with adjoining areas of Tamil Nadu and Karnataka. Through its unique geographical advantages, the region has remained well-integrated with global trade flows, with evidence of Roman traders and their wares having traversed its lands. Coimbatore and Tiruppur are globally recognized for their textile industry ecosystem, with many global brands having outsourced their production to the mills of these two districts.[76] The two districts have made a name for themselves in the export markets with a 54 per cent share in textile exports from India[77] and have the capacity to meaningfully diversify into geotextiles and specialized textiles. Coimbatore and its surrounding areas are also formidable components and capital goods manufacturing hubs, hosting the presence of both foreign and domestic majors. Ranging from industries for pumps and auto components to defence goods, the Coimbatore region is amongst the country's most developed industrial areas. Additionally, Coimbatore is attempting to become a major information technology hub.[78] Simultaneously, Kongu Nadu's climatic conditions have made it a well-established agricultural zone which specializes in cash crops and spices such as turmeric, coffee, tea, chilli, and rubber. If spun off into a state of its own, the state's high revenue can be invested in industrial support measures to scale up, consolidate, and upgrade its industries. Its access to talent, capital, and pre-existing industrial supply chains also makes it an ideal candidate for incubating robotics, automation, industrial design, and sunrise sectors.

- **Kashi**, which has had a political existence since the Iron Age, has been thought of as a separate state[79] since, alternatively, a state which would cover today's Purvanchal would be too populous, and hold within itself multiple peoples which are clearly identifiable as having different cultures. Holding within itself the twin centres of Varanasi and Gorakhpur, the state would act as the spiritual capital for all of the country. Kashi is a natural focus for religious tourism and acts as an important pilgrimage for not only Hindus but also Buddhists and Jains. Being located in well-irrigated plains, its tourism potential is not encumbered with environmental considerations of the order which one must be cognizant of in, say, Kedarnath or Kamakhya. The painstakingly constructed Kashi corridor alone has resulted in massive economic gains for the city, resulting in a broad-based increase in income.[80] Gorakhpur, meanwhile, is silently emerging as an engine of economic growth in an otherwise backward region of the country and has been consistently increasing its economic footprint.[81] Varanasi is also a growing manufacturing centre, with textiles and metal fabrication being its speciality; these industries remain largely informal in nature, and adequate support can enable faster growth in income as well. Varanasi's exalted status as a temple town, however, needs sustained state support for it to maximize its potential. What is often lost to commentators is that the city has faced repeated destruction at the hands of invaders, and there is hardly a temple in the entire city which has not been relocated or rebuilt after being destroyed. Many of these temples were reconsecrated in smaller forms to prevent the zealotry and greed of alien occupiers from targeting these temples again.[82] A large number of these temples were rebuilt with funds collected from the unnamed masses of all of Bhāratavarsha, not just kings or rich patrons. The entire city, including its many temples, requires a multi-decade restoration effort where its temples are reinstated with the grandeur they once commanded. Whilst prime amongst them is the Kashi Vishwanath temple,[83] the entirety of the city can and should be restructured to reflect its erstwhile splendour and infuse it with Indic modernity. This can take its tourism potential to the next level. Simultaneously, attempts at reviving education in the city, particularly on matters of law, architecture, culture, and spirituality can offer new avenues of nurturing a knowledge-based economy.

- **Nimar**, which corresponds to the south-western portion of Madhya Pradesh, is a land that is suffering from neglect due to its distance. Barwani and Khandwa districts are amongst the most backward districts in the country.[84] Simultaneously, Khargone district that housed the once-important industrial centre of Barwaha which is engaged in textile and ginning has been withering away. The region has a sizeable tribal population and performs poorly on most socio-economic indicators. However, the region has seen better days in the past—the entire region is dotted with temples and structures built from the Maratha era onwards, and with the Narmada flowing through it, it had some industrial centres. The region was a major cotton producer and processor, and has some minor mineral works such as for lime. It also hosted a route which was once known as the 'gateway to the Deccan'. The region, if turned into a state and thereby becoming a direct recipient of central funds, can invest in irrigation and measures across the cotton supply chain to revive its industry. It can also develop its touristic potential by systematically focusing on historical and religious sites and repurposing its historical havelis and palaces into luxury stays for people living in Gujarat, Maharashtra, and Madhya Pradesh looking for a quick getaway. Another important industry which it can focus on, by having its own legislation on forestry, is to engage in sustainable industrial forestry—the place suffers from large areas of land which are degraded and disproportionately impact tribal communities. Industrial forestry can supply readily accessible population centres with quality wood and wood products from the high-quality wood which grows there, most important of which are teak and sal, while improving its overall environmental circumstances. Statehood for Nimar can undoubtedly enable the region to turn its fortunes around and be a pilot project of sorts for similarly neglected regions of the country.

The Present Unemployment Crisis

The most pressing issue the nation faces today is its jobs crisis. India possesses a massive demographic dividend, yet its utilization remains alarmingly low. The conditions of employment remain distressingly dismal for the vast majority of the country, and the informalization of jobs within the already anaemic formal sector remains unabated as also underemployment, which is all but exploitative. In particular, the unemployment rates for various categories of educated youth masks the collective anxieties, frustrations, and precarity of young men and women who could have been contributing meaningfully to their families, communities, and nation. Despite a series of efforts to meaningfully ameliorate the situation, such as the government's focus on start-ups and manufacturing, the scale of the problem is much greater than the pace at which we, as a society, are able to address the problem. Employment is predominantly of poor quality, with stagnant or declining wages.[85] The longstanding neglect of serious education reforms and quality is taking a particularly vicious toll on the youth, impacting their job prospects and incomes. The human resource of this country is its greatest wealth, and a series of policy blunders both in terms of economics and education has made the situation very pressing. Meaningful employment is the need of the hour, and policy attention on the same is not possible without the states and the Union working closely.

Many of the low-margin, repetitive tasks on which the majority of Indians depend for their livelihood are under particular risk from automation with the advent of artificial intelligence and robotics. While the nation stares at such a grave cataclysm, the fact that vast stretches of Bhārat's landmass remain underutilized due to the country's political organization is nothing short of criminal. As discussed above, a big reason why economic policymaking and attention do not reach areas beyond the few dominant regions of a state is because of the way our states and constituencies are organized. Through the scheme of things proposed here, gains from specialization and impetus for wider state attention are expected to percolate across a far vaster area than before. New and different types of jobs will be created in a more dispersed, decentralized manner, and the absorption of labour flows will simultaneously raise wages. This will unlock geographical and human potential at a scale hitherto unimagined and raise the number and quality of jobs available throughout Bhārat. Nothing could cement Bhārat's civilizational destiny more than widespread prosperity, where ambition can be nestled in opportunity.

CHAPTER 5

Modus Operandi

'Laws and institutions must go hand in hand with the progress of the human mind. As that becomes more developed, more enlightened, as new discoveries are made, new truths disclosed, and manners and opinions change with the change of circumstances, institutions must advance also, and keep pace with the times. We might as well require a man to wear still the coat which fitted him when a boy, as civilized society to remain ever under the regimen of their barbarous ancestors.'

—Thomas Jefferson[1]

India's polity is no stranger to drastic constitutional changes. The systemic lethargy that has crept into Centre–state relations and governance is largely due to the fact that an unstable system favoured a number of political middlemen who stood to gain from such inefficiencies. The last major attempt at making India's polity work better came when the anti-defection law was instituted via the 52nd amendment to the Constitution in 1985.[2] The introduction of the goods and services tax (GST), including all the dextrous changes to the Constitution which made it possible, was commendable; but non-linear adaptations to the Constitution are a necessity in the realm of polity as well. There is nothing sacred (or even sensible) to assume that a system devised for India in 1950 by people who had experienced the world as it was back then will work for a Bhārat of 2025 and beyond. Much has changed since the Constitution came into effect—economically, socially, and politically. The fact that the constitution has been amended 106 times since its onset, implying an average of more than an amendment a year, makes it obvious that the document is an imperfect one which needs constant updating and reworking by the nation.[3]

If anything, the Constitution exists for the benefit of the nation and for it to appropriately devise systems for its all-round advancement. It is an evolving compact amongst the people of Bhārat where they tinker with the organization of and expectations from the state. The Constitution exists for and by the people, not the people for and by the Constitution—especially in a civilizational state.[4] The recent tendency to sacralize the Constitution and ossify it on arbitrary lines by invoking an amorphous, ideologically tinged 'basic structure' is deeply unhealthy and unnecessary. The Constitution is a mere instrument for progress and for reflecting the mechanism of achieving said progress on terms which the people deem fit. Understanding this and making the common people understand this is necessary if we want to improve the outcomes of the democratic process, both politically and economically. This is the highest objective and aspiration for Bhāratiyas.[5] To do what needs to be done, deep institutional changes are necessary.

Each Vote Same Value

The first of the two principles, namely, 'Each Vote Same Value', has no way of being realized with the present state boundaries and the current number and demarcations of constituencies in a state. The latter are fixed based largely on the population distribution of 1971, leading to inequalities between citizens in their single most important right, their vote. Merely increasing the number of seats proportionately from 543 to 888, or some such number,[6] is no solution because the skew ratios[7] between constituencies would remain unchanged and a vote from a smaller, more educated, and economically forward state would remain higher than a vote from a larger, less educated, and economically backward state. Since the devolution of funds from the common pool of taxation is also connected with artificially frozen population numbers, richer states are awarded more money per head than poorer states, which is a bizarre inversion of logic, ethics, and economics at once. Unfortunately, wealth has been indirectly encoded as a measure of worth under the current system of skewed representation. Simultaneously, the ratio of electors to the elected becomes so vast[8] that individual votes become meaningless, diluting the democratic principle itself and resulting in a flawed reflection of popular aspirations. If the first-past-the-post system is one where 51 per cent of the population (in real life, closer to 33 per cent) can impress its will on the naysayers, the problems caused by this would only be more when the constituencies are large.

A lot is being heard about the delimitation exercise which we are bound to carry out after 2026. Would the census which has been scheduled to commence sometime in 2025 be in time for a delimitation before the 2029 election? This would require the census to be completed by 2026,[9] or at the latest by mid-2027. While it is incumbent on the central government to schedule the next census as soon as possible, would this also involve caste enumeration?

The last such caste enumeration was in 1931. In a country where so much, official and unofficial, depends on caste, the least that young citizens are entitled to know is that caste reservations on which so much hinges with regard to their education and employment are based on numbers obtained in 1931, a clean sixteen years before Independence and Partition. This is a politically volatile issue and requires careful political navigation.

Does this mean we will not see a caste enumeration anytime soon? Karnataka carried out such an exercise some time back, but the numbers have not been released for nearly a decade. It is widely held that these numbers are a political hot potato, and this is the reason why successive governments have not made the results of the enumeration public.[10] Is this the reason why governments have been generally wary of a nationwide caste enumeration? Are they nervous about how many more Pandora's boxes would be opened all over the country if we were to carry out such an exercise? Politicians of all hues and colours swear by their loyalty to upholding caste reservations, some of them even to the extent of promising to increase them. Do they suspect that these reservations are based on caste data that is no longer accurate? Is this why they do not want to have a caste census now? The albatross of caste reservations is not going to be taken off our necks anytime soon, and as long as it hangs around in the present cacophonous manner, the goal of Vikasit Bhārat will remain elusive. The magic formula of quality with quantity is extraordinarily difficult to achieve. In a pluralistic democracy with a first-past-the-post parliamentary system like ours it is impossible to achieve anything unless we are given infinite time, which in itself is impossible. An inclusive, realistic, and measured national conversation on this prickly issue is necessary for both social and economic reasons.

We have devoted some space to discussing this caste and reservations issue in a book on delimitation because politicians, in the end, will be politicians. Any delimitation exercise will be planned, handled, and executed by them in large measure. In our opinion, the present political leadership is largely realistic and pragmatic—realistic about their opportunities and abilities to move Bhārat forward in a positive way, pragmatic about securing their electoral dominance in a parliamentary democracy with the first-past-the-post electoral system. It is vital for us, the people of Bhārat, in whose name the governance of this land is carried out, to ensure that the new delimitation boundaries are not gerrymandered to suit caste equations of special interest groups or the narrow compulsions of 'coalition dharma'. As the saying goes, politics is too important to be left to the politicians, and this is especially pertinent to the issue at hand.

In the name of diversity, the exercise of delimitation should not descend into keeping old wounds fresh for petty politics. We take our elections seriously. The entire process should not be retro-engineered by politicians to suit their present-day needs. Bhārat is a civilizational state. Any civilizational state inherently adopts long-term thinking and cannot prosper otherwise. 'Liberal democracies' of the Western type are addicted to short-termism. In such a context, the delimitation exercise must be of a type that takes a long-term view of what Bhārat will look like fifty and hundred years from now. Primacy has to be given to inclusive economics and holistic readings of identity. Essentially, the delimitation-cum-states' reorganization effort is a political reorientation of the country to enable it to achieve economic goals, and such an endeavour cannot be allowed to reproduce the ancient regime but with increased numbers, aided and abetted with dollops of corruption. The delimitation exercise which is to happen must be a break from the past and be based on new benchmarks which prioritize prosperity and composite identities. We lost a big chance in 1955. History should not be allowed to repeat itself.

Each State Same Heft

The second of the two principles, namely, 'Each State Same Heft', cannot be achieved unless all the states are of the same population, simply because constituencies are ideally demarcated on the basis of population. From the time of Ambedkar, a state population of 2 crore has been deemed to be optimal in terms of combining ease of governance with establishing a healthy connect between the people and those who they elect to legislate for them. We have shown in adequate detail that our present state boundaries are mostly the result of historical accidents, British proclivities, political chicanery, and sometimes quite simply quixotic perversity. This is no basis for delimitation of state boundaries in the largest country in the world, which finds itself poised to become a major power in the next half century. It is unacceptable that some states can be perpetually ignored while some get to goad the Union into submission on local issues, disturbing the economic and political division of power between the two levels of government.

The two principles for a healthy democracy in Bhārat are, therefore, fortuitously connected. The first principle cannot be realized without states of roughly equal population, namely, without the second principle. The second principle, namely, seventy-five states with a population of around 2 crore each and thereby having equal heft with the Union government, will provide the only level playing field for a nationwide delimitation, which is the only way of achieving the first principle, Each Vote Same Value. Here we have a conjoining of two important, nay essential, yet independent, requirements for a stable democracy, each of which may only be achieved with the other in place. *A system must be initiated which is stable to changes in the political dispensation at the Centre.* This is the least that we, the people of Bhārat, can give ourselves. Our Constitution begins with the words, 'We the People'. It does not begin with 'We the Politicians'.

A Roadmap for Transformation

The recent Lok Sabha election result has been exceptional in that the same pre-poll alliance, the NDA, has received a simple majority for the third consecutive time, only the second time this has happened in our history.[11] The prime minister has said in the recent election campaign that what he had done between 2014 and 2024 was only the trailer. The real movie would now follow. Would this movie run to full houses? Would it break records at the box office? Or would it crash? Who would be the main actors? Who would be the supporting actors? Who would be the guest actors? Who would be the heroes? Who would be the villains? Who would direct the movie? Would anyone prevent the screening of the movie? Above all, who would produce the movie? The answer to the last question would determine the plot, the story, and the outcome. The best outcome would be if the producers of this movie are the citizens of Bhārat, who have voted for the NDA and have endorsed the production of this movie.

Of the two central principles for constitutional reform and improvement outlined in this book, the first one, namely, Each Vote Same Value, is virtually mandated by the removal of the long fifty-year freeze on seat delimitation, which is coming to an end in 2026. It would be an act of extreme unwisdom on the part of the present dispensation to extend the freeze by another twenty-five years simply because it is a coalition government, which was the problem faced by Vajpayee in 2001.[12] Alternatively, and worse, the government may just go in for cosmetic delimitations in areas where local political and electoral problems are seen, the squeaky screw getting the oil as it were. The mandate is for reform, and a delimitation which is carried out afresh and unhindered is vital to balancing India's political and economic make-up.

The second principle that we have outlined, namely, Each State Same Heft, can only be achieved with states of roughly equal size. Without doing this, there is no rational solution to the north–south problem identified so clearly by Ambedkar back in 1955. There is no point in the assertion that there is no north–south problem and that India is one. Of course Bhārat is one, but the fault lines between the Hindi-speaking north and the non-Hindi-speaking south have existed since well before Independence, with West Bengal and Maharashtra being more than interested spectators, and it is important that any trace of this so-called north–south problem be removed from the country.[13] Unlike constituency delimitation, which is practically mandated on us now, there is no compulsion on the NDA government to initiate any move for a radical redrawing of state borders. However, and this point must be made clearly to politicians who might read this book—*there is no way a rational and fair nationwide delimitation of constituencies can be achieved without a complete redrawing of state borders*. Keeping present state boundaries while carrying out delimitation will be an almost futile exercise, since it will only compound existing problems that we have outlined in the previous chapters. What is encouraging about this redrawing is that it is totally permissible by Article 3 and would lie completely within the four corners of the present

Constitution, that too at the Parliament's sole and unilateral prerogative.

This leads to the next major sub-plot in the forthcoming movie. Would Bhārat be better off changing itself to a forward-looking economic powerhouse in a civilizational rubric within the present Constitution, or would a drastically changed Constitution be better or more efficient in effecting a quantum leap? This is a politically volatile question that needs cool and calm reflection instead of adherence to slogans from bygone ages.

A New (Constitutional) Deal

An important component of these changes in state boundaries leading to smaller, more uniformly sized states should be moves towards a healthier balance of power between the Union government and the state governments. The concerns of smaller states, such as those in the Northeast, have been sidelined due to their perceived lack of electoral importance, while larger states have managed to hold the Union hostage even in matters of foreign affairs.[14] A proper solution will be to make sure that the average size of states are small, and the difference between the largest and the smallest state in electoral terms is not the 80:1 absurdity as it stands today. In terms of population, the asymmetry becomes downright ridiculous, at 329:1. The ideal situation would be one where the Centre is politically strong while the states are economically strong—a time-tested model of decentralization which pervaded Indian history in times gone by, as we have described earlier.

In today's scenario, the Centre is financially strong while the large linguistic states are politically strong—an unhealthy mix, especially because the weak economic position of the states makes them want to flex their political muscle even more to wrest all sorts of concessions from the Centre. This phenomenon has undesirable effects on both the Centre and, eventually, the states themselves. Neither the Centre nor the states are able to deliver on their political and economic responsibilities in an adequate fashion.[15]

The seventy-five-states model would also have a direct bearing on the management of domestic supply chains, with increased efficiency gains (and incomes) from specialization, as also increased resilience due to multiple economic nodes specializing in similar production or processing activities for most goods or services. A new economic compact between states and the Union needs to be simultaneously implemented, where the states are able to generate enough revenue to fulfil an expanded economic mandate and utilize proceeds accordingly.

A thorough constitutional relook at taxation and its proceeds is in order along with a major reshuffling of Schedule VII, which contains three lists that divide zones of responsibility between the Union and states. Take, for example, salt; for archaic reasons, taxes over salt vest with the Union and an entire Central Engineering Service (the Indian Salt Service) runs for it, having a bizarre eleven sanctioned posts. Likewise, in a world where we have hot wars in cold spaces, that is, critical infrastructure and their public interfaces such as the power grid or social media are new battlefields for countries, having an artificial division between law and order (a state subject) and defence (a Union matter) is a grave weakness. A general rule of thumb ought to be that most revenue generating matters and points of economic policymaking ought to be transferred to the states. Meanwhile, subjects such as health and education ought to be on the concurrent list to enable the Union to set standards and for states to issue adaptations thereon. The Union should ideally transition into a role of a politically strong entity having much greater powers of supervising or politically directing state governments and an overseeing standards-setting agency on matters of economic importance, leaving the states to do most of the economic heavy lifting. On matters of communication, logistics, defence (including law and order), and similar subjects, the Union should remain untrammelled. What it means to be a state, thus, will be defined principally in terms of economics—a state is meant to nurture industry, raise incomes, and handle most affairs of public welfare—nothing more.

While the above may be achieved to a significant degree within the present paradigm of constitutional law, outcomes will be suboptimal at best. What the situation calls for is a new constituent assembly to thoroughly update our constitutional scheme. The reason why this is necessary is twofold. First, the sweeping, fundamental changes which are required for the state and the nation to deal with the challenges of the 21st century need dedicated deliberation. Second, there exists a severe aberration in the form of the Kesavananda Bhārati pronouncement of the Supreme Court in 1973. An indefinable 'basic structure', which changes as per the whims of the effervescent benches of the court, acts as an irrational straitjacket on any potential constitutional course corrections which an elected government may undertake. The underlying reason for the judgement, to grossly oversimplify, is that the power to amend the Constitution does not grant Parliament the power to change it to such an extent that it becomes a fundamentally new document. However, is the country the same as it was in 1950? Clearly not, and thus how can the same document, framed with the mechanisms and political ideologies which were in vogue seventy-five years ago, do any justice to the aspirations of the people as they are today? And when the first parliament of the country, which had droves of Constituent Assembly members as its members, found it fit to extensively modify the Constitution (including restrictions on fundamental rights), why was this clear intention of the makers of the Constitution sidelined? The basic structure doctrine has its roots in an overreaction to the excesses of the Emergency—with this historical context safely out of the way and an electorate that is far more mature, these artificial and undemocratic guardrails which grant precedence to unelected bodies ought to go.[16]

A rigorous and long-term solution to the delimitation conundrum, namely the conflict between Each Vote Same Value and Each State Same Heft cannot be obtained unless the constituent states of the Union of India are of nearly equal population. Currently, a voter in Dibang Valley is worth a whopping 1,382x the value of a voter in Thane. So what if Article 14 and the tall tales of equality over which much ink has been spilt? This is nearly axiomatic, and yet it was willfully or otherwise ignored by the Constituent Assembly, the States Reorganization Committee 1955, and the various Delimitation Commissions that were formed from time to time. The ill-conceived and pseudoscientific freeze which came in 1976 only compounded this unequalization of citizens.

Further discussion on the above point is instructive. To obtain the condition of Each Vote Same Value, the number of eligible voters in a constituency must be nearly the same all over the country. Now, if the states are of different populations, the above condition leads to the result that the number of constituencies in each state will be different. In this case, the larger states will have greater representation in Parliament, and thus the second condition of Each State Same Heft is defeated. In other words, the two most desirable conditions of Each Vote Same Value and Each State Same Heft cannot hold simultaneously if the states are of different populations. *On purely mathematical grounds, therefore, we conclude that the states of Bhārat must be of roughly the same size to obtain true electoral democracy.*

The advantages of having seventy-five smaller states with an average of nearly twelve or so MPs elected to the Lok Sabha from each of these states are many. Representation in the lower house of Parliament would be strictly according to population, which is the ideal in any democracy. A smaller state would be less likely and also less capable of harbouring fissiparous tendencies towards secession or separation from the Union of India. Mistreatment of the minorities by the majority community would be greatly reduced in a smaller state. The elected parliamentarians would be much more likely to attend to concerns of their constituencies and be in touch with the citizens in their boroughs. Because no new state has been defined in the above scheme with a distinctive caste identity, calls for caste-based benefits would decrease. No politician who appeals to voters on the basis of caste affinity would be able to create a *satrapy*. Regions within a state will not be able to capture the resources of the entire state and neglect regions that are not their own. The entire destructive idea of linguistic states would be buried forever.

We see today that some large states have developed regional and insular tendencies, with the ruling parties there making emotional appeals in the name of language and, in many cases, the Centre–state or the north–south divide. The businesses and industries in Tamil Nadu, West Bengal, and Maharashtra are particularly important for the progress and well-being of the nation as a whole. At the same time, businesses in these states are gravely dependent on their supply chain partners, labour, and customers which are spread across the rest of the country. These states also have maritime or land borders with foreign powers. They exercise an influence in national politics far beyond their capacities. They punch above their weight largely because of the importance they have been given as a result of the freezing of parliamentary constituencies since 1976.

The Centre already has a lot of authority to uphold the nation's integrity, and dealing with smaller states would be simpler. A rational division of Bhārat into seventy-five states might well put an end to the seditious demands that occasionally surface in some states. In the end, the Centre should not be held hostage by any one state, at least not in 2024. It appears that, rightly or wrongly, large non-Hindi speaking states with regional parties in power feel threatened by the Centre, mainly financially. As discussed before, this problem has its roots not in culture but in the approach undertaken by the States Reorganization Commission's 1956 recommendations, which, in the words of Ambedkar, balkanised the south and consolidated the north, causing large population differences in southern and northern states. Southern states claim, again rightly or wrongly, that Hindi-speaking states, who might also regularly have BJP state governments, are given preferential treatment by the Centre. In the end, Tamil Nadu might feel threatened by Uttar Pradesh, but Thondai Mandalam would hardly feel threatened by an Awadh of the same population. This alone would provide enough justification for the redrawing of state boundary lines so that we achieve seventy-five states with roughly 2 crore people, give or take, in each state.

Bhārat today is poised at an inflection point in terms of civilizational identity, economic take-off, and constitutional status. Politically speaking, there are two fundamentally different ways in which the country can navigate these inflection points, reflecting two essentially different ways in which Bhāratiyas look at themselves in their approaches to life itself. The first methodology would have the country going for incremental changes and amendments so that there is the least amount of local disturbance. In the other method, it would be held that incremental changes cannot bring about the drastic changes required in any realistic time frame. Practicality and time concerns would dictate that the political changes must be non-linear, capturing more effectively the nature of an inflection point itself. Small windows of opportunity demand big actions; an approach which was adaptive in one period of the country's evolution becomes maladaptive in the next. A Russian proverb holds that a big ditch cannot be crossed in multiple leaps—Bhārat faces this quandary today.

Taking a cue from science and the fact that Bhārat is a complex system, one would argue for the second approach and aver that electoral delimitation and states reorganization must be taken up together and at an all-India level. These are independent phenomena, and their synergy, which is the life and soul of any complex system (including the one under consideration), may only be achieved with a non-linear departure from existing paradigms and shibboleths. This country is committed to democracy. It deserves a robust and flexible system of constituency delimitation that automatically and simultaneously takes care of Each Vote Same Value and Each State Same Heft, without continuous political interference.

The preceding chapters have dealt with two independent concerns in the functioning of Bhārat as a viable democracy: the principle of Each Vote Same Value and that of Each State Same Heft. The former, essentially a reassertion of democracy's fundamental principle that the voice of each genuine eligible voter is the same across the country, is sought to be maintained through a procedure known as delimitation. This procedure is ideally carried out every decade or so, in order that the size of a parliamentary or assembly constituency is kept nearly equal to that of any other in the country. The latter is important in a large and diverse country because the basis for demarcating an area as a state of the Indian Union should be its true sociocultural identity. This alone allows genuine state concerns to be aired at the central government level so that no state becomes lesser than another in the eyes of the Union.[17]

Both these principles, namely, Each Vote Same Value and Each State Same Heft, have come under serious stress in Bhārat after seventy-five years of independence. This is disturbing in any democratic form of governance. India is special in that our governance structure also has many elements of federal structure in it. Constituency limits, largely frozen over the last fifty years, coupled with unequal population growth in different parts of the country have definitely resulted in the value of an individual vote becoming less in states where the population growth has been more. With regard to each state having the same heft and influence in determining national-level policies, the totally unequal sizes of our states have resulted in a half dozen large states having an unhealthy and dominant say in guiding the national agenda. This unequal influence is affected by the results of elections every five years, and as we know well, the results of these elections are unpredictable.

States should have some say in framing national policies, if at least to ensure that particular state interests are not compromised. This informal Centre–state dialogue has been going on with a greater or lesser degree of mutual satisfaction, and elements of a 'federal' structure have crept in imperceptibly into our polity. However, these happenings should not be confused with India being a federation. It is not. A federal polity is a system in which the constituents (states, Länder, cantons) are what come together to form a union, and this is virtually encoded within the constitution, say as in Canada, Germany, Switzerland, or the US.

Bhārat is not a federation. This is clearly deduced from the Constitution in which words like 'federation' and 'federal' are altogether absent. This needs to be borne in mind by our present opposition parties, notably the Congress and some regional outfits which depend upon xenophobic tendencies and economic anxieties for their survival. There was never any question of states coming together and negotiating a Union, as wrongfully asserted by a Congress MP last year.[18] Our states have no existence save at the wisdom of our Parliament. India is an indestructible union of destructible states, as Ambedkar had stated.[19]

Keep the Constitution or Change It?

There were consistent and shrill cries from certain quarters during the 2024 election that the Constitution was in danger. Equally vociferously, the prime minister maintained during the campaign that there was no question of changing the Constitution. It was said by the opposition that Modi would throw away Ambedkar's constitution, which is to raise the bogey of reservations being in danger.[20] This conflation of 'Ambedkar's constitution' with 'SC reservations' conveniently forgot that Ambedkar wished for reservations to continue for no more than ten years, that is till 1960. Likewise, many important stretches of Ambedkar's constitution lie in shambles, with no sight of redemption: implementation of

Hindi as the Union language, the right to property, and the main concern of this book, the delimitation commission and its corresponding mechanism. While the Constitution has been labelled a 'living document' *ad nauseam*, it seems that any and all constitutional evolution which does not adhere to neocolonial values mislabelled as liberalism and imposed largely by elites of a bygone era is verboten. The Constitution has been reduced to being a frozen book of commandments which has descended from the skies, instead of being a fluvial documentation of governance which adjusts as the nation forges its own path of progress. At the time of its inception, the makers of the Constitution did not have any misgivings as to its alterable nature. One need not look far: Nehru had stated that the Constitution was merely 'basis for further work', and Patel, in his characteristic terseness, had pronounced, 'This Constitution is for a period of ten years.'[21]

A constitutional revolution, whether it is done implicitly or explicitly, is a necessary phase of India's evolution that aims to change the nation's outlook and government to reorient it for the economic and social realities of today. The 1950 Constitution, with its numerous amendments, is a huge and unwieldy body of words that has long since outlived its practical utility.[22] It is more appropriate for a homogeneous nation state of the Amerisphere type, as it is modelled on a Western liberal democratic model and is based on the Westminster-style unwritten constitution of the UK. It fails to capture the developmental aspirations of the nation and the essence of dharmic governance systems that Bhāratiyas have been yearning and voting for.[23]

To achieve popular synergy and exponential growth in the economy, big constitutional changes are needed. One important component of these changes could be moves towards a healthier balance of powers between the Union and state governments. This would involve an organized delimitation of states, allowing for seventy-five states with roughly 2 crore people in each state. A new economic compact between states and the Union should be implemented, providing states with enough revenue to fulfil an expanded economic mandate.

Other changes that would need wide public debate include a wholesale re-evaluation of the role and powers of the judiciary,[24] a reworking of the balance between the legislature and the executive, and a restructuring of the civil services. This would allow the executive the latitude to include technocrats in government, selecting the best available talent from outside the legislatures. The present time might also be an opportune moment to initiate a debate on whether we really need the Rajya Sabha at all or alternatively whether we need it in its present form. Would a body more like the US Senate with a strictly equal representation for each state be more appropriate? With seventy-five states, this would mean an upper house with exactly 150 members, elected directly by the people. The book *Bhārat: India 2.0* written in 2022 by one of the authors of this book provides detailed justification for these changes.[25] A constitutional revolution inevitably leads to administrative and institutional revolutions, which are preconditions to make India resilient enough to benefit from the rapidly changing times in which we live.

1. The selection of a political executive (ministers) from a legislative assembly is an unstable arrangement in today's Bhārat. It leads to the legislature becoming a rubber-stamping body for the executive, defeating the very purpose of a legislature, and energies of legislators are often diverted to conspiratorial undertakings for them to

get executive portfolios. Thanks to the anti-defection law and the increasingly personality-driven trend of Indian politics, the legislature has become a mere appendage of the executive, resulting in shoddy legislation and indiscretion in demanding accountability from the executive. As the Indian electorate matures, it is more than capable of making a granular choice for levels and wings of government. It already elects state governments differently than national ones if deemed appropriate, even if state and national elections are spaced closely. For the sake of a better democracy, separately elected legislative and executive wings make perfect sense, since administration and legislation demand vastly different competencies. It is not logical to expect an elected parliamentarian who happens to get appointed, say, as minister for power transmission, to have a grip over the technicalities of the power transmission system. Getting elected and knowing all about power transmission are vastly different matters. Likewise, a chief executive is more like a policeman, whose job is to execute the law in light of the will and interests of the people—if allowed to frame the law itself, as is the case today, the legislature becomes hostage to the will of the chief minister and becomes incapable of placing a check on his exercise of powers. More preferable would be an American-style system, where one has a directly elected governor of a state (and correspondingly, president of the Union) having the freedom to head the executive and pick his own cabinet, with preference for technocrats who need not get elected. The job of the legislator may thus be pursued without the constant rush to become ministers. The resulting system will be more stable and efficient since domain experts will hold corresponding portfolios as opposed to professional politicians.

2. At the time the Constitution was drafted, strong winds of socialism were blowing across the global political landscape, which were reinforced when Indira Gandhi became prime minister. Soon after, the country was embroiled in a period defined by caste politics. What is common between the two systems of clientelism and today's demands of redistribution is that veiled political expediency gets the better of national economic interests. Focus shifts from all-round economic development to taking money from one's enemies and handing it over to one's (electoral) friends, with the difference being absorbed by a sprawling bureaucracy. This is a natural consequence of defining economics in terms of politics, something which has become encoded within the Constitution. Since roughly 2013, concerns about the economy have dominated political discourse; India's politics has been redefined in terms of economics. The Constitution needs to be updated to reflect these changed realities. In addition to granting more sources of revenue and economic powers to states as outlined in the foregoing paragraphs, a greater emphasis on economics needs to reflect in our constitutional scheme.
    a. The term 'socialist' is a shibboleth from a bygone era but is not vestigial—it must be removed. A string of judgements from the Supreme Court have been tainted with strained rationalization of how to characterize 'socialism' with respect to the economic changes of late. The term is loaded and taints our jurisprudence; it is an ever-present threat to the freedom to trade and for hardworking Indians to

retain the fruits of their labour. The right to property under Article 31 was the first casualty of an economic race to the bottom, whereby the said Article was abrogated and replaced with a draconian Article 31A, and the right to property was tucked away in a watered-down fashion in the form of Article 300A. All of Article 31A speaks about how the state may take away, practically at will, what it deems fit. The term 'socialism' must be dispensed forthwith; the directive principles of state policy must omit most of its socialistic content, and the right to property must be restored as a fundamental right. It is important to foster an all-round increase in incomes instead of relegating Bhāratiyas to being dependent on perpetual handouts. Gainful employment, raising incomes and standards of living, and making citizens self-dependent through industry should be the guiding principles which ought to be enshrined in the Constitution. Ambition, aspirations, and hopes must take the place of constitutionally endorsed dependency on handouts from a leviathan state.

b. In line with the above economic reorientation of the Constitution, a new generation of constitutional bodies needs to be set up. A Fiscal Responsibility Commission (FRC), somewhat similar in scope to the Office of Budgetary Responsibility in the United Kingdom or the US Congressional Budget Office, needs to be sanctioned by the Constitution. The principal role of the commission would be to sound the alarm on any measure by state or Union governments leading to a greater spend than revenue generated, save for essential welfare activities such as the provision of food and shelter, or on matters of strategic or defence interests. An independent watchdog, which can reduce information asymmetry and can effectively communicate to the people as to what the actual cost of any freebie will be, needs to exist for the people to make informed political choices. Thus, the fiscal consequences of moves like, say, Himachal Pradesh reinstating the old pension scheme in 2024 to benefit just 1.36 lakh pensioners by increasing the burden of taxation and debt on the entire population of the state[26] needed to have been clearly indicated to the people of the state in advance. The people need to understand the injurious nature of the real cost of such measures; current caution prevents later lament. The FRC would analyse proposals of policy changes, state and Union budgets, and party manifestos to act as an ombudsman for the people to be better economically informed before they make corresponding political decisions. For example, in each successive Union and state budget, a certain sum of taxpayer funds is granted to public sector undertakings. Today, 139 central undertakings and 330 state undertakings are defunct but lap up funds nonetheless.[27] No statutory body exists as of now that is empowered to meaningfully communicate such facts to the people. The FRC can fill this gap. The FRC can also analyse the functioning of schemes and publish the results of its operations in contrast to expectations as well. In a certain respect there is some overlap between the functions of such an FRC and the Indian Audit and Accounts Service or the Comptroller and Auditor General of India.

c. The salaries of ministers, legislators, and top bureaucrats need to be handsomely linked to economic metrics and particular metrics relating to their portfolio. A better performing economy ought to provide officeholders with a sizable bonus, while an economy that is stagnating should penalize those who do not act properly as the economy's stewards. Likewise, top officials for each department, say, water, should be rewarded handsomely for meeting targets for houses which have recently received taps, and conversely be made to suffer for failures. This pressure will not only incentivize better execution and policymaking but will also create a synergy between the legislature and the executive. The legislature would not normally harass the executive as this may have an impact on their own pockets and vice versa. It must be noted, however, that this system will only work with the elimination of corruption in politics, which is also a work in progress.

d. A business cycle is the sum of the time it takes for an economy to grow, peak, slow down, and then stabilize (before the cycle starts again). Before an economy peaks, it needs to be cautious, tighten monetary policy, and save up for bad times. When an economy comes off its peak, the government is required to loosen its purse strings to cushion the fall, and focus shifts to welfare from growth. On an average, when the Indian economy is generally in a good spot, Indian business cycles last around a year; when the times are tough in general, the time shrinks to nine months.[28] These numbers are important to politically factor in since an election cycle that is not in sync with business cycles will lead to confused mandates—one government may be responsible for fiscal profligacy when the times were good, but if its bad effects are left to a future government to bear, the people may misattribute tough times on the wrong party[29] and not make informed choices subsequently. Likewise, if a government racks up debt during tough times to fund fiscal expansion during a down-cycle (a generally good thing to do), and a future government during better times blames the previous incumbent on interest payments on said debt, it will be tantamount to misleading the people. Therefore, it is important to make sure that a government which has seen good economic times should remain incumbent when a slowdown inevitably arrives; or at least, each successive government should see both up-cycles and down-cycles in the same order as the government before it.[30] The current cycle of five years is completely out of sync with economic cycles, and thereby makes it difficult for the people to correctly attribute good and bad economic handling by a particular administration, and this weakens India's democracy. Therefore, the terms of governments ought to be increased to six years (the double of the lowest common multiple of twelve months and nine months, i.e., thirty-six months). To prevent this cycle from being broken, in case a government falls (that is, loses confidence or is dismissed by the president) before its term ends and is not replaced within six months of such an incident, the next elected government should last for only the remainder of the previous government's six-year term. The terms of the central and state governments would, in this manner, always be in sync as well. This is an economically and politically proper manner of implementing One Nation One Election.

e. We have made out the case earlier in this chapter that the Union needs greater political power, and the states need greater economic power. However, even if there is a rearrangement of entries between the three lists of Schedule VII of the Constitution, it would retain bizarre anachronisms. The Union list, for example, houses 'Courts of wards for the estates of Rulers of Indian States', while the state list contains 'Treasure trove'. There is no mention of trends which threaten to upend our lives—artificial intelligence, climate change, or even the internet. Clearly, the three lists need to be drafted anew. Likewise, the current default is that anything which is not placed in the three lists gets to be governed by the Union—this severely constrains the economic ambit of the states. By default, subjects not falling in any of the three lists ought to be concurrent subjects, and while the Union may regulate the same, economic benefits ought to mostly accrue to the states.

f. Inter-state migration and commerce, despite finding explicit mention in Schedule VII, remains a grossly under-regulated subject even though India's economy has steadily integrated itself. Assam's Muga silk readily finds its way to Delhi's showrooms, and Maharashtra's sugar finds a match in strong coffees being served with fragrant *dosais* in Chennai. Inter-state migrants are yet to have a formal division of responsibility between the states of origin and destination for their welfare. Clearly, constitutional protections and mechanisms need to be devised for the same. Likewise, there will be many states which must retain their forests for not only their local environment but also for all of India's carbon goals. States which bear a disproportionate environmental burden are not compensated monetarily for the same—perhaps a mechanism for green or carbon credit trading needs to be instituted where environmentally fragile and important states are financially compensated for the environmental value which they provide to the rest of the country.[31] Providing monetary incentives for states to maintain the environment they are blessed with will go a long way towards the nation's sustainability goals.

g. It is more than evident that India's vast bureaucratic complex, which decides everything from interest rates to the price of newspapers, has failed to live up to expectations.[32] The centralizing tendency of the higher echelons of the bureaucracy has often resulted in important warning signs being overlooked and with elected representatives feeling disgruntled over what is perceived as high-handedness. The problem that the bureaucracy faces is systemic and not individual. While much ink has been spilled on this subject by successive committees which have delivered their own diagnoses, our recommendations are of a limited nature. Civil servants should ideally be selected soon after school, before they can be moulded by our dystopian university ecosystem and before the inertia of age sets in. Attempts should be limited to only two, to prevent the loss of valuable years which can be better put to use elsewhere for the nation. All civil servants must retire around the age of forty-five at the deputy secretary or joint secretary level; all entries above this must be obtained by open competition (where the selecting body has a majority of non-civil service members) on a contractual basis where retired civil servants may also apply. These recommendations are not only to ensure that domain experts remain in charge of policy implementation but also to reduce rent-seeking, complacency, and gatekeeping, which have crept into the upper echelons of the services. Lastly, and perhaps bordering on the edge of being outlandish, paid coaching for civil services must be outlawed for it is an industry which exploits the hopes and aspirations of lakhs of young adults, sometimes even children, and wastes valuable years of our youth over a miniscule chance at making it into the civil services.[33]

3. Most importantly, and central to the core idea of this book, we need an immediate course correction to restore the proper and timely functioning of the delimitation commission as in Ambedkar's constitution sans the artificial dysfunction introduced in 1976 which has led to electoral distortions across the country. However, it is impossible to deliver Each Vote Same Value and Each State Same Heft without simultaneously carrying out states' reorganization. Delimitation and states' reorganization are two faces of the same coin—one cannot be achieved without the other. Likewise, their respective solutions, redrawing constituencies and redrawing state lines, are intertwined and cannot be mathematically executed without each other. Each citizen needs to be equalized electorally, and each state ought to be electorally meaningful enough to not

> be ignored by the Centre or overshadowed by large states. We have already described in some detail how simultaneous delimitation and states' reorganization will solve a number of prickly political problems, such as the north–south divide. A constitutional recognition of this concept, which will also introduce an actively adaptive mechanism to continuously reduce imbalances, would be to have a constitutional delimitation and states' reorganization commission, that is, a single constitutional body which carries out both delimitation and states' reorganization periodically, preferably every six years or so. Perhaps this body may also preside over states' delimitation commissions, which are responsible for drawing assembly constituency boundaries, so that all states have a common framework and timeline for delimitation while being insulated from partisan pressures. This overarching constitutional framework will ensure that differential population growth rates, migration flows, and changes in developmental status of places will not cause long-term underrepresentation or overrepresentation, which can fester into serious political problems in the future.

Constitutions have been readily rewritten (at times, replaced altogether) in other democracies, and it is also the duty of the present government to educate the people that a Constitution is only a plan, an idea of various actions that a country takes in order to provide maximum benefits for the maximum number of people, which is the democratic ideal.[34] The Constitution is not a holy book given by an unimpeachable and eternally valid body of men. It was written by educated nationalists as a document which was supposed to chart a course of action that was in the best interests of the India of 1950. There have been many amendments, 106 at the latest count, indicating that the Constitution is a document that is in need of constant correction. The question that really confronts the Bhārat of 2024 and its NDA government that the people of Bhārat have just elected is not a political and emotional one—it is an operational one. Have the changes and modifications brought about by all the amendments reached a point where it is in the better interest of the country to do a ctrl+alt+del on the Constitution and start again, while still retaining the most robust and time-tested parts of the existing document?

Without necessarily going into article-by-article discussion of our 1950 constitution and its 106 amendments, the following changes, as they should be called, may be accomplished without undergoing the exercise of writing a new constitution or, in other words, creating a constitutional assembly. Much of this could be carried out by the NDA government while keeping within the present Constitution. After all, the Constitution with a correct reading of Articles 368 and 13 enables the changing of practically every other article in the document (the understanding of the constituent assembly as well as the first parliament), another example of a complex system having an inherent self-correction mechanism.

1. Reconsideration of Article 15(4) that pertains to caste reservations.
2. Reinterpretation of Article 19(1)(a) and 19(2).[35]
3. Complete reconsideration of Articles 25 through 29 that deal with rights to freedom of religion; also with reference to the words 'profess' and 'propagate' in Article 25.
4. Freeing of Hindu temples from government control.

5. Reconsideration of Article 30 that gives the right to religious minorities to manage their educational institutions in a manner largely determined by them.
6. Removal of the word 'secular' from the preamble to the Constitution.
7. Removal of 'socialist' from the preamble to the Constitution and restoration of Article 31 that deals with the right to property.
8. Reconsideration of the concept of Basic Structure in particular and the Kesavananda Bhārati judgement in general so that a clearer definition of the judiciary's ambit in governance may be obtained.
9. Introduction of the UCC as recommended in Part IV as Article 44.
10. Redefinition of the term 'minority' and using the state and not the Union as the delimiter of such a classification.[36]
11. Reconsideration as to whether the Rajya Sabha is required.
12. Thorough and de novo approach to separation of responsibilities between states and the Union to concentrate economic powers in states and political powers in the Union.
13. Increasing government terms to six years from the present five years.
14. Having an independent constitutional Fiscal Responsibility Commission.
15. Linking remuneration of elected representatives and top bureaucrats to the performance of the economy in general and their own portfolio metrics in particular.
16. Revamping the civil services to ensure entry around the age of eighteen to twenty-one years and retirement by forty-five. Top bureaucratic posts to be all contractual and be allotted basis open competition, where retired bureaucrats may also apply.

17. Having an independent and single constitutional Delimitation and States Reorganization Commission, which will have the power to supervise and regulate states' delimitation commissions.
18. Reworking Schedule X of the Indian Constitution, known as the anti-defection law, to limit its ambit to votes of no-confidence and party splits or mergers.

If these items are considered and acted upon satisfactorily by the government, it would go down as the most important one in our history. No new constitution would be required to do any or all of the above.

A Civilizational Revolution

Returning to the main theme of the book, both delimitation and reorganization of state boundaries can be very well accomplished within the four corners of the present Constitution. Calls for a new constitution, however, come from quarters that are concerned with civilizational rather than arid administrative and electoral matters. These civilizational matters impinge on the theme of this book because the most efficient type of delimitation and governance involves smaller states that are most effectively defined on a civilizational basis.

Regrettably, our colonial mindset has persisted even after seventy-five years of independence. Many in the upper echelons of decision makers, that is, politicians and bureaucrats, were largely Macaulayist in their thinking, and sought to shape India in the image of what the West determined a nation ought to be, resulting in a continuous frontal assault on indigenous values and institutions which were far more suited to India and Indians along with the enforcement of mechanisms which are alien and maladaptive.[37] Dharampal, in his inimitable frankness, stated, 'As no fundamental changes were made at the existing centres of Governmental power, notwithstanding such insight, the reforms which came in 1920, met the same fate as earlier or later British attempts at reform. The post-1947 years, while greatly adding to the bulk, by the multiple increase in the departments of the Government as well as its personnel have merely added to its woodenness and frigidity… While all Governments everywhere do become somewhat wooden and their incumbents somewhat insolent, the extremeness of such phenomena (*or the mere harping on it*)[38] seems to be uniquely Indian.'[39] The diplomatic and organizational aspects of governance were, inter alia, gravely impaired. This had a direct impact on the way we handled our affairs, time and again compromising national interest for ideological reasons.

India is slowly coming to terms with its identity as Bhārat. The 2014 political shift has sparked a change in which a new nation is now proud of its civilizational values. The outcomes of the elections in 2014, and 2019 particularly, showed that Indians are rediscovering their culture. The 2024 result, mixed as it is, shows that Bhāratiyas desire that their long-lost identity, now newly found, is legitimized in formal documents and legalese of the state—a situation where the state, the *rājya*, has finally become subservient to the nation, the *rāshtra*. A majority in the Lok Sabha was thought to be unattainable for any one political party or pre-poll alliance. The shared element uniting the approximately 50 per cent of voters who have supported the NDA in the just concluded election needs to extend beyond political parties and the current political structure, even the BJP itself. We firmly believe that this sense of unity can only come from something more fundamental and deeper—namely, our identity as Bhāratiyas—a diverse but united *corpus aeternis*.

The issue of India's rediscovery and reconstruction as Bhārat, with its extensive literary and living legacy, stems from sanātana dharma, which is misleadingly and mistakenly called Hinduism. We direct readers to the foundational writings of Dharampal, Sita Ram Goel, and Ram Swarup. Moreover, Swami Vivekananda and Sarvepalli Radhakrishnan's writings are vital for gaining a theological and philosophical background because they both interpreted Bhārat in accordance with the Upanishads, particularly advaitic universalism, which is a set of ideas far more radical and practical than the French revolution's trite of 'liberty, equality, fraternity'. What is largely accepted among Indians is that from 1947 to 2014, we were under the grasp of incorrect narratives of what India is and what we Indians are meant to stand for. In a vast and vibrant democracy like ours, around 50 per cent of voters seem to share a specific viewpoint on some core issues, which sends a message that no one can ignore. India, or more accurately Bhārat, is a civilization with an unwaveringly dharmic foundation. Since it is dharmic, it can never turn into a theocracy; the internal diversity and dynamism of dharmic systems are so high that even prickly religious reform has emerged from religious quarters themselves—the history of the Arya Samaj and the various associations of the Bengal Renaissance come to mind.[40] For this reason, Indians have been consistently voting for a Hindu Rashtra, characterized by harmony and a vision of shared prosperity, as opposed to an exclusivist Hindu Rajya. The latter, basically a theocracy, is incompatible with sanātana dharma itself.[41]

Similar to Confucian ideals which are responsible for the survival and continuation of another ancient civilization, namely China, dharma is that which upholds any and all (the root of the word dharma, *dhr*, means 'to hold' or 'to sustain') and leverages deeply-rooted conceptions of justice, fairness, and appropriateness to govern the society in a spontaneous, decentralized, and duty-driven manner. Sarvepalli Radhakrishnan gave a very practical conception of dharma, free from dogma and abstraction: 'While the spontaneous activities of interest and desire are to be accepted, their full values cannot be realised if their action is unrestrained. There must be a rule, a guidance, a restraint. Dharma gives coherence and direction to the different activities of life. It is not a religious creed or cult imposing an ethical or social rule. It is the complete rule of life, the harmony of the whole man who finds a right and just law of his living. Each man and group, each activity of soul, mind, life, and body, has its dharma.'[42]

While entire shastras and their commentaries, ancient as well as contemporary, are dedicated to dharmic governance or the ideal of the Rāma Rājya, the one clear line is that religion, narrowly defined and understood, is not the pole star for any such system. Likewise, dharmic governance eschews political manipulations centred despotically around the state. Such machinations have been responsible for the massive destruction inflicted upon the world by colonialism and the wars which followed. Dharma also eschews solipsistic hyper individualism in which man debases himself and destroys the community as well as the environment.

Operationalizing, enshrining, and ultimately installing dharma as the source of state power and legitimacy of actions needs a fundamental shift away from the present conception, including the idea of what a constitution is and ought to do. In the words of G.V. Gundappa, 'Rama Rajya is the grandest conception of a Master Poet… where there are no fetters in the relationship between the ruler and the ruled…where Dharma doesn't depend on others for its functioning and is akin to breathing: effortless.' He similarly stated 'The verdict of those Pandits [wise and learned people] who have understood the nuances of tradition and act in a spirit of selfless service directed at the good of the country is Dharma....The ruler is subservient to Dharma; Dharma in turn is embodied in society. Therefore, the original home of the state's power emanates from the Dharmic feeling prevalent in the society. The seat of the ruler is just a mere implement or equipment that maintains and protects this Dharmic feeling.'[43] Thus, the state, nation, and politics itself are subservient to a higher sense of purpose and values, where each of the three play their role to continue to ensure the unrestrained flow of dharma. The state and its machinery become a mere instrument in the multifarious means in which dharma may be practised instead of being shackled to the stiff golden cage of laws or all-engorging impulses of tyranny. Legitimate actions are that which are in accordance with dharma, that is, are determined as just, moral, and in line with national interest.[44]

A more immediate development and one that directly touches on the question of a comprehensive all-India reorganization of states is, however, equally important. The nations that have achieved the highest levels of success in the previous 150 years have always had a very distinct sense of who they are and have unapologetically devised mechanisms which were in line with this identity. We believe that our civilizational revolution will primarily be the driving force behind India's transition from an era of linear to exponential economic growth, as the country begins to shake off this ambiguity. A recent example is the

Ram Mandir in Ayodhya—critics had made many a spurious extrapolation, such as the oft-repeated irrelevance of a temple to employment and the economy. However, the temple has led to a sustained and wide surge of quantifiable prosperity in Ayodhya, including a spurt in both the quantity and quality of employment available.[45] A full 1.5 lakh to 2 lakh jobs are expected to be generated over the coming five years thanks to the temple, apart from an all-round developmental burst in Ayodhya and surrounding areas.[46] By no means do the authors argue that temples are the only means of fostering development. What is instead being argued is that efforts of civilizational importance which are in line with the ethos and aspirations of the nation, independent of electoral ups and downs for any political party, are the key to boosting affluence equitably. Likewise, the planned restoration of the Martanda sun temple in Anantnag, and the ongoing clean-up of India's land ownership records to ensure the rights of indigenous peoples are steps in the right direction. Similar initiatives could include a serious reboot of the Nalanda University to run on Indian knowledge systems and methodologies, targeted revival of traditional textiles, and hybridizing indigenous varieties of grains to make adoption competitive. The government apparatus, which consists of judges, bureaucrats, and politicians, cannot by themselves lead a massive national endeavour that moves us towards our desired state of affairs in 2047. Above all, it requires that the people involved feel like close partners and stakeholders in this movement. We believe that this synergy can only arise when we all fully realize our civilizational identity.

The present time is a most important period in the history of Bhārat post 1947. The present electoral result has political, economic, social, and, above all, civilizational undertones and implications. This has not been an ordinary election. If 2014 was about change and 2019 about consolidation, 2024 is about continuity and accountability. The new Bhārat will be a complete reworking—a totally different concept of how this ancient land will embrace the modern world, going forward economically and geostrategically as it positions itself on an ancient bedrock of a 5,000-year civilization. The faded and tattered remnants of a particular 'idea of India' have all but been relegated to the sequestered abstractions of a greying commentariat. Bhārat is a *jivātmā*—a being which has remained alive and has adapted for millenia now, changing its form even as its core purpose and motivation of dharma (*mātrbhoomi, karmabhoomi,* and *punyabhoomi*) remain unblemished. Bhārat is not a mere idea. India might have been, but Bhārat is not.

At the risk of sounding provocative, the reduction of personalities like Gandhi, Ambedkar, and Nehru to mere snippets for use in trope-infested polemics is counterproductive. These eminent personalities were in their prime a century ago. Their contributions to the India of yore are undeniable and their places in history unshakeable. But today is another story. Anyone who ceaselessly trumpets these names will be reduced to an amusing oddity. The youth do not associate these political figures with current, active politics and see them as having ideas which were fitting only for their time, which has all but passed. This is a new world with ever shorter shelf lives for people, ideas, and achievements. The youth relate more to a cyber world with instant information, AI, rapid communications, and digital mechanisms being the new instruments of life. They are exposed to global ideas and trends on a live basis and are far less restrained in their inquiry of norms, ideas, and personalities. At the same time, men who expressed ideas which are eternal and valid at all times, such as Vivekananda, Aurobindo, Kabir, or Dostoyevsky are being absorbed, contended with, and reinterpreted constantly. Outmoded methods of political mobilization like socialism, communal appeasement, and casteism will give way to a positive and vibrant Bhārat that progressively abandons the detritus which had lodged into our minds through foreign rule, impoverishment, and the domestic confusion that followed.

In such a scenario, a country such as Bhārat that aspires to be a platform of global leadership must, as other world powers have done in the past, find a unique combination of that which is intrinsic to the land and that which is extrinsic and relevant to its dealings with the outside world. Democracy has been inherent to Bhāratiyas since time immemorial. It is also one of the best long-term models for governance because it is more humane and inclusive when compared to other forms. At the same time, all democratic mechanisms are an ongoing experiment and may be suitably tweaked without regard to ideas which may have been venerated by some as uncompromisable. The essence of democracy is meaningful representation of smaller groups of people, right down to the smallest minority of all, that is, the individual. Our model of seventy-five states emphasizes exactly this idea accompanied with the added advantage of delimitation of state boundaries following the time-tested and stable boundaries that have marked out smaller regions of this diverse land for millennia.

As for the West, it will need to observe and accept a rising Bhārat that does not seek Western approbation and approval for its existence. It will need to change its perception of hyper individualism and crass materialism as the supreme test of the foundation of liberal democracy because such perception excludes cultural and civilizational diversities that distinguish different nations and their democracies from the Western one.

Cultures and their values differ and retain the right to remain different in the way they approach political institutions. The West, if at all it admits Bhārat into the club of democracies, will do so grudgingly and only because it feels that we are the only available counter to China. This is neither a necessary nor a sufficient condition for the rise of Bhārat as a superpower in the next fifty or so years. As the authors have shown above, there is an important link between democracy and long-term economic growth as well as innovation. However, if the iteration of democracy being practised itself is undemocratic, that is, what the people think democracy ought to be like and what is being delivered to them are different, results will naturally be suboptimal. For achieving its goals, a silent revolution must happen from within. Bhāratiyas of all shapes, sizes, hues, religions, castes, and speaking all manner of tongues will need to formulate their unique set of laws, conventions, rules, and regulations that they feel will best suit their dominant identity as proud members of a five-millennium-old living civilization.

A delimitation-cum-states' reorganization which seems as drastic as the one we propose is bitter but necessary medicine for the folly of political short-termism stemming from rank opportunism effected through the freeze in 1976. If this book has demonstrated to the reader that this necessary exercise may only be rigorously and permanently achieved by redefining our states as seventy-five smaller units[47] with economic strength and civilizational resilience, we would have felt this endeavour to have been worthwhile.

A better democracy is one which can organize a political system that enables both rapid and sustainable economic growth. We hope to have provided a roadmap to this end and for the citizens of this country to iterate, improvize, and improve upon the ideas we have presented.

Notes

Preface

1 Not too many more vibrant democracies in the world than India: White House, *The Economic Times* (indiatimes.com), 2024.

2 https://www.firstpost.com/opinion/a-keralian-is-worth-1-8-rajasthanis-delimitation-is-the-final-barrier-to-real-democracy-in-india-13750354.html

Chapter 1: What Is Democracy?

1 Thomas Hobbes, *Leviathan*, The Project Gutenberg eBook.

2 Winston Churchill's observation on democracy will probably stand the test of time. 'Many forms of Government have been tried and will be tried in this world of sin and woe. No one pretends that democracy is perfect or all-wise. Indeed, it has been said that democracy is the worst form of Government except all those other forms that have been tried from time to time; but there is the broad feeling in our country that the people should rule, continuously rule, and that public opinion, expressed by all constitutional means, should shape, guide, and control the actions of Ministers who are their servants and not their masters.'

3 The antithesis of democracy is dictatorship and authoritarian rule by an individual or a group, where the individual rights of the people are partly or wholly taken away.

4 Thomas Jefferson encapsulated this well when he said, 'Every man cannot have his way in all things. If his opinion prevails at some times, he should acquiesce on seeing that others preponderate at other times. Without this mutual disposition

we are disjointed individuals.' Certain discordant forces in our country, including some political outfits, have stubbornly refused to consider these wise words.

5 D. Acemoglu and J.A. Robinson, *Why Nations Fail* (Profile Books, 2013).

6 Particularly relating to the performance of contracts.

7 *Political systems affect innovation*, LSE Business Review (2022).

8 Edwin Bryant, 'Early Indian Responses,' *The Quest for the Origins of Vedic Culture: The Indo-Aryan Migration Debate*, Oxford Academic (oup.com), (2001).

9 The Greeks and Indians share a multi-century shared history following Alexander, where the northwest of the subcontinent hosted a range of Indo-Greek kingdoms. Ashoka is said to have a Greek mother or grandmother, and Greek cultural influence such as fashion, sculpture, and even religious concepts saw give and take. Horashastra in Jyotish is said to have been derived from Greek studies, and Greek personalities such as Menander and Heliodorus came to contribute much to India. The feats of Krishna defeating demons and Hercules, for example, share curious similarities. One can find Greek presence up till modern-day Mathura.

10 The closest example which comes to mind of such a hotchpotch arrangement where a 'state', for the lack of a better word, is a matryoshka doll with many different kinds of smaller 'states', each having a different internal make-up and external relationship with its overlord and the unwieldy and somewhat fantastical arrangement known as the Holy Roman Empire which lumbered on from 800 CE to 1806 CE. The name, however, is flatly misleading, for it had little to do with the Romans of yore. Voltaire had famously quipped that the entity is 'neither holy, nor Roman, nor an empire'.

11 A republic is a state which is governed by an oligarchy, elected or otherwise. The antithesis of a republic is an absolute monarchy.

12 A striking recent example of this truism was seen in our Lok Sabha election result in 2014, where the people opted for a sharply different methodology of governance through a free and fair election.

13 'To define is to limit' — Oscar Wilde.

14 That socialism has little to do with democracy is brought out neatly in Alexis de Tocqueville's snippet 'democracy and socialism have nothing in common but one word, equality'. This should convince the reader about the oxymoronic nature of the amended preamble in our Constitution, which contains both these words.

15 Stefan Couperus, 'Democracy not lost? Functional democracy as a panacea for crisis in interwar Europe,' (*sagepub.com*), 2019.

16 Macaulay is long since gone but Macaulayism lives on in Lutyens' Delhi, Park Street in Kolkata, south Mumbai, and similar enclaves of crumbling privilege.

17 Translated to 'voice of the people, voice of god'. The phrase has a hallowed revolutionary pedigree; the phrase was supposed to have been uttered when the Archbishop of Canterbury brought charges in 1327 against the then King of England, Edward II, who was ultimately deposed. A Whig tract from 1709 uses the phrase as its title, and was a tour de force in unambiguously upholding the equality of all men and that 'mankind is at liberty to choose what form of government they like best'.

18 Dharma, righteousness, is the king of kings. *Dharmam kshatrasya kshatram*. It is the ruler of both the people and the rulers themselves.

19 The constitutional history of Britain over a millennium exemplifies to a tee Edmund Burke's dictum that 'We must all obey the great law of change. It is the most powerful law of nature.'

20 It is possible that this was accelerated by the fact that the monarchs in the House of Hanover were more comfortable speaking in German than in English. Through marriages into

the royal houses of Europe over 300 years, today's monarch King Charles III has a bloodline that is made up roughly half by German ancestors.

21 'The greatest calamity which could befall us would be submission to a government of unlimited powers' — Thomas Jefferson.

22 *World Bank halts new Uganda loans over anti-LGBTQ+ law*, bbc.com, 2023.

23 'The reason that Christianity is the best friend of government is because Christianity is the only religion that changes the heart' — Thomas Jefferson.

24 The introduction of a more recent term Fourth World, to contrast it from the newly aspirational Third World, appears to us to be even more meaningless. India's 2023 presidency of the G20 presents a suitable and fitting counter-narrative: one earth, one family, one future.

25 Phil O'Brien, *Chile: The Pinochet Decade: The Rise and Fall of the Chicago Boys* (JSTOR, 1983).

26 Theodore P. Gerber and Michael Hout, 'More Shock than Therapy: Market Transition, Employment, and Income in Russia, 1991–19951,' *American Journal of Sociology*, (uchicago.edu), vol. 104, no. 1.

27 *India: Another tryst with destiny*, https://www.theguardian.com/global/2014/may/18/india-narendra-modi-election-destiny, 2014.

28 Obviously, if the parameters chosen are the wrong ones, the outcome predictions will also be wrong. Say, if one takes the opinions of strongly anti-India experts living in the USA, for example, people of Pakistani origin, and then ask them to rate India as a democracy against Pakistan, the latter is likely to fare better in the overall rankings. Salvatore Babones has argued that in many cases of V-Dem democracy ratings for India, the experts chosen to adjudicate the matter are people, living in India, who are strongly prejudiced against the BJP and the

Modi government. They are also small in number, and this only tends to exacerbate the wrong outcomes predicted.

Salvatore Babones, *Inside the V-Dem Rankings,* https://www.indiancentury.org/research-papers/inside-the-v-dem-rankings.

29 How India helped Sri Lanka overcome economic turmoil: A review of 2023, *ET BFSI* (indiatimes.com), 2023.

30 'The cornerstone of democracy rests on the foundation of an educated electorate' — Thomas Jefferson.

31 S. Gurumurthy, *Random Thoughts 2021* (New Delhi: Vivekananda International Foundation, 2022). The term 'Rest' may be found in this book.

32 Samuel P. Huntington, *The Clash of Civilizations and the Remaking of World Order* (Simon & Schuster, 2011).

33 '*Dharmam kshatrasya kshatram*' — Brihadaranyaka Upanishad.

34 Alexander Dugin in Russia has made this point forcefully in several forums.

Aleksandr Dugin's Critique of Liberalism, Tsargrad Institute (katehon.com), 2021.

In this article that traces the beginnings of the resurgence of the civilizational spirit in India in the early 20th century, Dugin writes, 'In contrast, from the beginning of the struggle for independence, the main opponents of Congress believed that India was not just a country or a former colony, but the territory of a powerful and distinct civilization. Today we call it a civilizational state. This idea was first formulated by Kanaiyalal Munshi and referred to as "Akhand Bharat", "Undivided India" or "Greater India".'

35 Sebastian Conrad, 'Enlightenment in Global History: A Historiographical Critique,' *The American Historical Review* (2012).

36 Akhand Bharat Gross Indien, katehon.com (https://katehon.com/de/article/akhand-bharat-gross-indien), 2024.

37 Even with the telescoping of time scales in the modern world.

Chapter 2: Are Today's State Demarcations Good Identity Markers?

1 We refer here to the states configured after 1947.

2 The British Government's ouster of the East India Company was also a result of an economic tussle between sections of British society. The aristocracy and landed elites of Britain were deeply disturbed by the commercial upstarts of the Company using their wealth to enter into politics in Britain. Many of them were derisively called 'nabobs'. Robert Clive, who used the wealth he looted from India to purchase an Irish barony for himself, was vilified by his political rivals and was made subject to an inquiry in the elitist confines of the British parliament in 1772–1773, following which the parliament passed the Regulating Act of 1773 against the Company. There was also the added racial complication of the Company being dominated by the Scots and the Irish, who were looked down upon by the English, and the fact that many younger children of the nobility who could not inherit titles so long as their elder brothers were entering the service of the Company and getting a taste of power and military action.

3 Curious events such as Dalhousie's Doctrine of Lapse, this even from the days of the Company Bahadur, show that the British were always ahead in their strategic thinking and dovetailed it with their economic interests in India.

4 V.P. Menon, *The Story of the Integration of the Indian States* (Orient Longman, 1956), 546.

5 Hindol Sengupta, *The Man who Saved India* (Penguin Viking, 2018), 430.

6 This unfettered freedom to paint this canvas was given to Parliament by the simple and sweeping provisions of Article 3, which more than any other part of the Constitution, affirms the primacy of the Union vis-à-vis the states and removes any element of orthodox federal character in our polity. Any talk of pure federalism in India is only that—talk. Any element of

federalism in the governance structure given to the states is basically at the grace of the Union. It is not an inherent right of the states.

7 The formation of Telangana in 2014 is an example of a political decision that satisfied a legitimate demand, but the reasons behind this demand being ignored for at least forty years were purely political. The driving force behind the granting of statehood was the Congress party, but in the process, it became practically extinct in Andhra Pradesh. Delimitation decisions taken for political reasons have political ramifications and consequences. Decisions made on a more rational basis, like the granting of statehood to Uttarakhand, do not lead to political googlies and snafus for any of the parties involved.

8 The never-ending Kaveri river water dispute between Karnataka and Tamil Nadu is a case in point. A dispute between the two administrative entities, that is, the states, has morphed into a matter of communal tension between their respective denizens.

9 The more things change, the more they remain the same.

10 This is the reason we have said, at the beginning of this chapter, that the limits of Bhārat and India are mostly (but not wholly) congruent. The regions of incongruency are among the most interesting for Bhāratiyas today in terms of our foreign policy.

11 Kautilya, *The Arthashastra*, ed. and trans. L.N. Rangarajan (1992).

12 R.C. Majumdar, ed., *The History of Bengal, Vols. I and II* (The University of Dacca, Abinas Press, 1943), 1404.

13 These areas refer to modern-day western Uttar Pradesh and should not be confused with the subsequently created North-West Frontier Province, today's Khyber Pakhtunkhwa.

14 S.K. Dar, et al. *Report of the Linguistic Provinces Commission*, The Government of India Press, 1948.

15 F. Ali, et al. *Report of the States Reorganization Commission*, The Government of India Press, 1955.

16 Tilak was proven right when it came to the means being just as important as the ends, when post-Independence India went on a legal spree of contorting and secularizing the religious lives of sanātanis in the name of modernity.

17 In our opinion, this ascendancy of the moderates around the 1920s, culminating in the overall leadership of Gandhi, was a singular misfortune that postponed the reimagination of India as Bhārat by about a century.

18 Dharampal, *The Beautiful Tree: Indigenous Indian Education in the Eighteenth Century* (1983).

19 The high noon of the Maratha empire in the mid-18th century was symbolized by the well-known adage 'From Attock to Cuttack'. This saying was as well known in pre-Partition days as today's 'From Kashmir to Kanyakumari'.

20 Meenakshi Jain, *Flight of Deities and Rebirth of Temples: Episodes from Indian History* (Aryan Books International, 2019).

21 The famine was most definitely the result of British policy. T.E. Ravenshaw, the commissioner of Orissa, wrote in 1866 that 'Famine relief is at stand still. Public Works Department refuses to advance money to collectors to purchase rice. May I authorise advance for this purpose for Cuttack, Balasore and Puri.' Ravenshaw also disapproved collectors from distributing cooked food in relief centres, forcing people to take cash payments (which were useless considering little food was available for purchase in the first place). Many people voluntarily went to jail simply to have access to food.

Harihar Panda, *History of Orissa* (Kitab Mahal, 2008).

22 Troyer's Report dated 23 May 1817, Manuscript Vol. No. 387, Orissa State Archives.

23 *Utkal Dipeeka*, 22 October 1870.

24 *Utkala Bhāratinka Nibedan*, Sambalpur Hiteisini (5 March 1895).

25 Surasinha Patnaik, 'The Making of the Province of Odisha,' *Odisha Review* (2014). D:\backup\data\review\or-2014\f (odisha.gov.in)

26 Janmejay Choudhury, 'Political Awakening for Separate State and the Role of Maharaja Baikuntha Nath De,' *Odisha Review* (2015). D:\backup\data\review\or-2015\a (odisha.gov.in)

27 Viceroy of India, 1899–1905.

28 Andrew Frazer's report dated 15 October 1901.

29 Particular mention is warranted of pioneers such as Raja Rajendralal Mitra, Romesh Chander Dutt, and Benoy Kumar Sarkar who set the stage for nationalist historians to counter propaganda by well-patronized Imperialist and Marxist historiographers.

30 Let it not be forgotten that the British had their way in 1947 with the separation of East Pakistan from India.

31 Bipin Chandra, *The History of Modern India* (Orient BlackSwan, 2009).

32 K.L. Chattopadhyay, *Bengal Provincial Conference at Barisal: 14th & 15th April on JSTOR* (1906).

33 Bipin Chandra, *The History of Modern India* (Orient BlackSwan, 2009).

34 Some sections of the Indian political class have time and again attempted to recycle half-baked racial fantasies to pit Indian against Indian. During the British Raj, the terminology of such fraudulent ethnography flowed from the hallowed grounds of Oxford and Cambridge; identical attempts at fabricating racial divisions in the country to the benefit of foreign interests today have adopted the woke newspeak of diversity, equity, and inclusion which has been nurtured in the American Ivy League universities. At the time of writing, the former leader of opposition in the Lok Sabha has stated that 'In our Hindustan, we have Proto-Australian class, Negrito class, Mongoloid class.' Similarities with the Nazi official Albert Gorter's threefold division between 'Aryans', 'Mongolian (yellow)' and 'Negro (black)' are perhaps coincidental.

Adhir justifies Pitroda's 'racist' comments, says not everyone looks alike in India, Deccan Herald, 2024. https://www.

deccanherald.com/india/india-has-negrito-mongoloid-class-adhir-ranjan-chowdhury-backs-sam-pitroda-comment-draws-flak-from-bjp-3015342

Eric Ehrenreich, *The Nazi Ancestral Proof: Genealogy, Racial Science, and the Final Solution* (Bloomington: Indiana University Press, 2007). ISBN 978-0253349453.

35 Bipin Chandra, *The History of Modern India* (Orient BlackSwan, 2009).

36 In Bengal's case, for example, language was a matter of eclectic experimentation well into the British era. An artificial language known as Brajabuli, which was invented in the 16th century and is based on medieval Maithili having verb endings modified to resemble Bangla, was briefly revived by Rabindranath Tagore and Bankim Chandra Chattopadhyay. Such inconvenient histories have been expunged from Bhāratiya consciousness as a direct outcome of the politicization of language. Language as a fluvial, evolving means of cultural expression has become cribbed, canned, and constrained.

37 M.K. Gandhi, *Young India*, 18 February 1920.

38 Janmejay Choudhury, 'Political Awakening for Separate State and the Role of Maharaja Baikuntha Nath De,' *Odisha Review* (2015). D:\backup\data\review\or-2015\a (odisha.gov.in)

39 These disputations even go to the extent of maintaining that their version of Saivism is different from sanātana dharma and that the god Murugan or Velan (who they worship) is distinct from the so-called 'Aryan' Kartikeya or Subrahmanya. Some similarity may be found in the arguments of Lingayats in Karnataka that their community, the Veerasaivas, are not Hindus.

40 It is also not the case that Tamil and Sanskrit evolved separately from each other. Tamil borrows heavily from Sanskrit, particularly in terms of vocabulary, and Sanskrit has been theorized to have had significant borrowings from Dravidian languages, where Sanskrit phonology and syntax were

influenced by Dravidian languages. David Shulman, *Tamil.* (Harvard University Press, 2016), 17–19.

41 Daud Ali, 'Donors, Devotees, and Daughters of God: Temple Women in Medieval Tamilnadu,' *Reviews in History*.

42 The word 'Tenkasi' literally means southern Kasi.

43 *The dream that built Kashi of the south*, Indian Express (newindianexpress.com), 2020.

44 James Talboys Wheeler, *Madras in the Olden Time: Being a History of the Presidency from the First Foundation of Fort St. George to the Occupation of Madras by the French (1639–1748)* (Asian Educational Services, 1996).

45 Puzzling as it is, the name 'Madras' bears much more resemblance to the original name of the place, that is, Madraspatnam. The name 'Chennai' is more Telugu than Tamil. It was derived from Chennapatnam or beautiful place.

46 Richard De Smet, 'The Wide Range of De Nobili's Doctrine,' Review of Soosai Arokiasamy, *Dharma, Hindu and Christian, according to Roberto de Nobili, Vidyajyoti: Journal of Theological Reflection* 52/3 (1988): 159–164.

47 De Nobili Research Centre, Madras, *Interculturation of religion: critical perspectives on Robert de Nobili's mission in India* (Bangalore: Asian Trading Corporation, 2007).

48 N. Falcao, *Kristapurana: A Christian-Hindu Encounter: A Study of Inculturation in the Kristapurana of Thomas Stephens, SJ (1549-1619)* (Pune: Snehasadan, Anand: Gujarat Sahitya Prakash, 2003).

49 The 'secularization' of sanātani cultural attributes, which are then used to subvert and harm sanātana itself, is a process which has been taken forward with gusto by the intellectual descendants of colonizers. The recent opprobrium surrounding the award of Sangeeta Kalanidhi by the Madras Music Academy to the notorious T.M. Krishna is but one example—there are many more *shishyas* of the de Nobili *parampara* in Bhārat than one would imagine.

50 Blue-eyed, with blond hair and riding on horses all the way from Central Asia apparently.

51 *How the Dravidianists Destroyed Sanskrit in Tamil Nadu: A Slice from Real Life History*, The Dharma Dispatch (dharmadispatch.in), 2019.

52 Beschi was later turned into a hero for the Dravidian movement, and his statue (along with those of Caldwell and Pope) stand at Marina beach in Chennai. Strangely, he was christened 'Veeramunivar' by the Dravidians, which comprises two sanskrit words (veera and munivar)—something which Beschi himself would not have approved of.

53 The British had managed to do something of this sort in Nigeria, which, to this day, has more Anglicans than Britain itself.

54 It is quite interesting to note that the Mauryans themselves are subject to much anthropological speculation and may not have themselves fit into the meaning of the term 'Aryan' as understood by the Dravidianists.

55 The utterances of Udayanidhi Stalin calling for the eradication of sanātana dharma is nothing new, being a continuation of the work of de Nobili.

56 Mountstuart Elphinstone Grant-Duff, 'An Address Delivered to the Graduates of the University of Madras' (25 March 1886).

57 The legendary Carnatic music composer Tyagaraja stands at the fore of this list of Telugus who assimilated themselves fully within the Tamil lands.

58 Visweswaraya hailed from a Telugu-speaking family settled near Chikkaballapura on the outskirts of Bengaluru.

59 Fort St. George Gazette No. 40 (5 November 1895).

60 Dravidianism's spearheads include last names such as Thevar, Naicker, Naidu, Reddiyar, etc., which cannot be considered economically or socially backward.

61 Eugene F. Irschick, *Politics and Social Conflict in South India* (1969), 134–135.

62 Pi. Ci Kaṇēcan, *C.N. Annadurai* (2003), 25. Naicker was engaged in public desecration of Ganesha idols as recently as 1953 as a form of campaigning.

63 The subsequent splitting of the AIADMK from the parent DMK in 1970 is in our view a mere technicality arising from personality conflicts. Both these dominant parties are two sides of the same Dravidian coin.

64 Venkataraghavan Subha Srinivasan, *The Origin Story of India's States* (Ebury Press, 2021).

65 Ashok Lahiri, *India in Search of Glory* (Penguin Random House, 2022).

66 Ibid.

67 Nalin Mehta and Mona G. Mehta, 'Gujarat Beyond Gandhi: Notes on Identity, Conflict and Society', *South Asian History and Culture* 1, no. 4 (2010): 467–479

68 P.R. Rao, *Ancient and Mediaeval History of Andhra Pradesh* (Sterling Publishers, 1993).

69 Perhaps it is more than coincidental that these four states along the Coromandel coast constitute a continuous strip of land where neither the BJP nor the Congress have ever been strong enough to have captured political power at the state level in the last thirty years or so. The artificial linguistic identities seem to have swamped any national ethos of a deep and sustained type. Only now has the BJP managed to enter coastal Odisha in force, which is perhaps a sign of changing times and thoughts.

70 'I do not say, but I have my fears that if Karnataka is created as a separate province, it would be a province of all the Lingayats against everybody else' — B.R. Ambedkar's speech in Bombay, 1938.

71 Modern European history has a curiously comparable situation when the same Habsburg wore the crowns of Austria and Hungary after 1867 in what was called Austria-Hungary. Franz

Joseph was Emperor of Austria and King of Hungary from 1867 to 1918.

72 There is a snarky saying in Tamil lands, which ought to be taken as friendly banter between the denizens of its great cities, but also as a marker of the identitarian distinctions between their respective regions—The Tamil language was born in Madurai, attained perfection in Tanjore, and died in Madras.

73 'Despite years of effort, economic growth concentrated around Bengaluru: Report,' *Times of India* (indiatimes.com), 2022.

74 Akhil Goyal, *Vidarbha: Regional Imbalance and Creation of a New State,* 2023.

75 These problems associated with a mega city in an otherwise impoverished state are further exacerbated by the fact that this mega city is both the business and political capital of the state. The US is a much richer country than India but even they have ensured that many of their largest cities are not the political capitals of the states in which they are located. New York City, Chicago, Dallas-Fort Worth, and Los Angeles are not the capitals of New York, Illinois, Texas, and California, respectively.

76 *CEC flags-off first consignment of Ladakhi apples to different states of the country*, The Administration of Union Territory of Ladakh, 2021.

77 Ruchir Sharma, *The Rise and Fall of Nations* (Penguin Random House UK, 2016).

78 The rationale for the name is strictly historical—the 1928 Nehru report, which involved both Motilal and Jawaharlal, contained the first constitutional exposition of linguistic statehood. Prakasam was Andhra Pradesh's first chief minister and kicked off the kind of linguistic state politics which the country continues to grapple with.

79 Without attempting to be exhaustive, one might mention Yadavs in Bihar, Muslims in Uttar Pradesh and West Bengal, Marathas in Maharashtra, Christians in Kerala, and Thevars and Gounders in Tamil Nadu.

80 This situation was worse in places under direct British administration as opposed to the princely states.

Abhijit Banerjee, Lakshmi Iyer and Rohini Somanathan, *History, Social Divisions and Public Goods in Rural India*.

https://economics.mit.edu/sites/default/files/publications/History%2C%20Social%20Divisions%20and%20Public%20Goods%20in%20Rura.pdf

81 Naicker 'reformed' the Tamil alphabet, which was then imposed throughout by the dominant castes which drove the Justice Party. A new form of de-Sanskritized and contrived Tamil called Senthamizh was also deployed to wipe out Tamil Nadu's innate internal diversity.

82 One may also count EVMs in such technologies, as the phenomena of booth capturing and missing ballot boxes were important ingredients in identitarian political strategy.

83 CAD Vol. VII (4 November 1948).

84 We shall emphasize again here that India is not a federation but a union of states, and that the terms of reference for the construction of this union lies exclusively with the Union of India, in other words, with the Parliament of India.

85 In practical terms, this means that there is an increasing tendency among Hindus in India to consider Muslims in India and Pakistan as being different.

86 These deleterious consequences of large states exercising an unhealthy influence on Centre–state relations have also been felt in the other large states, say, in Maharashtra, Bihar, West Bengal, and Tamil Nadu, but nowhere are the effects as bad as in Uttar Pradesh, which by itself could qualify to be the fifth largest country in the world on the basis of population. This outsize effect of Uttar Pradesh has once again been revealed in the 2024 election.

87 We prefer the term 'decentralized' to 'federal'.

88 The Maurya, Gupta, Byzantine, Ming, Mughal, and Habsburg dominions were only approximations of empires by this token.

Chapter 3: Why Does Bhārat Need Delimitation of Electoral Constituencies Today?

1 In the early days of electoral democracy in England, the aristocracy (which was losing influence as the voter franchise kept expanding), evolved various mechanisms to protect their interests. This included setting up constituencies which had a tiny population but had some historical settlement to justify its continuation so that aristocrats could keep getting elected to parliament without genuine democratic competition. These were known as 'rotten boroughs'. Another technique was to set up 'pocket boroughs', where most of the voters were simply tenants of an aristocrat who could control them. An example of a rotten borough was Old Sarum in Wiltshire, which was an abandoned citadel in ruins atop a hill having a total of seven registered voters, but which sent two parliamentarians to the House of Commons. Another was Dunwich in Suffolk, which was once a town but had fallen off into the sea and continued to send two parliamentarians with thirty-two voters. The Reform Act, 1832, mooted by the 2nd Earl Grey (of Earl Grey tea fame) removed such oddities by carrying out a major delimitation exercise similar to the one we recommend in this book.

2 This point is of note as delimitation in all territories formerly ruled by Maharaja Hari Singh in Jammu & Kashmir till 1947 will sooner or later need to come within the ambit of the Indian state, and any future delimitation exercise will need to take into account considerations such as those which applied in Germany upon reunification. Specifically, Gilgit, Baltistan, and PoK will need to have a proper delimitation exercise. The status of Chitral is yet another question. Jammu and Kashmir will be discussed later in this chapter in the context of constitutional changes after the revocation of Article 370 in 2019. The matter will also be discussed in the next chapter with regard to how exactly five new states may be carved out of the original pre-1947 Jammu & Kashmir.

3 A.K. Verma, 'Delimitation in India: Methodological Issues', *Economic and Political Weekly* 41, no. 9 (2006): 794–799

4 Lebanon and Kenya share this dubious distinction with India.

5 How India pulled off its first general election, *The Indian Express*, 2024.

6 The seemingly irrational objection that the opposition parties today have to One Nation One Poll perhaps arises from some fear that the BJP, which is in an unassailable position with respect to the Lok Sabha, will concomitantly capture most if not all the state assemblies, because of voter indifference. They forget that the Indian voter is astute and that on many occasions has voted for different parties in the state and at the Centre when the elections are held simultaneously or within a small interval of time. Odisha in 2019 and 2024, Haryana in 2019, and Andhra Pradesh in 2024 are recent examples.

7 This would lead to some voters having an increased say in who gets to be a member of Parliament and would obviously be relevant only in very special constituencies. It is a theoretical possibility but need not be dismissed out of hand in our view.

8 India's Emerging Crisis of Representation, *Carnegie Endowment for International Peace*, 2019.

9 Dierk Herzer, Holger Strulik and Sebastian Vollmer, 'The long-run determinants of fertility: one century of demographic change 1900–1999', *J Econ Growth* (2012) 17: 357–385.

10 Some argue that the rate of population increase was comparable everywhere but to start with the northern states were more populous. In this sense, Bihar and Tamil Nadu might simply be outliers.

11 Bihar and Tamil Nadu make an interesting comparison. In 1971 their populations were nearly the same, 4.2 and 4.1 crore. By 2011, Bihar at 10.4 crore had far outpaced Tamil Nadu at 7.2 crore. The reader will note that not all northern states have the same rate of population increase, and likewise not all southern states do either. Put another way, fertility rates

have decreased at different rates in states, both in the North and in the South. See also https://www.news18.com/opinion/opinion-delimitation-final-barrier-to-real-democracy-in-india-8821760.html

12 B.R. Ambedkar, *Thoughts on Linguistic States*, 1955.

13 This is hardly possible. Uttar Pradesh, our largest state, has 25.7 crore people while Sikkim, our smallest state, has 6.1 lakh, making for a population differential of 421.

14 We also do not have an institution like the US Senate where each state has the same representation of two senators, whatever be the population. Also, and most significantly, the two components of the US Legislature, namely the Senate and the House of Representatives, are of equal importance. All bills, including money bills, need to be passed by both the House and the Senate. This is not the case in India where the lower house is much more important than the upper house. Further, and to exacerbate our situation, larger states have a proportionately higher representation in the upper house. So, any comparison between the Rajya Sabha and the US Senate is specious.

15 Election Commission, pib.gov.in/PressReleaseIframePage.aspx?PRID=1947865, 2023.

16 Malkajgiri in Telangana and Bengaluru North with 31.5 and 24.01 lakh voters are staggeringly large constituencies. They are also of sprawling size.

17 A.K. Verma, 'Delimitation in India: Methodological Issues', *Economic and Political Weekly* 41, no. 9 (2006): 794–799

18 It is amazing that just one amendment caused so much systemic havoc in so many spheres of constitutionality and governance. The facts that it was rushed through Parliament at a time when almost all political opponents of Indira Gandhi were in jail and that the Janata Party government that followed her did not repeal the entire amendment in toto need to be considered carefully by all students of Indian political history. The institutional erosion which happened around the time

of the Emergency and the maladaptive responses to these distortions which followed require proper historical treatment.

19 Population Foundation of India, *Towards Population Stabilisation in India: Why Stringent Control Measures Do Not Work*.

20 The Janata government, elected after the Emergency, undid much of the damage of the 42nd Amendment through the 43rd and 44th Amendments, but they did not reverse the changes to Articles 81, 82, and 170. Essentially, delimitation continued to be frozen.

21 Vajpayee rejoined the NDA alliance in 1999 as prime minister, bringing with him the Telugu Desam Party (TDP) and the DMK, two states that would lose parliamentary representation if the 1971 census freeze was lifted. There was also uneven population increase within the states. There was a push to split Madhya Pradesh and Bihar into smaller states, and the BJP has long supported this idea. Furthermore, there was criticism over the unequal distribution of parliamentary seats among the SC/STs, which are required under the Constitution to be allocated based on population (Article 330). Thus the Vajpayee-led NDA opted for a compromise and continued the delimitation freeze. The present coalition dispensation at the Centre should not see a repeat performance of 2001 with another twenty-five-year delimitation freeze—this would essentially make a mockery of any kind of sensible electoral democracy in our diverse country.

22 How Uttar Pradesh is key to forging India's economic and political path, *The Times of India* (indiatimes.com), 2022; Uttar Pradesh outpaces Tamil Nadu to become the second-largest economy in India: Report, *ET BFSI* (indiatimes.com), 2023.

23 The size of each constituency varies by state in India, and the sizes are diverging rather than converging, While the economy has been more liberalized since 1991, and while this has increased growth rates in every state, those in the south and

west had greater growth, and since 2001, the disparity between some northern and southern states in terms of fertility rates has widened even further.

24 Ram Madhav, 'Don't rewrite the Constitution', *Indian Express*, 26 November 2023. https://indianexpress.com/article/opinion/columns/samvidhan-diwas-baba-saheb-bhim-rao-ambedkar-constitution-day-colonial-constitution-rewriting-of-constitution-9041229/

25 In the heat and dust of Indian politics, even redrawing state boundaries slightly by the BJP, fully conforming to the provisions of Art. 3, will be deemed anti-constitutional and anti-democratic by the opposition.

26 Technically, Article 370 has not been revoked; Article 370 permitted the Union government to extend parts of the Constitution to Jammu & Kashmir. In 2019, the Union government simply declared that all of the Constitution will apply to the erstwhile state, rendering its special status nugatory. Nonetheless, for both reasons of approximating the practical outcome of this action as well as for convenience, the terms 'revocation' and 'abrogation' have been commonly used to refer to this proclamation and the acts which followed it. Thus, this book will continue to refer to Article 370 being revoked or abrogated, notwithstanding such an appellation being technically inaccurate.

27 Ladakh had and continues to have one Lok Sabha constituency.

28 The Jammu region had 54 lakh inhabitants according to the 2011 census while the Kashmir Valley had 69 lakh inhabitants. For comparison purposes, PoK has 40 lakh people while Gilgit-Baltistan has 14 lakh people. The latter would necessarily come into the picture in some future delimitation exercise. See Table 4 in Chapter 4.

29 J&K Delimitation Commission issues final notification, reserves 43 Assembly seats for Jammu, 47 for Kashmir, *The Indian Express* (2022).

30 A Roadmap to Representation: The Case for Gilgit-Baltistan, *Global Order* (globalorder.live), 2020; What the Constitution Amendment Bill for Gilgit Baltistan might look like, *Global Order* (globalorder.live), 2020

31 Shruti Rajagopalan, 'Demography, Delimitation, and Democracy', 2023 (substack.com).

32 This has been defined as the ratio of the total number of eligible voters in the five top constituencies by population to the corresponding number in the bottom five. This ratio now stands at 15.6 in India, showing a considerable skew.

33 A.K. Verma, 'Issues and Problems in India's Delimitation Exercise', *The Indian Journal of Political Science* 63, no. 4: 371–388.

34 In our opinion, even 888 seats are insufficient for the lower house in a country with such a large population. Around double this number would be more reasonable.

35 Ambedkar used the word 'fantastic' to describe the size disparity in India's states in his 1955 document.

Chapter 4: Identities, Small States, and Delimitation

1 The Pakistani impetus of 'one unit' and the imposition of Urdu along with upper-caste Muhajir culture (coupled with the suppression of the cultures which had hitherto prospered there) was also a brazen and brutal attempt to enforce post-Westphalian political systems on peoples which are fundamentally non-Westphalian in their politics. Of course, that entire country may be described as a fully artificial nation state. It is no coincidence that Pakistan has retained the internal boundaries of its four provinces as they existed in 1947.

2 One People One Country One Leader.

3 We refer here to Africa and the Middle East.

4 Is India a country or a continent? *The Economist* (economist.com), 2017.

5 The ultimate reality in the sanātani tradition, Brahman, is the underlying conscious oneness of all.

6 Taittiriya Upanishad, 2.6

7 States Reorganization Commission Report, 1955, 45.

8 States Reorganization Commission Report, 1955, xx.

9 The separation of Kasaragod taluk from Mangalore district in the erstwhile Madras presidency and its inclusion in the new state of Kerala continues to be a sore point in Karnataka till today. Ostensibly this was done in exchange for Kerala yielding Kanyakumari, a part of the erstwhile princely state of Travancore, to Madras state.

10 Vikash Vaibhav, 'State-size and economic growth: evidence from state reorganization in India', *Indian Economic Review* 59 (2023): 177–204.

11 B.R. Ambedkar, *Thoughts on Linguistic States*, 1955.

12 This is so because minorities by their very nature will tend to be scattered here and there in a state and are not uniformly distributed everywhere.

13 Divide and Conquer: Are Smaller States the Answer in India? *Knowledge at Wharton* (upenn.edu), 2011.

14 The populations of the seventy-five states do vary around a mean of 1.88 crores. Small populations are found in geographically isolated places (Banaskantha and Ladakh) or where the culture is unique (Kodagu and Indrakil). Large populations arise when mega cities are located in these states. The difference in population between the largest and smallest of our seventy-five states, Mithila and Ladakh, is 276 as opposed to the corresponding number 327 for our present twenty-eight states, where UP is the largest and Sikkim the smallest. Since outliers would bias such data, it is more helpful to note that thirty-five of our seventy-five states have populations between one and three crores. See Figure 3.

15 A study of the creation of new states in present-day Gujarat over the past twenty years is illustrative. Gujarat had twenty-five

districts in 2011. Today it has thirty-three. A number of new districts like Aravalli, Mahisagar, Chota Udaipur, Morbi, Dwarka, Gir Somnath. Amreli, and Botad have been created by delimitation and transfer of taluks from one or more of the earlier districts. The reasons for such delimitation appear to be cultural and economic. Our present proposal is practically a repeat of this exercise at an all-India level. Only Gujarat has gone ahead and created so many new districts in a relatively short period of time. The reader will note that creation of new districts within a state is exclusively within the powers of the state government.

16 It may be noted that even these various demands to split smaller states off from larger existing states usually arise because of economic considerations.

17 The 2021 book *Bhārat: India 2.0* by one of the present authors provides an earlier version of this map. The present version takes into account the many useful comments and suggestions made by readers of this book, and we are thankful for these inputs. These changes are, by and large, minor. What is important is the idea of seventy-five or so somewhat equally sized states as opposed to the present condition in which we have twenty-eight states with wide differences in population.

18 This refers to the districts of Bihar in 2011 because the latest census data is only available for this date.

19 Azamgarh, Jaunpur, Gorakhpur, Varanasi, Ghazipur, Kushinagar, Ballia, Deoria, Maharajganj, Siddharth Nagar, Mirzapur, Mau, Chandauli, Sonbhadra, Sant Ravidas Nagar.

20 Our new Gilgit state is made up of Gilgit, Nagar, Hunza, and Ghizer districts in the Gilgit division, Chitral district from Khyber Pakhtunkhwa province, as also Diamer, Darel, and Tangir districts of Diamer division.

21 The long and complicated history of Chitral has been outlined by us previously, and we reiterate here that it is legally a part of the Union of India. https://organiser.org/2023/12/06/209641/opinion/chitral-pojk-part-1-time-to-reclaim-the-lost-

territory-and-expand-footprints-in-the-region/#google_vignette https://organiser.org/2023/12/12/210562/bharat/chitral-pojk-part-ii-time-to-intervene-as-hindus-are-vulnerable-to-attack-by-islamists-in-pakistan/

22 The reader will note that the present-day Ladakh UT consists of two districts Leh and Kargil. Leh is retained (includes Aksai Chin and Siachen) in the new Ladakh state that also contains Lahaul-Spiti and Kinnaur districts from today's Himachal Pradesh. Kargil district is transferred to the new Baltiyul state.

23 Baltiyul, essentially Balitistan in the local language, comprises Skardu, Shigar, and Ghanche districts from today's Baltistan, Astore, and Kharmang districts from Diamer division, and Kargil district from today's Ladakh UT.

24 Sikkim CM P.S. Tamang stresses cultural unity, says Sikkim and Darjeeling must preserve language and heritage Sikkim: 'Collective efforts required from society to develop Nepali language', says CM Prem Singh Tamang - Sikkim: 'Collective efforts required from society to develop Nepali language', says CM Prem Singh Tamang (indiatodayne.in)

25 Our concept for UT Delhi closely follows the structure of Washington D.C. which is a small government enclave sandwiched between the states of Maryland and Virginia. Inhabitants of the US capital vote in the presidential elections but have no representation in the Congress.

26 The available map is from *Seminar*'s June 1978 issue, which replicated the April 1973 issue map. Raj Thapar and Romesh Thapar, *Seminar* 164, 1973.

27 Data is taken from the 2011 census. Indian Districts by Population, Sex Ratio, Literacy 2011 Census and the reader may suitably extrapolate these population figures to today's numbers.

28 Gilgit-Baltistan: Districts & Places—Population Statistics, Maps, Charts, Weather and Web Information, City population (citypopulation.de).

29 These four largest states in our scheme are (in descending population order) Mithila, Kashi, Gauda, and Awadh. It is worth considering whether these four states may be further subdivided for administrative convenience in the future.

30 The irrational demarcation of the present-day Maharashtra continues to influence local events that often dominate large national issues. Elections in the richest state in India are still dominated by caste and regional issues. The state contains four disjointed parts, Mumbai-Konkan, Western Maharashtra or Desh (comprising Pune, Satara, Kolhapur, Nashik), Marathwada, and Vidarbha. The existence of no less than six major political parties claiming the forty-eight Lok Sabha seats in Maharashtra is possible because each of these parties attracts voters in different parts of the state and from different castes, clearly indicative of distinct micro-identities. The big differences between Lok Sabha and assembly election results in Maharashtra also reveal this fragmented structure of this large state. The results of the Maharashtra Assembly election in late 2024 show that electoral outcomes can swing suddenly: the NDA alliance did much better in the state-level election than it did in the Lok Sabha election in mid-2024. The only factor that seems to hold this state together is the Marathi language, about which the inhabitants have a fierce and frenzied loyalty, which is almost bizarre.

31 The broad concepts in both Bengal and sanātana dharma owe to the fact that the same land nurtured religious approaches as diverse as those propagated by Sri Chaitanya Mahaprabhu, Sri Bamakhepa, and Sri Atisa Dipamkara.

32 It is interesting to note that the list of titles adopted by the Gajapati kings of Odisha include Gaudeshvara but not Vangapati.

Bhaskar Mishra, 'The Traditional Role of Gajapati Maharaja in Shri Jagannath Temple', *Orissa Review*, 2011. (odisha.gov.in)

33 R.C. Majumdar, *History of Ancient Bengal* (G. Bhardwaj & Co., 1971).

34 R.C. Majumdar (ed), *The History of Bengal, Volume I, Hindu Period* (University of Dacca, 1943).

35 Any region with latitudinal expanse without a corresponding longitudinal stretch is more likely to show a higher diversity of population.

36 Kerala was unusual in former times in that there was more maritime interaction with foreign powers than overland interaction with the inhabitants of Bhāratavarsha. The only regions through which any kind of land interaction would have been possible were the extreme north, namely, the area around Kasargode, the Palghat gap in the middle, and the far south between Thiruvananthapuram and Kanyakumari. The rest of the eastern part of the Malayali region was densely forested and mountainous.

37 Tyagaraja, Muthuswami Dikshitar, and Syama Sastri, all of whom lived in the general period 1760–1835, are referred to as the Musical Trinity of Carnatic music because of their overwhelming contribution to the art and practice of today's Carnatic music. Swathi Thirunal was influenced in his composition style by his court musician Vadivelu, a violist, who was a pupil of Muthuswami Dikshitar.

38 The exact quote is 'was there ever a sillier thing than what I saw in Malabar? The poor "Paraiah" is not allowed to pass through the same street as a high caste man, but if he changes his name to a hodge-podge English name or to a Mohammedan name, it is alright. What inference would you draw that these Malabaris are all lunatics, their homes so many lunatic asylums, and they are to be treated with derision by every race in India until they mend their manners and know better. Shame upon them that such wicked and diabolical customs are allowed.' *From Colombo to Almora: Vivekananda's Notes*, 1904. While Swami Vivekananda uses

the term 'Malabar', which would usually be taken as north Kerala, he was in all likelihood talking about Travancore–Cochin. There also exists a historical debate as to whether Swami Vivekananda used the words 'lunatic asylum' or did he instead use the term 'madhouse' for the region.

39 Thiruvananthapuram makes global list of twenty-four 'out-of-the-box' emerging tech locations, *The Indian Express* (newindianexpress.com), 2023.

40 Thrippati Danam: A Ritual by which the Rulers of Travancore became 'Padmanabhadasas', *The Hindu Post* (hindupost.in), 2018.

41 While being classified as a zamindari and not a princely state within the British Empire, the exact status of the Raj Darbhanga is a cause for much debate. It enjoyed much greater powers and autonomy than many princely states and had its own administrative setup.

42 The decline (and wipeout) of these industries have been largely due to political reasons. Under Indira Gandhi, important holdings such as the British Indian Corporation were nationalized, which held a number of large mills in its portfolio. The Partition led the Bengal National Bank, one of whose founders was the Maharaja of Darbhanga, to its ultimate demise. The last straw came when the maharaja's two newspapers, *Indian Nation* and *Aryavarta*, delivered some less than stellar reporting about Jagannath Mishra, the Congress chief minister of Bihar. Mishra proceeded to use the state machinery to undermine industries connected to the erstwhile zamindars and fomented a succession crisis which has all but hollowed out the family, with many important industries becoming collateral damage.

Darbhanga provides a classic study of the decline and fall of India's feudal ruling class, *India Today*, 2014.

43 Bihar Sugar Industry: Long Tale of Sweet Memories, Bitter Truth, *NewsClick*, 2020.

44 Industries minister: Mithila region to get 2 ethanol production plants soon, *The Times of India* (indiatimes.com), 2021.
45 The Maithili movement, *Frontline* (thehindu.com), 2018.
46 H. Jha, (ed.), *Courage and Benevolence: Maharajadhiraja Kameshwar Singh (1907–1962)*, Darbhanga: Maharajadhiraja Kameshwar Singh Kalyani Foundation, 2007.
47 Santosh Kumar Chaudhary, 'Mithila State Movement: History', Encyclopedia MDPI
48 Devanand Kamat, 'The Voice of Mithila Mihir: The Making of the Idea of Mithila', *Nidān: International Journal for Indian Studies* 8, no. 2 (2023): 31–44 (uni-heidelberg.de)
49 The name 'Darbhanga' is derived from a combination of Dwara and Bhanga, that is, the door to Bengal.
50 Rayalaseema organisations step up stir for irrigation water in Andhra, *The Indian Express* (newindianexpress.com), 2023.
51 Informally these ceded districts were also called backward districts or BACK by the British, an acronym for Bellary, Anantapur, Cuddapah, and Kurnool.
52 The birth of Rayalaseema, *The Hindu*, 2016.
53 Apart from being a politician, he was the owner of *Andhra Patrika*, a publication which was at the forefront of the demands for Andhra Pradesh, and the founder of Amrutanjan Healthcare Limited (of Amrutanjan pain balm fame).
54 While the Sribagh Agreement is the basis for the union between coastal Andhra and Rayalaseema, the so-called Gentlemen's agreement of 1956 forms the basis for the union between Telangana and coastal Andhra-Rayalaseema. Now that the Gentleman's agreement has come undone, perhaps the Sribagh Agreement is next. Why Andhra Pradesh, being born of two separate agreements between three distinct regions, was not considered a federation is a question of both academic and practical consequence.
55 Case for High Court in Rayalaseema, *The Hans India* (thehansindia.com), 2018.

56 Environment in elections: Andhra's Rayalaseema battling drought conditions for 4 years, but ignored in poll manifestos, *Down to Earth* (downtoearth.org.in).

57 Rayalaseema gave six chief ministers to Andhra Pradesh, but it still cries for attention, *News18*, 2019.

58 Rayalaseema backwardness attributed to lack of political will, *The Hindu*, 2021.

59 Rayalaseema in a state of discontent, *The Hindu*, 2015.

60 Rayalaseema can become a prosperous state if made separate, *The Indian Express* (newindianexpress.com), 2013.

61 How a sliver of Korea took root in a village of Andhra Pradesh is a story of globalisation, *The Hindu*, 2022.

62 The reader may note that the small coastline of the proposed new Rayalaseema includes Sriharikota.

63 Donald L. Horowitz, '6. An Economy of Antipathy: Target Selection and the Imperatives of Violence', De Gruyter (degruyter.com).

64 Reetika Revathy Subramanian, 'A Tale of Two Cities: Reconstructing the "Bajao Pungi, Hatao Lungi" campaign in Bombay, and the Birth of the "Other"', *Subversions* 3, no, 2 (2015) (tiss. edu).

65 Why Meghalaya is rattled by exposure of its shameful persecution of non-tribals for decades, *Swarjya* (swarajyamag.com), 2020.

66 'Bearing Witness': The Impact of Conflict on Women in Nagaland and Assam, Centre for North East Studies and Policy Research, 2011.

67 For 1991 riot survivor, the nightmare returns, *Bangalore Mirror* (indiatimes.com), 2016.

68 3.3 lakh people migrated from Uttarakhand from 2018 to 2022, says report, *The Times of India* (indiatimes.com), 2023.

69 In the end, this is the basis for our Varna system that is based on professional competence.

70 N. Gregory Mankiw, 'Chapter 3, Principles of Economics, sixth edition', Cengage Learning, 2012.

71 All of these products have been granted the geographical identification (GI) tag under the Geographical Indications of Goods (Registration and Protection) Act, 1999.

72 Paradise on Earth: How beautiful roses, lavenders can be an economic miracle for Kashmir, *Firstpost*, 2023.

73 Unravelling the economic odyssey of Jammu & Kashmir, *Kashmir Reader*, 2024.

74 With core assets in Khavda & Mundra, Kachchh becomes central to Adani's green ambitions, *The Indian Express*, 2024.

75 G.R. Desiraju, 'Sun, solar energy and the climate change challenges', *Firstpost*, 2024. https://www.firstpost.com/opinion/sun-solar-energy-and-the-climate-change-challenges-13681142.html.

76 Coimbatore, Tirupur will spur textile export growth: Minister, *The Times of India* (indiatimes.com), 2022.

77 How can India replicate the success of Tiruppur in 75 other places? *Business Standard* (business-standard.com), 2022.

78 Coimbatore to get Rs 1,100cr IT Park, library and science centre, *The Times of India* (indiatimes.com), 2024.

79 In our scheme, the new state of Kashi would have fifteen districts from present-day U.P. and seven from present-day Bihar.

80 How renovated Kashi corridor is proving to be a boon for Varanasi's economy, *Zee News*, 2023.

81 Rise of Gorakhpur, fall of Mathura – How UP's temple towns contribute to economy, *The Print*, 2022.
https://theprint.in/opinion/rise-of-gorakhpur-fall-of-mathura-up-temple-towns-economy/826234/

82 Meenakshi Jain, *Flight of Deities and Rebirth of Temples: Episodes from Indian History* (Aryan Books International, 2019).

83 Meenakshi Jain, *Vishwanath Rises and Rises: The Story of Eternal Kashi* (Aryan Books International, 2024).

84 List of 112 Aspirational Districts (niti.gov.in).

85 India Employment Report 2024: Youth employment, education and skills (ruralindiaonline.org).

Chapter 5: Modus Operandi

1 Dobbs: Wise words from Thomas Jefferson on constitutional change, *The Denver Post*, 2016.

2 This law, however, caused other problems as members of the ruling party or coalition, who did not hold executive positions, namely, ministerships, were rapidly reduced to rubber stamps forced to obey the diktats of their political party bosses, and unable to make objective comments on proposed legislation in a free parliamentary debate. The concept of a parliamentary backbencher (considering we like to say that we have modelled our governance system after the UK) has now all but vanished.

3 Amendments mean 'changing the Constitution', and so the shrill cries during the recent election that the Constitution is under the danger of being changed mean nothing. The Constitution has been changed 106 times since 1950, mostly by parties which today occupy the opposition benches.

4 The preamble begins with 'We the people of India…', and concludes with 'hereby adopt, enact and give to ourselves this constitution'. It is fairly apparent through both the constitutional understanding which prevailed at the time of the first parliament as well as the wording of the preamble that the Constitution was to be easily modified by the people (acting through the Parliament).

5 Indeed, the general elections serve as the best possible occasions when the people decide the terms they deem fit for their governance. This is the kernel of democracy and implies, nay even mandates, change as the circumstances and conditions that the nation finds itself change.

6 Recently there has been some talk of increasing the number of Lok Sabha constituencies flat out across the country, to achieve

a total of 888 seats. This decreases the number of voters sending a single member to the Lower House but has no effect on Each Vote Same Value. The value of a vote remains just as unequal as it is now and the existing disparities continue, perhaps in a magnified way.

7 To recapitulate, the skew ratio is the ratio in population between the largest and smallest constituency in a group.

8 The reader is reminded that on average, 17.86 lakh crore voters send a single MP to the Lok Sabha today.

9 It is speculated that the next census will probably be a two-year-long exercise, from January 2025 till December 2026.

10 Informally, it is understood that the percentage of the politically dominant Vokkaliga caste is not 14 per cent as conventionally understood but closer to 8 per cent.

11 Nehru obtained a majority for the Congress in the Lok Sabha in 1952, 1957, and 1962. The percentage of votes polled by the Congress in these three elections increased from 45 per cent to 47.8 per cent in 1957 but declined to 44.7 per cent in 1962. The BJP has secured a majority in 2014, 2019, and 2024, but the vote percentage has been increasing from 31 per cent in 2014 to 37.36 per cent in 2019 to 41.36 per cent in 2024. Considering the fragmented nature of the Indian polity, these latter numbers are impressive. There were far fewer political parties in Nehru's time.

12 Let it not be forgotten that Vajpayee had to capitulate in 2001 with regard to delimitation.

13 Let it not be forgotten that it was Rajaji's imprudent introduction of Hindi in the educational curricula of Madras presidency in 1938, following Gandhi's equally obstinate insistence on Hindi in the national discourse, that allowed the Justice Party to morph into the secessionist Dravidar Kazhagam whose illustrious offspring, the DMK, has continued to enjoy unbridled sway with its isolationist Dravidian ideology till the first signs of its breach were seen in the 2024 election. Rajaji

further distinguished himself by allying his Swatantra Party in 1968 with the DMK and against the Congress, an election that brought into power the DMK and began an unbroken stretch of Dravidian party rule in that state for fifty-six years. This has been a costly price for the nation to pay for one man's failings.

14 Two examples of larger states causing a compromise on national interest are quite recent. Tamil Nadu's DMK, an alliance partner of the then-United Progressive Alliance (UPA) government, had forced the prime minister to not attend the Commonwealth summit because it was being held in Colombo. Likewise, the TMC had derailed water-sharing arrangements and exchange of enclaves with Bangladesh for years.

DMK's Karunanidhi welcomes PM's decision to skip CHOGM meet in Sri Lanka, *India Today*; India-Bangladesh ink first water treaty in years but Teesta pact still elusive—Why Mamata must relent, Explainers News, *Times Now* (timesnownews.com).

A third example is the erstwhile state of Jammu & Kashmir, but here domestic and international issues are so inextricably intertwined that after a time it became impossible to determine what influenced what. After the abrogation of Article 370 on 5 August 2019, the situation became somewhat clearer, but there are still bridges to cross—the recent flare-up in PoK, which is an integral part of Bhārat, could be a prelude to more serious developments. However, and in the context of the present book, it may be noted that as many as twenty-six seats in the J&K assembly have now been allotted to PoK and Gilgit-Baltistan.

15 The absurdly high 69 per cent cap on reservations wrested by the Tamil Nadu Chief Minister J. Jayalalitha in 1994 and further included in the Schedule IX at her insistence so that it may not even be reviewed unless we give ourselves a new constitution is a prime example of how a politically powerful

state may influence important national-level questions in a coalition regime, simply on the strength of its local political compulsions. The effect of this debilitating legislation is seen even today in the hesitant country-wide implementation of the New Education Policy 2020, which the Dravidian parties oppose tooth and nail.

16 Basic structure doctrine: It is a poor fix for the Constitution's flaws, *Scroll* (scroll.in), 2023.

17 Shloka 12 of the Shiva Tandava Stotram comes to mind. 'Towards different imageries in the world, towards snakes and garlands/towards a lump of clay and a valuable jewel, friends and enemies/seeing a grass-like eye and a lotus-like eye, towards commoners and their rulers/When will I worship Sadashiva with equanimity in conduct?'

18 This MP made the further mischievous, even treacherous, suggestion that the word 'union' in the preamble suggests that the states were sovereign entities that came together for a negotiated settlement. He also made the ludicrous statement, in the same speech in Parliament, that India is not a nation. All this is blatantly false and must be called out in all forums. The word 'union' was used instead of 'federation' in our Constitution to show the contrast between these two terms. A union is just that—the union is carried out by parliament that glues together the pieces it has fashioned. There were no states as we understand them today on 15 August 1947. The Parliament created all our states and called their union the Union of India. The Parliament may just as easily fragment, dissolve, reshape, and reassign any state in any manner it wishes using the provisions of Article 3, and it would strictly be within the four corners of our present constitution.

19 The 'Union government' has a unifying effect, *The Hindu* (2021).

20 Whatever the phrase 'Ambedkar's constitution' means. Politicians seem to like the phrase *Babasaheb ka samvidhaan.*

21 Basic structure doctrine: It is a poor fix for the Constitution's flaws, *Scroll* (scroll.in), 2023.

22 It would do us well to remember what James Madison said about lawmakers that 'it would be of little avail to the people that the laws are made by men of their own choice if the laws be so voluminous that they cannot be read, or so incoherent that they cannot be understood'. Our Parliament should probably study these words carefully.

23 'Dharmic' is a term which is neither religious nor theocratic. Arguing otherwise is to take a colonial lens to the idea.

24 'To consider judges as the ultimate arbiters of all constitutional questions is a very dangerous doctrine indeed, and one which would place us under the despotism of an oligarchy.' — Thomas Jefferson

25 G.R. Desiraju, *Bhārat: India 2.0* (Vitasta Publishing, 2022).

26 Himachal Pradesh government has raised VAT on diesel to cover OPS cost: Hardeep Singh Puri, *The Tribune India*, 2023.

27 Public sector undertakings: A tragedy of errors, *Swarajya* (swarajyamag.com), 2022.

28 Economic Survey 2019–20, Department of Economic Affairs, Ministry of Finance, Government of India, Volume II, Chapter 1: State of the Economy, p. 6 (2020).

29 To some extent this happened in 2009 when the UPA was re-elected. It had ridden piggyback on the long-term beneficial actions of the Vajpayee government—the economy was at a peak between 2004 and 2009. However, the fiscal profligacy of UPA between 2009 and 2014 had consequences that Modi 1.0 had to mop up.

30 Dambisa Moyo, *Edge of Chaos* (Little, Brown, 2018).

31 One may refer to the Green Credit Rules, 2023, issued by the Ministry of Environment, Forest, and Climate Change on 12 October 2023 for a conceptual understanding of green credits.

32 This discounts some very stellar officeholders who have rendered yeoman service to the nation and many of whom go unrecognised.

33 The Central Consumer Protection Authority's Guidelines for Prevention of Misleading Advertisement in Coaching Sector, as well as its suo motu action against coaching centres, shows an incipient understanding of how deleterious the coaching industry is to the youth. Ministry of Consumer Affairs, Food & Public Distribution, https://pib.gov.in/PressReleaseIframePage.aspx?PRID=2073013, 2024.

34 Ambedkar was unambiguous about this when he said that 'the nature of the Union of India expresses only an idea. It does not indicate an achievement…' in his 1955 document on 'Thoughts on Linguistic States'.

35 G.R. Desiraju and D. Bhattacharya, 'India's Constitution and internal unrest', *Swarajya*, 2023. https://swarajyamag.com/blogs/indias-constitution-and-internal-unrest

36 A Muslim would not be a member of a minority community in, say, Kashmir, Kamtapur, or Malabar.

37 The more recent spectacle of bureaucrats, pretend academics, and self-professed public intellectuals parading in Indian gear in fashionable Delhi salons and spouting what they consider to be politically convenient native lines and at the same time retaining an inner Anglophilic and Macaulayist core is not what Bhārat needs at the present juncture. Even more irrelevant to the people of Bodinayakanur, Siliguri, and Buxar are the absurdly large number of podcasts featuring these individuals in their narcissistic echo chambers.

38 Authors' italics.

39 Dharampal and Pawan Gupta (ed.), *Rediscovering India* (Society for Integrated Development of the Himalayas and Dharampal Shodh Peeth, 2022).

40 Subrata Dasgupta, *The Awakening: The Story of the Bengal Renaissance* (Random House India, 2011).

41 These demands include, for example, disenfranchisement of Muslims.

42 Sarvepalli Radhakrishan, 'Dharma: The Individual And The Social Order in Hinduism', *Swarajya* (swarajyamag.com).

43 DVG's Profound Commentary on the True Essence of Rama Rajya, *The Dharma Dispatch* (dharmadispatch.in), 2020.

44 Legislators, including those in the executive (both political and bureaucratic) and even the judiciary, have not conducted themselves in a manner which instils any sense of decency, let alone confidence, in the people. If anything, the technicalities of the law and the many opaque whims which have marred the justice system have been weaponized by each of these wings of government—to the detriment of the nation. Chief ministers have been running ministries from jail while facing damning credible allegations ranging from corruption to anti-national activities. Judges appoint themselves to the highest forum of adjudication, where family names and lineages run across benches. Corruption and red-tapism by elements in the bureaucracy have maligned the entirety of the institution. Clearly, the law and how institutions view it is not doing justice to the people. The situation reminds one of mediaeval England, where courts of law had become so encumbered, even perverted, by the strictures of law that a separate system of courts which followed equity or moral determinations based on then-prevailing religious sensibilities were set up. Sir Thomas Moore quipped in this regard that 'one court to do injustice and one court to give justice: courts of law and equity'.

45 Ram Mandir: From spiritual centre to economic hub: Ayodhya's rise after Ram Mandir construction, *The Economic Times* (indiatimes.com), 2024.

46 Abhishek Dixit, 'The Ayodhya opportunity: Economic implication scenarios after the Ram Temple construction in Ayodhya: A multi-sectoral analysis', *IJRCT* 12, no. 4 (2024) (ijcrt.org).

47 Seventy-five is in our view an ideal number but the economic, social, cultural, and political arguments advanced here could just as well hold for delimitation into anything between fifty to hundred smaller states.

Index

About the Authors

Gautam Desiraju is one of the foremost scientists in India with an H-index of 104 with seminal contributions to the fields of crystal engineering and hydrogen bonding. He is Professor Emeritus at Indian Institute of Science, Bengaluru, and Distinguished Professor at UPES, Dehradun. He was the president of International Union of Crystallography between 2011 and 2014. Desiraju is a recipient of several international awards, such as the Humboldt Research Award and van der Waals Prize. He is the author of *Bhārat: India 2.0*, which advocates constitutional reform in India to bring it more in tune with its civilizational nature.

Deekhit Bhattacharya is an Associate at Luthra and Luthra Law Offices India, Delhi. He has economics and law degrees from the University of Delhi. His interests and publications focus on the interface between state, society, business, and technology. He was associated with the S20 Secretariat of the G20 at the Indian Institute of Science with Prof. Desiraju.

About the Authors